Software Development

with (**Visual Basic**)

For the E-Quals IT Practitioner Diploma – Level 2

Peter Blundell, Alan Jarvis, K. Mary Reid and Charles Smart

Series Editor – Jenny Lawson

www.heinemann.co.uk
✓ Free online support
✓ Useful weblinks
✓ 24 hour online ordering

01865 888058

Heinemann

Inspiring generations

Heinemann Educational Publishers
Halley Court, Jordan Hill, Oxford OX2 8EJ
Part of Harcourt Education

Heinemann is the registered trademark of
Harcourt Education Limited

Text © Jenny Lawson, Alan Jarvis, Peter Blundell, Charles Smart, K. Mary Reid 2004

First published 2004

09 08 07 06 05 04
10 9 8 7 6 5 4 3 2 1

British Library Cataloguing in Publication Data is available
from the British Library on request.

ISBN 0 435 47152 X

Typeset by 𝅺 Tek-Art, Croydon, Surrey

Original illustrations © Harcourt Education Limited, 2004

Cover design by Wooden Ark
Design by Wooden Ark
Printed in the UK by Bath Press Ltd
Cover photo: © Harcourt Index/Corbis

Acknowledgements
Every effort has been made to contact copyright holders of material reproduced
in this book. Any omissions will be rectified in subsequent printings if notice is
given to the publishers.

Screenshots reprinted by permission from Microsoft Corporation
Screenshot on page 241 reproduced with permission from Tesco.

Websites
Please note that the examples of websites suggested in this book were up to
date at the time of writing. It is essential for tutors to preview each site before
using it to ensure that the URL is still accurate and the content is appropriate. We
suggest that tutors bookmark useful sites and consider enabling students to
access them through the school or college intranet.

Tel: 01865 888058 www.heinemann.co.uk

Contents

Introduction

The City & Guilds Level 2 Diploma for IT Practitioners is a collection of two related qualifications:

- Diploma for IT Practitioners (ICT Systems Support)
- Diploma for IT Practitioners (Software Development)

There are three books in this series, designed to meet the needs of these City & Guilds qualifications:

- Systems Support – Level 2
- Software Development with Visual Basic – Level 2
- Software Development with Java – Level 2

Units in this book

This book contains material to cover one core unit (204 *Create software components with Visual Basic*), Unit 206 (*Test software components*) and two other units from the bank of nine units (208 *Website design* and 209 *Create designs for software components*). It therefore provides enough units to complete the award for the Diploma for IT Practitioners (Software Development).

	Systems Support – Level 2	Software Development with Visual Basic - Level 2	Software Development with Java – Level 2
Core units	401 Maintain equipment and systems	201 Create software components using 'C'	201 Create software components using 'C'
		202 Create software components using 'C++'	202 Create software components using 'C++'
		203 Create software components using Pascal	203 Create software components using Pascal
	402 Customer support provision	204 Create software components using Visual Basic	204 Create software components using Visual Basic
		205 Create software components using Java	205 Create software components using Java
		206 Test software components	206 Test software components
Optional units	403 Install and configure equipment and operating systems	207 Operating systems	207 Operating systems

	Systems Support – Level 2	Software Development with Visual Basic - Level 2	Software Development with Java – Level 2
	404 Install, configure and maintain software	208 Website design	208 Website design
	405 Systems testing		
	406 System monitoring and operation	209 Create designs for software components	209 Create designs for software components
	407 Repair centre procedure		
	408 Networking		

Assessment

Assessment is carried out by City & Guilds.

For all units, you will be expected to complete at least one timed class-based assignment which is set by the examination body. These assignments assess practical activities in the core units, and underpinning knowledge as well as practical activities for the optional units.

In addition, there are examinations which are designed to test knowledge and understanding of each core unit. These tests are 40-item multiple-choice questions, delivered on-line.

As with City and Guilds E-Quals awards, if you don't pass an examination or an assignment, you are welcome to make another attempt, at a new examination paper and/or a new assignment.

Create designs for software components

The chapters in this unit contain information about how to implement software features in both the Visual Basic and Java programming languages. You should refer to unit 2 for full details of how to write programs in one of these languages. The subject of program testing is part of this unit, but it is covered fully in unit 3.

Outcomes

◆ Describe the common features of high-level programming languages

◆ Specify data types and data structures

◆ Develop a software component design specification

◆ Validate the completed design specification

1 Describe the common features of high-level programming languages

Writing all but the simplest of computer programs is a complex process that requires planning. When building a house, the first step is for an architect to produce a detailed design. In the same way, when creating software the first step also involves designs.

A **program** is a set of instructions that tells the computer what to do. Whatever function you want a computer to perform, all you have to do is write the program.

A program is a little like a recipe for cooking a meal. A recipe lists, in detail, the steps you must follow to make the meal. Recipes are written in English, to be understood by humans, and they assume a level of common sense from the cook.

Computers, on the other hand, do not have common sense. They require a very precise set of instructions. The microprocessor or chip at the heart of a computer can understand instructions only in the form of binary codes (made up of 1s and 0s). But binary codes are very difficult for humans to understand, so all modern programming is done using **symbolic languages** with English-like statements, known as high-level programming languages. Over the years, many different high-level programming languages have been developed, each with its own set of features. Some of the best known are listed in Table 1.1.

Table 1.1 *High-level programming languages*	
Language	**Features**
C++	Low-level technical programming
Cobol	Traditionally used for business applications (stands for COmmon Business Orientated Language)
Fortran	Traditionally used for complex scientific programming (stands for FORmula TRANslation)
Java	Designed for Internet programming
Pascal	Often used for teaching programming
Visual Basic	Easy-to-use Windows programming language, developed by Microsoft

Table 1.2 shows a very simple program written in two different languages, Basic and Pascal.

Table 1.2 **Sample programs**	
Basic	**Pascal**

Dim num1 as integer
Dim num2 as integer
Dim answer as integer
Print "Calculator Program"
Print "Enter first number"
Input num1
Print "Enter second number"
Input num2
answer = num1 + num2
Print "The answer is ", answer
	program simcalc(input, output);
	uses crt;
	var
	  num1 : integer;
	  num2 : integer;
	  answer : integer;
	begin
	  writeln ('Calculator Program');
	  writeln ('Enter first number');
	  readln (num1);
	  writeln ('Enter second number');
	  readln (num2);
	  answer := num1 + num2;
	  writeln ('Answer is ', answer);
	  delay (5000)
	end.

Once the program has been written using the high-level language, a piece of software known as a **compiler** is used to convert the high-level language into the binary instruction codes that the computer's microprocessor can understand.

Although there are many different high-level programming languages, they all share similar main features. However, there are many detailed differences between computer languages. This means that an expert in one language would not be able to use another without retraining.

1.1 Syntax and keywords

Programs are made up of **instructions** or **statements**. Each statement is written on a line on its own, using a text editor which is normally part of the programming IDE (integrated development environment), which also includes a compiler and other tools. The rules governing how these instructions are written are called the **syntax**. Each high-level language has its own syntax. If the syntax rules are broken when the program is written, when the compiler attempts to convert the instructions into binary codes, it will produce an error, telling you that it cannot convert the program into binary because you have made a syntax error. Figure 1.1 shows an example.

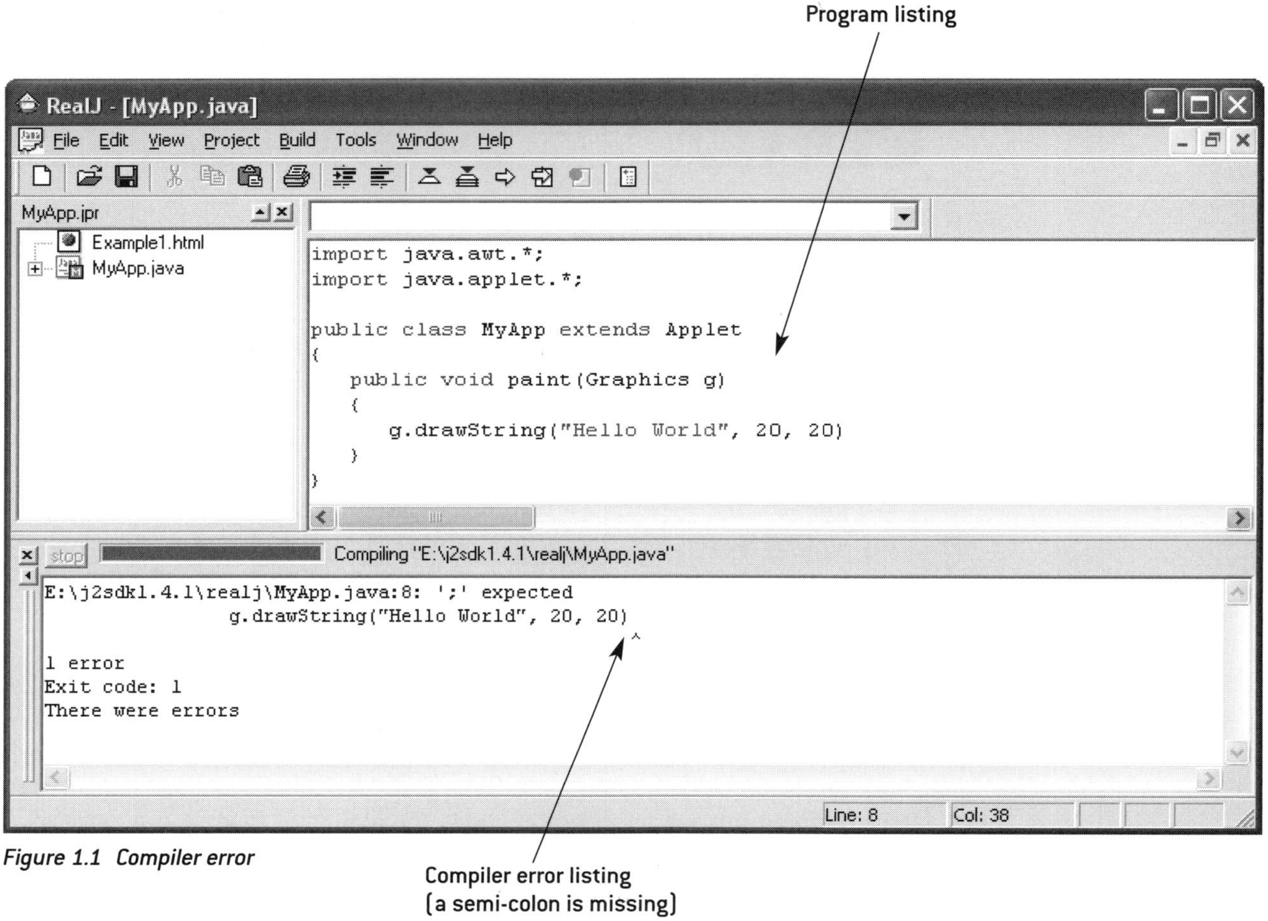

Program listing

Figure 1.1 Compiler error

Compiler error listing
(a semi-colon is missing)

Program statements are made up of a **keyword** – that is, the actual instruction – and one or more **parameters** or **arguments** which qualify the keyword. For example, in the Basic programming language, if you want to display the words 'Hello World', the instruction would be:

```
Print "Hello World"
```

In this case, *Print* is the keyword and Hello World (placed between double quotes in the code) is the parameter which qualifies the keyword, showing what is to be printed. Programming languages have several hundred keywords, and part of learning how to use any language involves learning what the keywords are used for and the exact syntax of how they are used.

Part of the syntax of any language is the spelling of the keyword. So, for example, if you spell the Print keyword incorrectly (perhaps Pritn instead of Print) you have made a syntax error; the statement would be rejected by the compiler and it would issue an error message such as 'unrecognised keyword'.

The same statement in the Java language looks a little different:

```
System.out.print("Hello World");
```

Java has a rather more complex syntax than Basic. It is **case-sensitive**, which means that not only must you spell the keywords correctly, but the capitalization must be correct too – so both *System.Out.Print* and *system.out.print* would be incorrect.

Also, Java, C++ and Pascal require that you add a semi-colon at the end of each statement to show where one statement ends and the next begins. Omitting it will produce syntax errors when the program is compiled. COBOL, on the other hand, requires a full stop at the end of each statement. Basic does not use any punctuation at the end of each statement. Instead the lines are numbered, although if you want to put two statements on the same line you can do this, separating them with a colon.

PRACTICAL TASK 1.1

What programming language skills are most in demand in the job market? It is important that you develop your own skills in an area where you are most likely to get a job.

1 Carry out your own survey on which programming languages are most in demand. Go to some computing job websites (such as www.computing.co.uk/careers or www.totaljobs.com – select IT and Internet) and search for Java, Basic, C++ and other programming languages. How many jobs can you find for each language?

2 Make a list of the most popular languages and skills.

1.2 Comments

Although programs are intended to be understood by computers, it is important that humans can understand them too. Programmers often need to modify or correct programs, so it is good practice to include comments in your programs.

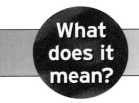

Comments are plain English explanations of what parts of the program do. These comments are ignored by the compiler.

It is not necessary to add comments to every statement in the program. But comments should be added as often as required to explain what the statements that follow mean. The more complex the program, the greater the need for detailed comments.

So that the compiler knows where the comments are, they are preceded by a special character. In Basic, this a single quotation mark (') (or the keyword *rem*), while in Java and C++ it is two slashes (//). Table 1.3 shows two examples.

Table 1.3 *Sample programs with comments included*

Basic	Pascal

Rem Declare variables
Dim num1 as integer
Dim num2 as integer
Dim answer as integer
Print "Calculator Program"
Print "Enter first number"
Rem Accept first number
Input num1
Print "Enter second number"
Rem Accept second number
Input num2
Rem Add two numbers together
answer = num1 + num2
Rem Display the answer
Print "The answer is ", answer
	program simcalc(input, output);
	uses crt;
	// declare variables
	var
	  num1 : integer;
	  num2 : integer;
	  answer : integer;
	begin
	  writeln ('Calculator Program');
	  writeln ('Enter first number');
	  // accept first number
	  readln (num1);
	  writeln ('Enter second number');
	  // accept second number
	  readln (num2);
	  // add two numbers togther
	  answer := num1 + num2;
	  // display the answers
	  writeln ('Answer is ', answer);
	  // wait before closing window
	  delay (5000)
	end.

Comments should also be added at the beginning of the program stating who wrote the program, along with a brief description of its purpose and the date when it was last modified.

1.3 Variables and constants

Programs need to be able to store data.

- That data may be input from the user of the program or it may be the result of a calculation.
- The data may vary or it may be constant.

Programs store data that varies using what are called **variables**, and these are areas of the computer's memory allocated to the program. Variables have three attributes:

- a name
- a data type
- a value.

To refer to the variable, a **name** is given to it. The name is chosen by the programmer.

◆ All programming languages require variables to start with an alphabetic character.

◆ No programming language allows variable names to contain spaces.

◆ The variable cannot have the same name as one of that language's keywords. This is because each language has a list of so-called **reserved words**, which cannot be used as variable or constant names or as program or procedure names.

So, for example, *Print*, *22* and *my variable* would not be valid variable names (why not?), but *x* and *myvariable* would be valid. It is good practice to give a variable a name that tells something about its purpose. So, a variable used to store the score in a computer game might be called *score*.

The **data type** determines the data that can be stored in the variable. For example, a variable that holds someone's name will need to have a *text* data type, while a variable that holds their age will have an *integer* (that is, whole number) data type. Different languages allow different data types and give them different names, although all languages allow for **text**, **integer number** and **real number** data types. (A 'real number' is a number with a decimal point in it.)

The **value** is assigned during the program execution, and may depend on a number of things, such as user input. The value stored in a variable varies – hence the name 'variable'.

As well as allocating memory storage for values that vary, many programs need to store fixed values, or **constants**. For example, a program that needs to store the maximum score in an exam or the mathematical value of pi (3.14176…) would store these values in a constant, which – unlike a variable – does not change during the execution of the program.

Before either variables or constants can be used, they must be **declared**. The syntax of declaring variables depends on the programming language. For example, with the Basic language, to declare an integer variable called *mynumber* the instruction uses the *Dim* keyword:

```
Dim mynumber as Integer
```

What does it mean?

*An **integer** is a whole number, such as 3 or 25, without a fractional part. When declaring a variable in Basic, the **Dim** keyword is used to indicate that this is a variable declaration.*

With Java, declaring variables is a little simpler:

```
int mynumber;
```

Assigning a value into a variable is done using the **assignment operator**, the equals sign (=). So, to assign a value to the mynumber variable, using Basic, the statement would be:

```
mynumber = 2
```

In Java it would be:

```
mynumber = 2;
```

These assignments put the number 2 in the *memory area* called mynumber.

Constants also need to be declared. In Basic, the statement would be:

```
Const Pi = 3.14176
```

In Java (*float* is the data type for real numbers) the statement would be:

```
Final float Pi = 3.14176
```

Go out and try!

Find out how variables are created in Basic, Java and another language of your choice. Find out what data types these languages support, and what ranges of values can be stored in the different data types.

1.4 Arithmetic operators

Having assigned values to variables, it is often useful to carry out arithmetic using the usual four operators, as listed in Table 1.4.

Table 1.4 **Arithmetic operators**	
Operation	**Operator**
Addition	+
Subtraction	−
Multiplication	*
Division	/

Arithmetic operators can be used with actual numbers, or with values contained in variables or constants. So, in the Basic version of the example program shown in Table 1.2 (page 3), the instruction:

```
answer = num1 + num2
```

took the values contained in the variables *num1* and *num2*, added them together and placed the result in the variable called *answer*. The instruction:

```
answer = num1 * 2
```

would multiply the value in num1 by 2.

Parentheses allow you to change the order of precedence – that is, the order in which the different arithmetic operations are normally carried out. For example, you might imagine the calculation:

    10 + 5 * 2

would give the result 30, but operators are *not* evaluated from left to right. Multiplication is done before addition, so the result would be 20 – with 5 multiplied by 2 first (giving 10), and then the 10 is added to give 20.

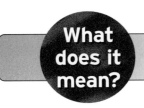

What does it mean?

Parentheses are rounded brackets, like this ( ). Calculations within parentheses are done first.

There is a simple mnemonic to help you remember the order of mathematical precedence, which is 'BODMAS'. This stands for:

- **B**rackets
- Powers **O**f
- **D**ivision ⎫
- **M**ultiplication ⎭ working from left to right
- **A**ddition ⎫
- **S**ubtraction ⎭ working from left to right

So anything in brackets is done first, followed by division and multiplication, and then any addition and subtraction as necessary.

To get the result of 30 in the earlier example, the expression would need to be written as:

    (10 + 5) * 2

To raise a number to the power of a certain value, the **^ operator** is used. For example, the formula to find the area of a circle is:

$$a = \pi r^2$$

Therefore the following instruction, using two variables called *radius* and *area*, would implement this formula:

    area = 3.14 * radius ^ 2

The **modulus operator** in Basic is *Mod*, and in Java it is %. So for example, in Java, 8 % 3 has the result 2.

What does it mean?

The modulus is the remainder left over after division. For example, 13 divided by 4 is 3 remainder 1 – so 1 is the modulus in that case.

What results will these formulae produce?

112 – 4 * 5

2(12 – 4) * 5

315 / 2

415 % 2

53.14 * 6 ^ 2

1.5 Program constructs

Programming languages provide a wide range of functions, with hundreds of keywords. Different programming languages, as already mentioned, have different syntax for writing instructions using these keywords. However, all programming languages provide instructions that control the program flow. These instructions allow blocks of code (i.e. a number of instructions which carry out a particular task) to be executed in different ways. The different ways block of code can be executed can be broadly divided into:

◆ sequence

◆ selection

◆ iteration.

These terms are sometimes called **program constructs** or **program control structures**, because programs are constructed out of blocks of code that are executed in one of these three ways.

Sequence is when the program statements are followed one after the other. An example might be doing a calculation or accepting some input from the user.

Selection is where a choice is made as to which set of instructions to carry out next. The choice is made based on a criterion such as an option the user has selected. In most programming languages, selection is done using the *if* keyword.

Generally, selection constructs take the form:

```
If (condition) then
    (
    statements to be executed if the condition is true
    )
else
    (
    statements to be executed if the condition is false
    )
end of selection construct
```

The exact syntax of the construct depends on the language in use.

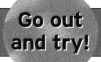

Go out and try!

Find out what syntax is used in Java, Basic and one other language for creating if...else constructs.

Iteration is where instructions are repeated either a certain number of times or until some condition is met. An iteration construct is sometimes called a **loop**.

What does it mean?

*A **loop** is a part of a program that is repeated. For example, if you want a program that prints out a times-table from 1 to 12, the most efficient way to write the program would be with a section of code that repeats (loops) 12 times.*

Iteration can be implemented in a program in a number of different ways. In a *fixed* iteration construct, the loop is repeated a fixed number of times and is often implemented using the *For* keyword. However, there are situations in programming where the statements need to repeat until some condition is met, rather than a fixed number of times. This is often implemented using the *While* keyword, which takes the general form:

```
While (condition)
    (
    statements to be repeated while the condition is true
    )
```

With this type of loop, the condition is tested on entry into the loop. So, if it is not true at the start of the loop, the statements inside the loop will not be executed at all. A slightly different version of this loop has the condition at the exit point of the loop, which takes the form:

```
Repeat
    (
    statements to be repeated
    )
until (condition)
```

In this case, the statements within the loop will always be executed at least once because the condition is not tested until the end of the loop.

Check your understanding

Find out what different types of loops can be used in Java, Basic and one other language. In each case, find out what the syntax is for each type of loop.

Procedures

A common technique for dealing with complex programming problems (such as controlling a space rocket or producing a computer game) is to divide the problem up into sections. To start with, these can be large sections covering broad areas. Then, further detail can be added bit by bit to each of the sections until a detailed solution has been designed. Program design takes the same approach. Faced with a complex program to design and write, where do you start?

The first step is to divide the program up into sections, which in programming terminology are called **procedures** and **functions**. Within each procedure, the next step in the 'divide and conquer technique' of problem-solving is to identify which of the programming constructs are needed, and in which combination, to achieve the required functionality.

PRACTICAL TASK 1.2

Think of a task you are familiar with, such as completing a piece of course work. Break the task down into sections which involve different activities (just as you would break a programming task down into procedures), such as finding relevant library books. For each section (procedure), further subdivide the section and decide for each subsection what parts need doing in sequence (such as typing up the course work), making selections (finding suitable books) and repetition (refining and proof-reading your final document).

1.6 Relational and logical operators

Selection and some iteration constructs rely on a condition to decide how to proceed. This condition takes the form of a test, which needs to evaluate true or false, and is known as a **Boolean condition**. Here are some examples of Boolean conditions:

◆ Is this person over 18?

◆ Are there any seats free on the plane?

◆ Has a student achieved 80% attendance?

Boolean conditions use relational operators, such as equal to, greater than and less than. Table 1.5 shows the relational operators with their equivalent symbols for both Basic and Java.

More complex relational conditions can be put together using the logical operators, as listed in Table 1.6.

Table 1.5 *Relational operators*

Relational condition	Java operator	Basic operator
Equal to	==	=
Not equal to	!=	<>
Less than	<	<
Greater than	>	>
Greater than or equal to	>=	>=
Less than or equal to	<=	<=

Table 1.6 *Logical operators*

Logical condition	Java operator	Basic operator
AND	==	=
OR	!=	<>
NOT	<	<

Boolean logic was developed by an English mathematician call George Boole, hence the name. Boolean logic is actually very simple and involves combining conditions with the AND, OR and NOT operators. For example, a condition such as 'male AND over 30' would select all people who are both men and over 30. The condition 'male OR over 30' would select people who were either men or over 30 (i.e. including all men of any age and women over 30).

Logical operators allow relational operators to be combined:

◆ Is this person over 18 AND under 60? – In this case, both conditions must be true for the expression to evaluate to true.

◆ Are there any seats free on the plane OR is there another flight the same day? – Here, either condition can be true.

In real-life applications, multiple combinations of conditions like these can introduce a considerable degree of complexity. In these situations, **decision tables** are sometimes used to identify the different conditions and associated actions.

A decision table is used to model complex series of conditions and the actions that are taken in each situation. Many real-life applications have complex conditions. For example, issuing a bus pass may depend upon a number of conditions, such as the age of the applicant, where the person lives and whether he or she has a recent photograph. Decision tables are described on page 30.

13

Check your understanding

Write an *If* instruction (using the language of your choice) that will carry out one action if the value contained in a variable called *personsAge* is over 18 and under 60, and another action if it is not.

1.7 Structured programming

The concept of breaking a large and complex program into separate procedures has already been briefly introduced. Creating a program using this so-called structured approach has a number of advantages:

◆ Structuring a program in this way is an effective way of dealing with complexity.

◆ Since the same function is often required a number of times within the program (for example, when validating user input such as a date), creating a separate procedure to carry out this task avoids duplicating code and may create general-purpose procedures that can be re-used in other programs.

◆ In a large programming project, which may employ many programmers, by dividing the program up into procedures, each programmer can work independently on one or more procedures.

When program control is passed to a procedure from the main program, the main program can pass parameters to the procedure which the procedure then uses in its processing. For example, if a procedure is written to validate a date input by the user, the main program will pass the date the user entered. Once the procedure has carried out its task, it can return a value to the calling program. In the example of the data validation procedure, the procedure could return a Boolean value set to 'true' if the date was valid and 'false' if it was not valid.

1.8 Naming conventions

Just as adding comments to programs is considered good practice, so using consistent, meaningful names for variables, procedures and files is also good practice and helps to make programs more understandable. Remember that you cannot use any of the language keywords as variable or procedure names, nor can you have spaces in variable names. Where you want to use a meaningful variable name made of several words, just join them together leaving out the spaces, as in *dateOfBirth*. Note that it is a widely used convention to start variables' names with a lower-case character and, where it is made up of several words, each of those has an initial capital.

In a Windows programming environment, as well as naming variables, the window components such as text boxes, command buttons and list boxes also need names. This can easily lead to confusion! For example, you might have a text box used to enter someone's surname and decide to call the text box 'surname'. The value entered into this text box may need to be transferred to a variable, but what name do you choose for this variable? You cannot call both the variable and the text box the same name. It is therefore good practice to precede window component names with something that identifies not only that they are window components but also what type of component they are. Text boxes, for example, can be preceded with 'txt', so the name for the surname text box would be *txtSurname*. Table 1.7 shows suggested prefixes for the most common window components.

Table 1.7 *Component name prefixes*	
Component	**Suggested prefix**
Command button	cmd
Text box	txt
List box	lst
Label	lbl
Check box	chk

Chapter summary

This chapter has covered all the practical activities listed under the first outcome in the specification, including:

◆ the main features of programming languages

◆ the use of arithmetic operators

◆ the program constructs of sequence, selection and iteration

◆ relational and logic operators

◆ structured programming

◆ naming conventions.

2 Specify data types and data structures

The concepts of variables and data types have already been introduced (see page 6). This chapter looks in more detail at different data types and introduces some more advanced topics such as arrays and file handling.

2.1 Data types

In general, a variable or constant can hold data of only one particular type. There are two fundamental data types – numbers and text – but many variations of these types exist, which, for example, hold numbers of different sizes. Table 1.8 describes the common data types in more detail.

Table 1.8 *Data types*

Data type	Allows for	Example	Java declaration	Visual Basic declaration
Integer	Whole numbers	5	Int age;	Dim age as integer
Floating point	Numbers with a decimal point	5.5	Float price	Dim price as single
Character	Single characters	m	Char gender	Dim gender as string
String	Strings of characters	John	String name	Dim name as string

Most languages provide different versions of the same data type to store different ranges of numbers. For example, the *Integer* data type in Visual Basic can only store numbers in the range −32,768 through to +32,767, while the *Long* data type can store numbers in the range approximately −2 million through to +2 million. The difference is due to the amount of memory used to store the variable – Integer uses 2 bytes (16 bits) whereas Long uses 4 bytes. Both Visual Basic and Java provide a floating-point data type called *Double* that can store very large numbers, which might be used in scientific calculations.

2.2 String manipulation

Most programming languages provide a number of built-in string manipulation functions. Some of the Java and Basic string manipulation functions are listed in Table 1.9.

There is a wide range of applications where string manipulation may be required. An example is the processing and validation of postcodes or other codes which contain combinations of alphabetic and numeric characters. The first four characters of a postcode contain a code which identifies the area of the country to which the postcode belongs, while the final three characters identify the street. In a program that sorts mail, the first step would probably

Table 1.9 *String manipulation functions*

Description	Basic function	Basic example	Java function	Java example, where string str contains 'Hello'
Returns the length of a string	Len	Len("hello") returns 5	length	str.length() returns 5
Converts a string to upper case	UCase	UCase("hello") returns "HELLO"	toUpper	str.toUpper() returns "HELLO"
Converts a string to lower case	LCase	LCase("HELLO") returns "hello"	toLower	str.toLower() returns "hello"
Returns a number of characters from the middle of a string	Mid	Mid("Hello", 2, 3) returns "ell"	substring	str.substring(1, 3) returns "ell"

Note that in Visual Basic the Mid function counts the characters in a string from 1, but the Java function substring counts from 0.

be to divide the mail into areas of the country. So, if the postcode were contained in a variable called *postcode*, the following instruction would move the area part of the postcode into a separate variable called *area*:

```
area = postcode.substring(0,2)
```

PRACTICAL TASK 1.3

What do the following Basic string functions return?

1 UCase("basic")

2 Len("what's for tea?")

3 Mid("String manipulation", 6,5)

2.3 Passing parameters and return values

Procedures are commonly passed one or more variables as parameters to process, and they then return a value when they have finished their task. Procedures, of course, have a name, and the general form of calling a procedure is as follows:

Procedure_name(parameter1, parameter 2, etc.)

The previous section on string manipulation introduced some built-in functions, provided as part of the programming language, which are passed parameters and which return values. Programmers can, of course, write their own functions or procedures. So, for example, if a procedure is required to validate a date, it might be called *vDate* and it is passed three integer variables, called *day*, *month* and *year*. Having validated the date, the procedure returns an integer which indicates whether the date was valid – or, if it was not valid, where the problem lies. In this example, the return value is placed in a variable called *isValid*:

```
isValid = vDate(day, month, year)
```

The scope of variables

One question that arises when designing procedures is whether the variables that exist in the main program can be accessed by the procedures (known as the scope of variables).

The answer is that it depends on how the main program variables are declared. If they are declared as **global variables**, then they can be accessed and used by the main program and all the procedures. If they are declared as **local variables**, then they cannot be accessed in that way.

> ### What does it mean?
>
> The **scope** of a variable refers to the extent to which the variable is available within the program. In a program that is spilt into different procedures, variables within the main program may or may not be available within the procedures.
>
> Variables that are available is both the main program and the procedures are know as **global** variables, while those which are not are known as **local** variables.

It is generally accepted that global variables are not a good idea and should be avoided if possible. The problem with them is that it is easy to make mistakes and misuse them. This is especially the case if several programmers are working on the same program. One programmer may use a global variable in a procedure for one thing while another programmer may use it in a slightly different way. Another reason is that global variables make maintaining large programs difficult. For example, it may be decided that a particular global variable needs to be changed from an integer to the real data type (see page 7). This would mean that all the procedures using the global variable would need to be changed.

Data hiding

Using only local variables within procedures is sometimes called data hiding, because all the data (variables) are hidden within the procedure. The only way data can be put into and taken out of the procedure is by using the parameters that are passed and the return value, and this is called the **public interface** of the procedure.

In the example of the date validation procedure, the variables used as parameters for the procedure contain the values which are passed to the procedures for processing. This is known as passing parameters **by value**. In some circumstances, the parameters passed do not contain the values themselves; instead they are a **pointer** to the actual value. A pointer contains the memory address of the variable or object that is being passed. This is known as passing parameters **by reference**. An example of this can be found in Windows programming where objects such as a command button are created and then passed as parameters to the procedure which adds them to the current window. In this case, the procedure is not passed a simple variable containing a value, but is being passed the name of an object, the name being a way to refer to the object itself.

The concept of passing parameters by reference is often a difficult one to grasp. An analogy can be drawn with a treasure hunt. You may be led to look under a stone, and under the stone you might find the treasure itself (by value) or you might find a clue which tells you where to look for the treasure (by reference).

2.4 Arrays

Mostly, variables are used to store a single value. However, there are situations when variables are needed to store a number of related items. For example, consider a program that records and processes the number of hours of sunshine each day in a week. Seven variables could be created, one for each day of the week, such as (in Basic):

```
Dim sunshine1, sunshine2, sunshine3, sunshine4, sunshine5,
                            sunshine6, sunshine7 as single
```

The problem with this approach is that when the program does any processing with this data it needs to process each variable separately, rather than use a loop to process them. For example, if the program needs to print out each variable it would need seven separate Print statements.

The solution to this problem is to use an array. An array is a special type of variable that can store a collection of items all of the same data type. Arrays are declared in a similar way to normal variables, except that the number of **elements** in the array (that is the number of items it can store) must be indicated. So the array needed to store the number of hours of sunshine in a week would be declared, in Basic, like this:

```
Dim sunshine(6) as single
```

Array elements are numbered (or *indexed* to use the proper term) from 0. So sunshine(6) produces a seven-element array – sunshine(0) through to sunshine(6).

All the array elements can now be printed using a loop; for example:

```
For i = 0 To 6
Print sunshine(i)
Next i
```

Here the loop counter (the variable *i*) is used as a **subscript** to access each element of the array.

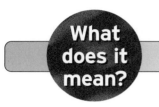

A **subscript** *is a number that is used to access an individual element of an array.*

The data in an array sometimes needs to be searched or sorted. Searching through an array for a particular value, such as the largest or smallest, involves looping through the array to find the required value, using a *For* loop. For example, suppose the program for recording sunshine hours needs to find the day with the highest number of hours. This Basic code shown provides the required value and stores it in a variable called *Highest*:

```
Highest = sunshine(0)
For i = 1 To 6
    If sunshine(i) > Highest Then
        Highest = sunshine(i)
    End if
Next i
```

Sorting involves putting the items in an array in some order, such as ascending numeric order. There are many sort algorithms available, and the topic of designing efficient sort routines is a subject within itself.

A **sort algorithm** *is a method or technique for sorting a number of items into some kind of order (usually ascending or descending numerical order).*

A simple, but not particularly efficient, sorting algorithm, called the **bubble sort**, is described here. With this type of sort, the program uses a loop to check each element in the array to see whether it has a higher value than the next element. If it has, it swaps the values in the two elements.

The bubble sort is best explained by an example. Suppose the array shown in Figure 1.2 is to be sorted into ascending order.

Array element	0	1	2	3	4	5	6
Value	9	7	8	3	6	5	2

Figure 1.2 Starting array

The loop would first compare elements 0 and 1, and – noting that they are in the wrong sequence – it would swap them. Then it would compare elements 1 and 2 – they would be out of sequence too, so they would be swapped; and so on. Figure 1.3 shows the results of the first loop through the array with the swapped values shaded.

Array element	0	1	2	3	4	5	6
Start values	9	7	8	3	6	5	2
Loop 1	7	9	8	3	6	5	2
Loop 2	7	8	9	3	6	5	2
Loop 3	7	8	3	9	6	5	2
Loop 4	7	8	3	6	9	5	2
Loop 5	7	8	3	6	5	9	2
Loop 6	7	8	3	6	5	2	9

Figure 1.3 First loop

As can be seen, at the end of the first loop through the array the highest value (9) is in the correct place, but the rest of the array is not sorted. The loop must be executed for as many times as there are items in the array, using another loop.

The sample Basic code below would sort the array holding the number of sunshine hours:

```
For j = 0 To 6
   For i = 0 To 5
   If sunshine(i + 1) > sunshine(i) Then
      temp = sunshine(i)
      sunshine(i) = sunshine(i + 1)
      sunshine(i + 1) = temp
   End If
   Next i
Next j
```

Sorting is a very common data-processing function, and efficiency is important because the more efficient the sort, the quicker it can be done. While speed may not be an issue with just seven data items, real-life data-processing sorts may involve tens of thousands if not millions of data items. The bubble sort code shown above would prove particularly inefficient if that data was already partially sorted with perhaps just one or two items out of sequence. This is because it goes on looping through the array even when no swaps are required.

This could be avoided by using a variable as a **flag**. A flag is an indicator used to tell whether an event has occurred or not. The flag could be set to 0 at the beginning of the inner loop, and set to 1 if a swap is needed. At the end of the loop, the flag could be inspected to see whether it was still zero. If it was, this would indicate that no swaps had taken place, so the array must now be sorted in order and no further iterations through the outer loop are required.

Go out and try!

As mentioned earlier, there are many other – more efficient – sorting routines. Some of these are highly complex. Two relatively straightforward ones that you can investigate are the *insertion sort* and the *merge sort*.

2.5 File manipulation

Variables provide storage for data while the program is running, but once the program ends all the data held in variables is lost. For permanent storage, data must be written to a file saved on the computer's disk.

Data written to **files** must be structured in some way. For example, suppose a program is written to record details of students enrolled on a course. The students' details are written to a file, and the data for each student is held in a **record**. The individual items of data recorded for each student, such as name, date of birth and address, are held in **fields**. Each record contains a complete set of fields. This example is illustrated in Figure 1.4.

ID	Surname	First name	Address	Postcode	Date of birth
1	Jones	Rose	123 High Street	N14 6BS	19/06/1983
2	Gibson	Colin	12 Wood Green	N22 5LT	04/11/1970
3	Sheruncle	Bob	10 Hill Side	LU6 3QW	10/02/1964
4	Smith	Wendy	33 Station Road	MK6 1RD	30/12/1982

A file · *Field names* · *A record* · *Field*

Figure 1.4 Sample file structure

Serial files

The simplest type of file is a serial file. With this type, records are written to the file as they arise naturally, and so may be in no particular order. While this makes writing records to the file simple, finding a particular record within a serial file can be very inefficient. Since the records are in no particular order, each record must be read one at a time until the required one is found. This may work reasonably quickly for files with just a few hundred records, but it would be impossibly slow for larger files.

Sequential files

In a sequential file, the records are written in a particular order, based on one of the fields – which is known as the **key field**. The key field should uniquely identify each record on the file, so the field chosen is often a code such as an account number or product code. Before a series of records can be written to a sequential file, they must be sorted into key order – hence the importance of sorting routines.

Using sequential files presents a number of issues. Finding a particular record in the file could be done by simply reading through the file one record at a time until the required one is found, as with a serial file. However, as the records are in key order there is a more efficient way.

PRACTICAL TASK 1.4

Imagine a file used to store details of all the music CDs in your collection. What fields would the file need? What would you use as a key field?

Imagine a sequential file of outstanding orders that has 200 records. The order numbers (the key field) on the file run from 110 to 550 and order number 250 is the one that is required. The quickest way to find the required record would be to read the record at the middle of the file (record number 100) and check what order number that record has. Since the records are in order number order, if the record in the middle of the file has an order number greater than 250, then the required record must lie in the lower half of the file; while if the middle record has an order number less than 250, the record must lie in the upper half. Let us assume that the middle record has an order number of 325, so the required record is in the lower half. The next step is to read the middle record in the lower half of the file – record number 50 – and check the order number of that record. The same logic applies to this record: if its order number is over 250, the required record is in the lower half of this section of the file; if not then the required record must be in the upper half. This routine is followed until the actual record is found, each time halving the number of records under consideration.

Inserting new records

Another issue with sequential files is inserting new records. If the record(s) to be inserted have key values higher than any of the existing records, then there is no problem because the record can be inserted at the end of the file. However, many applications will require that new records with key values within the range of existing values be inserted. In these situations, complex processing is involved to allow space to be made in the file to allow the new record to be inserted in the correct place among the existing records.

Using sequential files places a considerable burden on the programmer, requiring complex programs to be written to deal with finding, inserting and deleting records. For this reason almost all modern applications use a database management system (such as Microsoft's *Access*) which deals with all these issues. Database management systems (DBMSs) provide a programming interface using a special database language called SQL.

What does it mean?

SQL (structured query language) allows programs to be written that issue a procedure call to the database management software, sending an SQL statement as a parameter.

Database management systems and the SQL language are a complex topic, on which whole books have been written. They are beyond the scope of this unit.

PRACTICAL TASK 1.5

Find out about a database management system such as *Access*, *mySQL* or *Oracle*. Could you store your CD collection database using these systems? Will they allow you to search for matching records using only the key files, or can you search on any fields? Do you need to know SQL to use these database management systems? Can programs be written to interface with these systems?

2.6 Binary and ASCII

Computers store and process all data and instructions as binary codes – that is, numbers that contain 1s and 0s only. In the decimal number system, each digit in a number (from the right) represents an increase in magnitude of ten. So, for example, the number 234 represents:

◆ 4 ones

◆ 3 tens

◆ 2 hundreds.

In a binary number, each digit (from the right) represents an increase in magnitude of two. So a binary number such as 10011 represents:

◆ **1** one

◆ **1** two

◆ **0** fours

◆ **0** eights

◆ **1** sixteen.

You can easily convert this number to decimal by adding up the one, two and sixteen, which gives 19.

Converting a decimal number to binary involves repeatedly dividing the number by two:

```
19 divided by two gives:
9 remainder 1
    9 divided by 2 gives:
    4 remainder 1
        4 divided by 2 gives:
        2 remainder 0
            2 divided by 2 gives:
            1 remainder 0
                1 divided by 2 gives
                0 remainder 1
```

Then read the remainders off *from the bottom*, which gives: 10011.

The decimal numbers 1 to 10 and their binary equivalents are shown in Table 1.10.

Table 1.10 **Decimal table**				
Binary				**Decimal**
$8 = 2^3$	$4 = 2^2$	$2 = 2^1$	$1 = 2^0$	
0	0	0	1	1
0	0	1	0	2
0	0	1	1	3
0	1	0	0	4
0	1	0	1	5
0	1	1	0	6
0	1	1	1	7
1	0	0	0	8
1	0	0	1	9
1	0	1	0	10

Check your understanding

1 Convert 101100 from binary into decimal.

2 Convert 93 from decimal into binary.

All the characters you can print or display, plus many more control characters, are encoded into groups of seven binary numbers using **ASCII codes** (pronounced *askey*). The complete set of ASCII character codes is shown in Table 1.11. So, for example, the ASCII code for the letter 'a' is 97, while the code for 'z' is 122. The upper-case characters have different codes, so the code for 'A' is 65.

When comparisons between character values are done (using an If instruction, for example), the comparisons are done using the ASCII values. This means that when validating user input the program will need to test for both the upper-case and lower-case characters, since they will not be considered as the same.

You can print out the ASCII code of any character using the *Asc* function in Basic. The instruction:

```
Print Asc("z")
```

will print 122.

Table 1.11 ASCII table

Binary pattern	ASCII code	Hex code	Character	Binary pattern	ASCII code	Hex code	Character	Binary pattern	ASCII code	Hex code	Character
00000000	0	00	Null	00101011	43	2B	+	01010110	86	56	V
00000001	1	01	SOH	00101100	44	2C	,	01010111	87	57	W
00000010	2	02	STX	00101101	45	2D	-	01011000	88	58	X
00000011	3	03	ETX	00101110	46	2E	.	01011001	89	59	Y
00000100	4	04	EOT	00101111	47	2F	/	01011010	90	5A	Z
00000101	5	05	ENQ	00110000	48	30	0	01011011	91	5B	[
00000110	6	06	ACK	00110001	49	31	1	01011100	92	5C	\
00000111	7	07	BEL	00110010	50	32	2	01011101	93	5D	]
00001000	8	08	BS	00110011	51	33	3	01011110	94	5E	^
00001001	9	09	HT	00110100	52	34	4	01011111	95	5F	_
00001010	10	0A	LF	00110101	53	35	5	01100000	96	60	`
00001011	11	0B	VT	00110110	54	36	6	01100001	97	61	a
00001100	12	0C	FF	00110111	55	37	7	01100010	98	62	b
00001101	13	0D	CR	00111000	56	38	8	01100011	99	63	c
00001110	14	0E	SO	00111001	57	39	9	01100100	100	64	d
00001111	15	0F	SI	00111010	58	3A	:	01100101	101	65	e
00010000	16	10	DLE	00111011	59	3B	;	01100110	102	66	f
00010001	17	11	DC1	00111100	60	3C	<	01100111	103	67	g
00010010	18	12	DC2	00111101	61	3D	=	01101000	104	68	h
00010011	19	13	DC3	00111110	62	3E	>	01101001	105	69	i
00010100	20	14	DC4	00111111	63	3F	?	01101010	106	6A	j
00010101	21	15	NAK	01000000	64	40	@	01101011	107	6B	k
00010110	22	16	SYN	01000001	65	41	A	01101100	108	6C	l
00010111	23	17	ETB	01000010	66	42	B	01101101	109	6D	m
00011000	24	18	CAN	01000011	67	43	C	01101110	110	6E	n
00011001	25	19	EM	01000100	68	44	D	01101111	111	6F	o
00011010	26	1A	SUB	01000101	69	45	E	01110000	112	70	p
00011011	27	1B	ESC	01000110	70	46	F	01110001	113	71	q
00011100	28	1C	FS	01000111	71	47	G	01110010	114	72	r
00011101	29	1D	GS	01001000	72	48	H	01110011	115	73	s
00011110	30	1E	RS	01001001	73	49	I	01110100	116	74	t
00011111	31	1F	US	01001010	74	4A	J	01110101	117	75	u
00100000	32	20	space	01001011	75	4B	K	01110110	118	76	v
00100001	33	21	!	01001100	76	4C	L	01110111	119	77	w
00100010	34	22	"	01001101	77	4D	M	01111000	120	78	x
00100011	35	23	#	01001110	78	4E	N	01111001	121	79	y
00100100	36	24	$	01001111	79	4F	O	01111010	122	7A	z
00100101	37	25	%	01010000	80	50	P	01111011	123	7B	{
00100110	38	26	&	01010001	81	51	Q	01111100	124	7C	ı
00100111	39	27	'	01010010	82	52	R	01111101	125	7D	}
00101000	40	28	(	01010011	83	53	S	01111110	126	7E	~
00101001	41	29	)	01010100	84	54	T	01111111	127	7F	del
00101010	42	2A	*	01010101	85	55	U				

Numbers 0 to 9 have an ASCII code, the code for 0 is 48, 1 is 49, etc. However, representing numbers as ASCII code is treating them as text, rather than numbers with which you can do arithmetic. For example, if you enter the Basic instruction:

```
Print "1" + "2"
```

it will print 12 – that is, the text string "1" joined together (or *concatenated* to use the correct term) with the text string "2". If you enter:

```
Print 1 + 2
```

you will be given the result 3, which is the numbers 1 and 2 added.

What does it mean?

Concatenate is a technical term which means to link or join together. When you concatenate two strings (such as 'cat' and 'dog'), they are linked together in a single string, to become 'catdog'). Both Java and Visual Basic use the + sign to concatenate strings.

Therefore, while characters can be stored on a computer only as binary numbers using the ASCII encoding scheme, numbers can be represented either by their binary equivalent or as their ASCII value. So, the number 5 can be represented as its binary equivalent, 101, or as its ASCII value 53, which in binary is 0110101.

Chapter summary

This chapter has covered all the practical activities listed under the second outcome in the specification, including:

- ◆ **identifying the basic data types**
- ◆ **string manipulation methods**
- ◆ **local and global variables**
- ◆ **the use of arrays**
- ◆ **file manipulation**
- ◆ **binary and ACSII representation of numbers.**

3 Develop a software component design specification

Before a program can be written, a design must be produced. Structured programming design techniques involve two main steps:

1 Modularise the program. As already mentioned, this involves breaking the program down into smaller parts, or procedures, each of which performs a particular task.

2 Design how each of the modules will work.

The procedures of the program can be graphically illustrated using a **structure chart**. This is a diagram showing the overall structure of the program, how it will be split into different procedures, and how the procedures will interact.

A number of different design techniques are used to identify how the procedures themselves will work. Two techniques will be described here in detail.

◆ **Decision tables** are useful where there are a lot of different options to choose from and you want to identify what happens in each circumstance.

◆ **Program design languages**, such as flowcharts and pseudo-code, are more detailed techniques, often used in the later stages of the design process.

In addition, the input, output and storage requirements of the program must be identified, and suitable file layouts, input screens and output report formats must be designed.

3.1 Structure charts

Structure charts are simple diagrams that identify how the program will be spilt into procedures, what order the procedures will be called in, what parameters will be passed to each procedure, and what values will be returned. The chart is drawn with a box containing the name of the main program at the top. Each of the different procedures is shown in a box below, connected to the main program by a line. An arrow is drawn pointing into each procedure box showing the parameter to be passed to the procedure. Another arrow is drawn pointing back into the main program box showing the value to be returned by the procedure. This is shown in Figure 1.5.

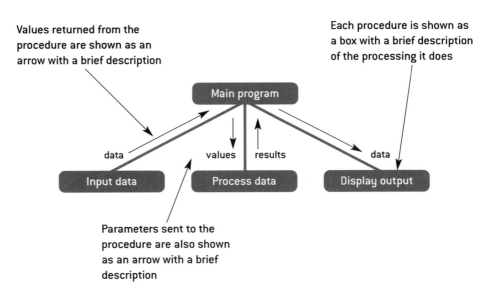

Values returned from the procedure are shown as an arrow with a brief description

Each procedure is shown as a box with a brief description of the processing it does

Parameters sent to the procedure are also shown as an arrow with a brief description

Figure 1.5 Sample structure chart

CASE STUDY

Northgate College

Northgate College requires a program that will accept a student's details before they are recorded on a database. The program needs to validate the student's date of birth and postcode, and return a code to indicate whether the validation has been successful – or if not, what the error was. The program could be divided into three procedures: a date validation procedure, a postcode validation procedure, and a procedure to display the meaning of an error code returned by either of the two other procedures. The structure chart for this arrangement is shown in Figure 1.6.

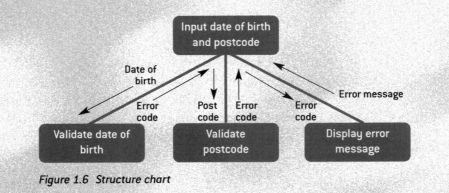

Figure 1.6 Structure chart

PRACTICAL TASK 1.6

You are planning to write a program to allow you to search for CDs on your CD collection database by their catalogue numbers. The program needs to accept a catalogue number, check that it is in the correct format (e.g. numeric), and then search for a matching catalogue number on the file. It then has to return the CD details if found, and an error code if not. Draw the structure chart for this program.

3.2 Decision tables

Another design tool that is useful where the processing in a program includes a range of true or false values is a decision table. A decision table has two parts – **conditions** and **actions**. All the possible combinations of conditions are listed at the top of the table. For example, consider an application which plans the food deliveries for a supermarket. Part of the program decides what type of lorry the food will be sent by. This choice is based on two conditions:

1   Is the food perishable?

2   Is the journey over 3 hours?

The top part of the decision table for this application therefore lists the four possible combinations, shown in Figure 1.7.

Conditions	Rule 1	Rule 2	Rule 3	Rule 4
Perishable food?	Y	Y	N	N
Journey over 3 hours?	Y	N	Y	N
Actions				
Normal lorry		X	X	X
Refrigerated lorry	X			

Figure 1.7   Decision table

The actions (i.e. what to do in each condition) are listed in the lower part of the table. In the supermarket delivery example, there are two possible actions – using a refrigerated lorry or using a normal lorry. If the food is perishable and the journey time is more than 3 hours, a refrigerated lorry is used; in all other cases a normal lorry is used. Therefore, the lower (actions) part of the decision table shows which type of lorry is used for each rule.

Decision tables make it easy to see that all the different possibilities have been covered, and they also help to design the code for the rules. The top half of the table makes up the If conditions, while the lower part shows what to do in each situation.

CASE STUDY

Ezee Klaim

Ezee Klaim is an insurance company. The company requires a program for insurance claims handling. The various rules that apply to how claims are authorised are shown in a decision table (Figure 1.8).

Note the pattern of Ys and Ns when the table is extended from two conditions to three conditions.

◆ Draw up a decision table describing a series of rules that apply in a situation you are familiar with – for example, the rules regarding bus pass applications, coursework hand-in rules, eligibility for allowances or benefits, and so on.

Data	Claims handling rule numbers							
Rules	1	2	3	4	5	6	7	8
Policy valid?	Y	Y	Y	Y	N	N	N	N
Claim below £10k?	Y	Y	N	N	Y	Y	N	N
No claims in last 6 months?	Y	N	Y	N	Y	N	Y	N
Actions								
Authorise	X							
Send inspector		X	X					
Refer to manager				X				
Refuse					X	X	X	X

Figure 1.8 Insurance claims handling decision table

Check your understanding

Northgate College

Northgate College has rules about how much students must pay to do a course.

◆ Overseas students must pay the full college fees.

◆ Home students receiving Jobseeker's Allowance (JSA) do not pay anything.

◆ Home students not on JSA and over the age of 21 pay 50% of the full fee.

◆ Home students not on JSA and under 21 pay 25% of the full fee.

Draw up a decision table for these rules.

3.3 Program design language

The design process having been started with the structure chart, a program design language then provides a way to add much more detail to the design for each procedure. There are a number of different program design languages that can be used. Two are described here: flowcharts, and pseudo-code or structured English.

Flowcharts

As the name suggests, a flowchart is a diagram showing the steps that must be taken to carry out some task. (Flowcharts can be used to design all sorts of processes, not just programming ones.) A flowchart is a good tool to use at the early stages of understanding how a particular procedure will work as it produces an easy-to-follow graphical representation of the processing involved.

Using a flowchart, the different programming constructs (sequence, selection and iteration) required to complete the required task within a particular procedure can be identified.

Flowcharts use a variety of symbols, linked by arrows to indicate the type of step involved at each stage. A sample flowchart is shown in Figure 1.9, which shows the steps for bubble sorting an array.

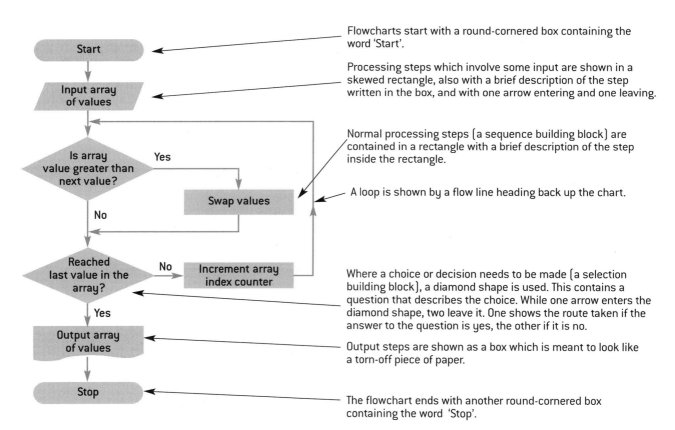

Flowcharts start with a round-cornered box containing the word 'Start'.

Processing steps which involve some input are shown in a skewed rectangle, also with a brief description of the step written in the box, and with one arrow entering and one leaving.

Normal processing steps (a sequence building block) are contained in a rectangle with a brief description of the step inside the rectangle.

A loop is shown by a flow line heading back up the chart.

Where a choice or decision needs to be made (a selection building block), a diamond shape is used. This contains a question that describes the choice. While one arrow enters the diamond shape, two leave it. One shows the route taken if the answer to the question is yes, the other if it is no.

Output steps are shown as a box which is meant to look like a torn-off piece of paper.

The flowchart ends with another round-cornered box containing the word 'Stop'.

Figure 1.9 Sample flow chart

Flowcharts are a good introduction to program design methods. However, they are not good for complex problems because the flowcharts themselves can become complex and difficult to follow. Furthermore, although they give a good idea of the general processing tasks required, they do not bear a particularly close resemblance to the code that will eventually be written.

CASE STUDY

Northgate College

A flowchart showing the process of validating a student's date of birth is shown in Figure 1.10.

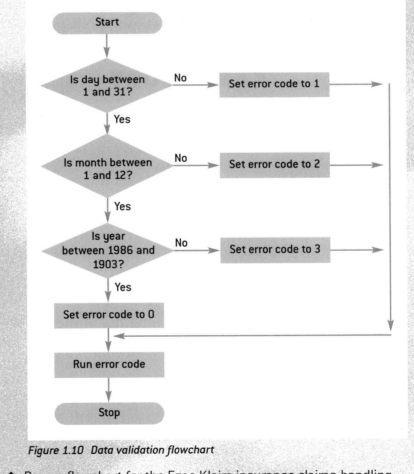

Figure 1.10 Data validation flowchart

◆ Draw a flowchart for the Ezee Klaim insurance claims-handling decision table example shown earlier in Figure 1.8.

Pseudo-code or structured English

Pseudo-code (sometimes called structured English) is a 'half-way house' between written English and programming code. It is sometimes used as the final stage in designing the processing involved, and allows a detailed design of the programming code to be produced without worrying too much about the exact syntax of the language. Pseudo-code uses typical program instructions and common programming keywords to implement control structures, such as:

- *If* to implement selection
- *Do while* and *Repeat until* to implement iteration.

There are no standards for pseudo-code, so common sense and a knowledge of programming languages are required. Instructions should include active verbs such as read, calculate or update, rather than vague phases or words like 'process'.

CASE STUDY

Ezee Klaim

The decision table for Ezee Klaim's claims-handling procedure (Figure 1.8) could be further developed by writing the pseudo-code:

```
If Valid = 'no' Then
    Print 'Reject'
Else
    If claimValue > 10 Then
        If noClaims = 'yes' Then
            Print 'Send inspector'
        Else
            Print 'Call manager'
    End If
Else
    If noClaims = 'no' Then
        Print 'Send inspector'
    Else
        Print 'Authorise'
End If
```

◆ Draw up the pseudo-code for the Northgate College decision table you created earlier.

PRACTICAL TASK 1.7

Write the pseudo-code for the date validation routine shown in the flowchart shown earlier in Figure 1.10.

3.4 File layouts

The way files need to be organised into records and fields has already been discussed (see page 22). The exact details of this arrangement must be designed and recorded using a table (sometimes called a **data dictionary**) which shows the fields contained in each record, the name of the field, its length and the type of data it stores.

Check your understanding

You decide to write a simple program – called My Contacts – that will be used to record contact details of your friends and relations. The file used to store the data could have a layout as shown in Figure 1.11. What field would you use as the key field?

Field name	Length	Data type
First_name	20	Alphabetic
Surname	20	Alphabetic
Home_phone	15	Numeric
Mobile_phone	15	Numeric
E-mail_address	15	Alphanumeric
Birth_date	8	Date (dd/mm/yy)
Address	20	Alphabetic
Town	20	Alphabetic
Postcode	7	Alphanumeric

Figure 1.11 File layout

PRACTICAL TASK 1.8

Create a file layout for the 'students file' of Northgate College.

3.5 Screen layouts

Most of the design methods looked at so far concentrate on the internal working of the program. The data to be input into the program will probably have been identified, but now it is time to design how the input screens will look to the user, and how the input data will be validated.

Data validation

Validation of data is important. You must make sure that only correct data is accepted, because incorrect data may cause problems when you try to process it. For example, a text value input when a numeric one is expected may cause the program to crash. Incorrect data such as a wrong postcode or invalid date of birth is useless. Two main types of validation check can be done.

◆ A **range check** checks that numeric data is within a valid range of values. Date checking is an example of this. Month numbers, for example, must be in the range 1 to 12. Any value outside the range is invalid and should be rejected.

◆ A **type check** tests input to ensure it is the correct data type. A person's surname, for example, must contain only alphabetic characters, while a quantity of items purchased must be numeric.

Check digits

Code numbers such as account numbers or ID numbers need to be correct. But unlike with data such as people's names, mistakes are not easily seen. To reduce errors, these code numbers sometimes have a check digit included.

A check digit is a value that is calculated from the other numbers in the code number. When the code number is input, the check digit is recalculated and compared with the number that is input. If the calculated check digit is different from the one that the user has input, then an input error must have been made. Many commonly used code numbers have check digits — credit card numbers, supermarket bar codes and ISBN numbers are examples.

Every book has an ISBN (International Standard Book Number), which is ten digits long plus a final check digit (or letter X, standing for 10). The ISBN number of the *BTEC First for IT Practitioners* course book is 0-435-45469-5, so the check digit is 5. To calculate an ISBN check digit, two steps are required.

◆ The first nine digits of the ISBN are multiplied by weighted values which correspond to the digit's position. So the first number (from the left) is multiplied by 1, the second by 2 and so on. All these values are then added together.

◆ The resulting value is divided by 11, and the check digit is *the remainder*.

So, using the ISBN for the book mentioned above, the check digit is calculated as follows:

$$0 \times 1 = 0$$
$$4 \times 2 = 8$$
$$3 \times 3 = 9$$
$$5 \times 4 = 20$$
$$4 \times 5 = 20$$
$$5 \times 6 = 30$$
$$6 \times 7 = 42$$
$$6 \times 8 = 48$$
$$9 \times 9 = 81$$

On adding these together we obtain a total of 258. When divided by 11 this leaves a remainder of 5 — which is therefore the check digit required.

Check your understanding

1 What check digit should be added to this ISBN number: 0-131-90190-?

2 A user has entered an ISBN number as 0-19-861200-3. Recalculate the check digit to find out whether the number has been input correctly.

Screen design

The layout of the contents of a screen is important because it forms the main user interface. If a screen is not labelled correctly or clearly, or is inconsistent or illogical in the order of the fields, users may find the program confusing and difficult to use. If the screen layout is messy, and contains spelling errors, users may come to the conclusion that the software is of poor quality.

Screen designs consist of three main parts:

◆ the screen layout showing the position of the various controls such as labels, input boxes and buttons

◆ the input data table, showing what data is input to each input box and how it is validated

◆ a table showing the error messages to be displayed if the validation of input data is unsuccessful.

The screen layout can be hand-sketched, or drawn using a graphics program, or laid out using a form design tool, such as that included in Visual Basic. Screen layouts must be clearly labelled, with the various controls placed in a neat and consistent way, with proper horizontal spacings and vertical alignment. The controls should be in a logical order; that is, they should be in the order the user is most likely to use them, from the top of the screen to the bottom.

CASE STUDY

Northgate College

The screen layout for the Northgate College student records system is shown in Figure 1.12.

The input data table for this screen is shown in Figure 1.13. Note that because this data is to be recorded on a file, the information about the field name, type and length will be the same as shown in the file layout.

The validation error code, along with the messages displayed, is shown in Figure 1.14.

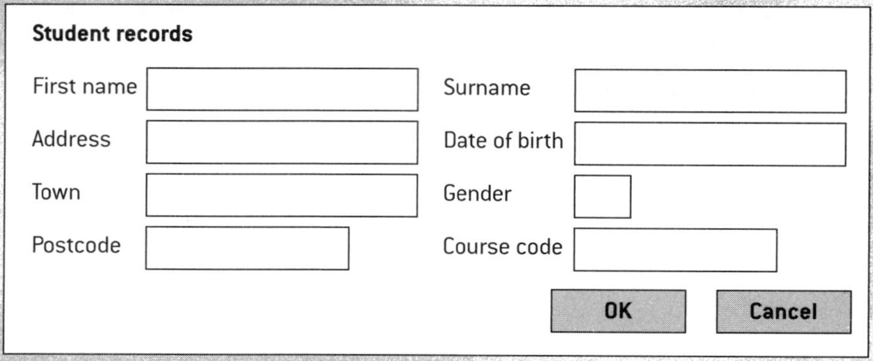

Student records

First name		Surname	
Address		Date of birth	
Town		Gender	
Postcode		Course code	

OK   Cancel

Figure 1.12 Student records input screen

Field	Field type	Field length	Validation
Surname	Alphabetic	20	Must be entered
First name	Alphabetic	20	Must be entered
Address	Alphabetic	20	Must be entered
Town	Alphabetic	20	Must be entered
Postcode	Alphanumeric	8	Must be in the format: AA99-9AA
Date of birth	Date (dd/mm/yy)	8	Must be a valid date
Gender	Alphabetic	1	Must be M or F
Course code	Numeric	4	Range 0001 to 1750

Figure 1.13 Input data

Error code	Error message
0	No error (no message displayed)
1	"Surname missing"
2	"First name missing"
3	"Address missing"
4	"Town missing"
5	"Postcode missing or invalid"
6	"Date of birth missing or invalid"
7	"Gender must be M or F"
8	"Course code missing or invalid"

Figure 1.14 The meanings of error codes

◆ What other information about the design for the screen would be useful?

Check your understanding

Create a data input screen layout for the My Contacts program data file, shown earlier in Figure 1.11.

When designing data input screens you must try to think of all the possible error conditions that could occur. Validation of the input data using range and type checks have already been mentioned. These are important and should prevent your program crashing because data input is of the wrong type. Also, they can help prevent invalid data getting into the system. Remember, too, that certain *combinations* of input data may be invalid. For example, imagine a program that allows users to order a new car on-line. If a user selects the convertible (open-top) version of a car, he or she should not be allowed to choose a sunroof as one of the optional extras!

Error conditions

Error conditions that cause a program to crash unexpectedly are clearly important to avoid. The main sources of these types of error are described below.

◆ **Invalid data type.** An example is trying to put a text value into a variable that has a numeric data type. Type checks should be used to prevent this type of error.

◆ **Arithmetic errors.** Certain types of calculation are invalid and will cause the program to crash, such as an attempt to divide a number by zero. Range checks should be used on input data to ensure zero values cannot be used in calculations using division.

◆ **Index number errors.** If a program attempts to access an array index that is greater than the size of the array, then the program will crash. For example, if a program has a ten-element array and a loop within the program attempts to access the eleventh element, the program will crash. Loops need to be carefully inspected and tested to ensure there are no circumstances in which this kind of error can occur.

◆ **File error.** If the program reads or writes to files, there are a number error conditions that can occur. The file may have been deleted or moved, the disk may be full, or some other kind of disk input/output (I/O) error may occur. The program must also never attempt to read records beyond the end of the file. Some of these types of error may be beyond the control of the programmer, so when carrying out file I/O tests, it is wise to use the error detection methods built into many programming languages to catch unexpected errors. Visual Basic has the 'on error goto' construct, while Java has 'try ... catch'.

Making sure a program is as error-free as possible is the purpose of program testing, covered in detail in the section on testing (see page 48).

3.6 Print layouts

Much of what has already been said about screen layout design applies also to printed reports. These, too, must be clear, neat, consistent and logical, with informative titles. Printed reports often include lines of information listed down the page. This information often needs to be listed in a particular order and perhaps grouped in some way. The field names of the data to be printed must be either drawn from the fields in the file layout or generated at print time.

CASE STUDY

Northgate College

A printed report that lists all the students, grouped by course number and sorted alphabetically within the course by surname, is required by the students record system. The layout for the report is shown in Figure 1.15.

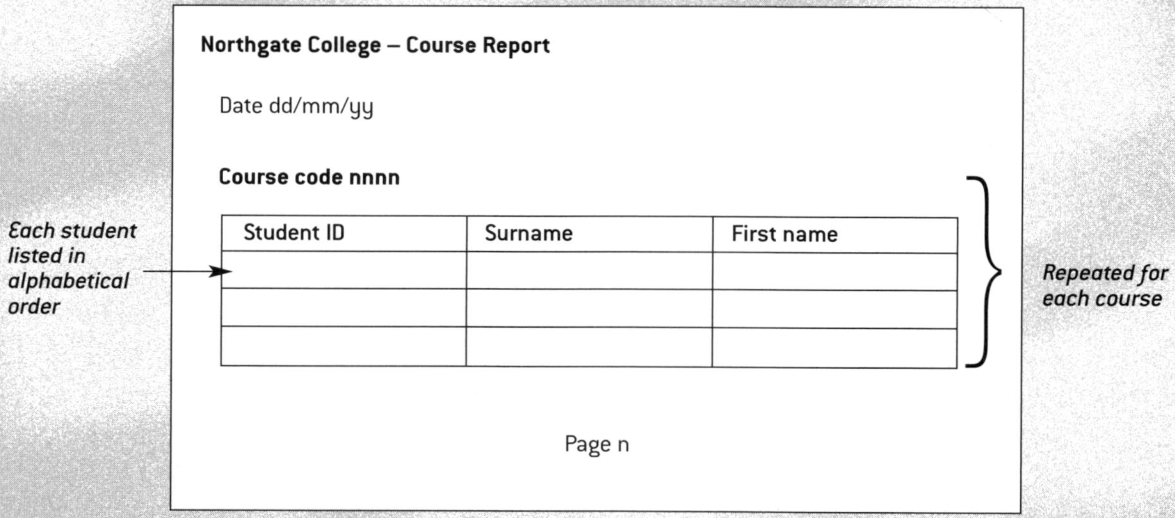

Northgate College – Course Report

Date dd/mm/yy

Course code nnnn

Each student listed in alphabetical order →

Student ID	Surname	First name

Repeated for each course

Page n

Figure 1.15 Print layout

◆ What other information about the design for the report would be useful?

3.7 A worked example

This section shows how the various tools described in the previous sections can be used to design a simple system. The system to be designed is a payroll system used to calculate monthly salaries based on rates of pay and hours worked.

Structure charts

The initial stage in the design is to decide what main functions the program will have. Information about this may well come from the people who will use the program – and will be detailed in the program specification. This program will have three main functions.

1 Add new or modify existing employee details.

2 Add details about hours worked.

3 Print salary slips.

These functions can be described in a simple structure chart as shown in Figure 1.16.

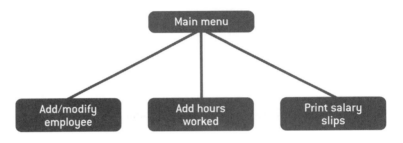

Figure 1.16 Structure chart for the payroll program

Detailed structure charts will be produced here only for the 'Add hours worked' and 'Print salary slips' modules.

A structure chart for the *Add hours worked* procedure is shown in Figure 1.17, in which there are three modules:

◆ *Find employee.* This module will have passed to it the employee's ID as a parameter, and it will search the data file containing the employee's details. It will return the employee's name (if found) or an error code (if not found).

◆ *Input details of hours worked.* This module will accept and validate the number of hours worked by the employee and the week number that the hours apply to.

◆ *Write hours worked to file.* This module will write the employee's ID and hours worked to the hours-worked data file. It will return a result code to indicate whether it was successful.

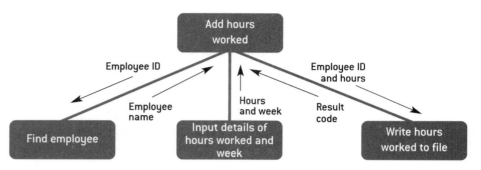

Figure 1.17 Structure chart for the procedure to add hours worked

It now becomes clear that *two* data files will be needed: an employee file and an hours-worked file. The layouts for these files will be defined later.

The structure chart for the *Print salary slips* procedure is shown in Figure 1.18. This procedure also has three modules:

◆ *Find employees and hours worked*. This module has passed to it the week number for which payslips are to be produced. It then searches through the hours-worked files to find records relating to this week. When it finds matching records, it will place them in an array and return that array to the main program when it reaches the end of the file. A *two-dimensional array* will be needed, containing the employee ID and the hours worked.

◆ *Calculate salary*. This module has passed to it the array created by the previous module and calculates the money due to each employee based on the hours worked. This data is placed in another array which is returned to the main program.

◆ *Print salary slips*. This module takes the two arrays created by the previous two modules (containing the employee details, hours worked and salary due) and formats the data into a printed payslip.

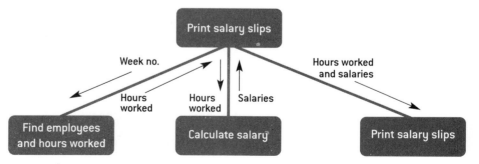

Figure 1.18 Structure chart for the procedure to print wage slips

Detailed designs

Now that the structure diagrams have identified the overall structure of the program, detailed designs should be produced for each module that has been identified. In this worked example, detailed designs will be produced only for the *Find employee* and *Calculate salary* modules.

First let us tackle the design for the *Find employee* module. When an employee's hours worked are being entered, the employee's ID number is used to identify the person. The purpose of this module is to check that the ID is valid and is the correct one. Having completed a validation check on the ID (more about that later), the program needs to loop through all the records in the employee file, checking to see whether a match can be found for the ID number that has been passed to the program. If no match can be found, then an error code is returned. If a match *is* found, the employee's name is copied from the file and returned to the main program. The flowchart for the program is shown in Figure 1.19.

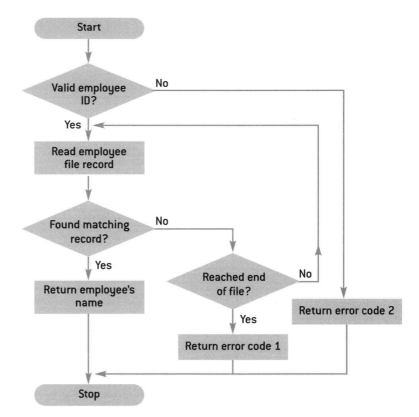

1.19 Find-employee flowchart

Next, the *Calculate salary* module has to take the number of hours worked and calculate how much to pay the employee. This company has two rules about salary calculations.

◆ If the employee is a supervisor, he or she is paid £9 per hour regardless of how many hours worked.

◆ If the employee is not a supervisor, he or she is paid £7 per hour. However, if the person works more than 35 hours in the week, he or she is paid £7.40 per hour.

These rules are summarised in the decision table shown in Figure 1.20.

Conditions	Rule 1	Rule 2	Rule 3	Rule 4
Supervisor?	Y	Y	N	N
Over 35 hours worked?	Y	N	Y	N
Actions				
£7 per hour				X
£7.40 per hour			X	
£9.00 per hour	X	X		

Figure 1.20 Calculate wage decision table

The flowchart which implements the rules shown in the decision table is shown in Figure 1.21.

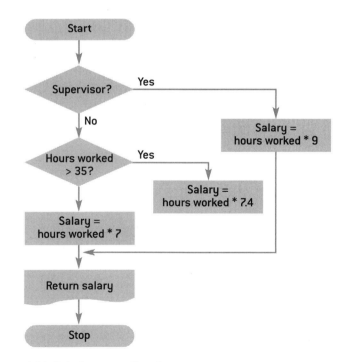

1.21 Calculate wage flowchart

File layouts

File layouts for the employee and hours-worked files are shown in Figure 1.22.

Employee

Field name	Datatype	Length
Employee_ID	Integer	6
First_name	String	25
Surname	String	25
Address_1	String	25
Address_2	String	25
Town	String	25
Postcode	String	7
Home_phone	String	12
Bank_AC_no	Integer	20
Supervisor	Boolean	-

Hours-worked

Field name	Data type	Length
Empolyee_ID	Integer	6
Week_number	Integer	2
Hours_worked	Integer	3

Figure 1.22 File layouts

Input and output specifications

An **input specification** will be produced here for only the 'Add hours worked' procedure. From the structure chart (Figure 1.17) it can be seen that this procedure is made up of three sub-procedures. However, a single input screen can be used to input details of the employees' IDs for whom the hours are to be added, the week number and the actual hours worked. The screen form layout is shown in Figure 1.23.

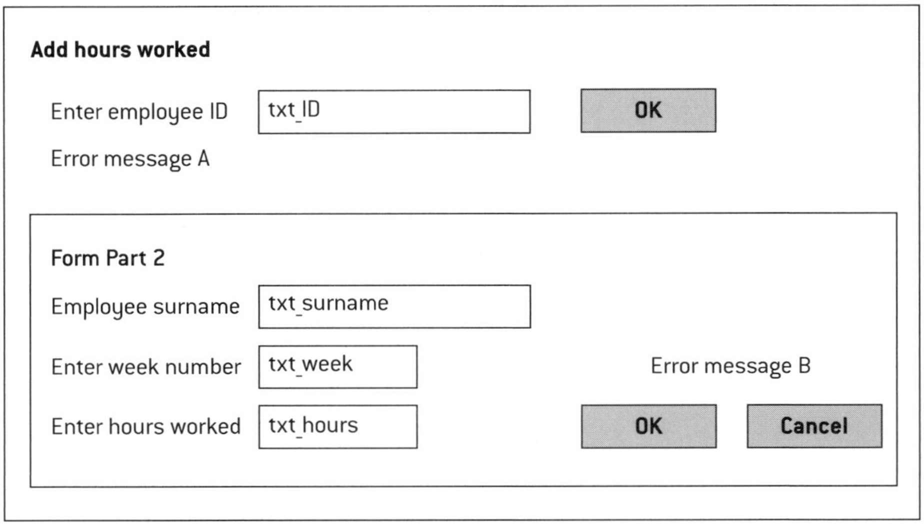

Figure 1.23 Add-hours-worked screen design

This is a two-part form. An employee's ID is entered in the first part and the OK button is clicked. If a valid employee ID is entered and that employee exists on the employee file, then the second part of the form appears, with the employee's surname shown in the *txt_surname* text box. Figure 1.24 lists the fields on the form and the validation rules applied.

Field name	Type	Validation
txt_ID	Input	Numeric, 6 digits
txt_surname	Ouput	-
txt_week	Input	Numeric, range 1 to 52
txt_hours	Input	Numeric, range 1 to 120

Figure 1.24 Fields on the form

There are two error message fields, detailed in Figure 1.25. Error message A is used to display any errors relating to an employee's ID, while error message B is used to display errors relating to the week number or hours worked.

Error message A	
Code	Message displayed
0	(no error)
1	Non-numeric employee ID
2	Employee ID not 6 digits
3	Employee ID not on file
Error message B	
0	(no error)
1	Non-numeric week number
2	Week number must be in range 1 to 52
3	Non-numeric hours worked
4	Hours worked must be in the range 1 to 120

Figure 1.25 Error messages

An output specification (print layout) will now be produced for the salary slips. These are simple printed sheets that are given to employees to show how much they are being paid and how it was calculated. The layout of the sheet is shown in Figure 1.26.

Salary slip

Date: dd/mm/yy

First name   Family name

Hours worked	Hourly rate	Total salary
n.n	£n.nn	£nnn.nn

Figure 1.26 Print layout for wage slips

PRACTICAL TASK 1.9

Complete the design for this system.

Chapter summary

This chapter has covered all the practical activities listed under the third outcome in the specification, including:

- structure charts
- decision tables
- flowcharts and pseudo-code
- data validation
- error conditions.

4 Validate the completed design specification

Having completed the design for the program, there are two important steps to be take before the program is actually written.

4.1 Verify the design

The design must be verified against the specification. The program specification lists what the users of the program want. It tells the designer what the program will do, what features it will have, what data it will accept or reject, and what calculations it will carry out. The program designer should use the specification as a type of guide book for writing the program.

However, sometimes the designer may forget or misinterpret some features listed in the specification and the design produced may not match the specification as closely as it should. Therefore, once the design is complete the designer (or if possible someone who has not worked on the design – since it is sometimes difficult to spot one's own mistakes) should go through the specification line by line checking that all the features and functions required have been covered in the design and that the design is *complete*.

As well as checking that the design conforms fully with the specification, it is also important to check that the design is *consistent*. **Consistency** covers a wide range of areas. It includes, for example, making sure that a sensible naming convention is used, making sure screen layouts have a uniform design, and ensuring that the design from the high-level structure diagrams through to the low-level pseudo-code is consistent – and in particular that there are no functions mentioned in the structure diagram for which no lower-level design exists.

4.2 Testing

Testing is a vital (though often unpopular!) part of software development. The users of the software would not be very impressed if the program produced the wrong answers, nor would they be happy if the program kept crashing. Testing is the process of checking that all the functions of the program work as they should and give the correct results. The definitions of terms like 'work as they should' and 'correct results' need to come from the original program specification that was agreed by the users and the developers before the program was written.

As well as checking that the program works correctly when used correctly, the software developer also needs to check that the program is robust and can withstand being used incorrectly to a great extent without crashing. The reason why this is important is because the users of the program are unlikely to be computer experts. They may misunderstand how the program is supposed to be used, they may also make mistakes when using the program – pressing keys or clicking buttons in error or making inappropriate entries in a text box.

The final testing of the program cannot be fully completed until the program is written. However, at this stage two aspects of the testing can be done.

1 **Test data** can be prepared.

2 **Dry-run testing** can be used to test the logic of the design.

Test data

Test data is input data that will be used to find out whether the program deals with it correctly. This involves choosing some input values and then manually working out what output the program *should* produce with these chosen inputs (the *expected outputs*). The program is then run using these input values and the expected outputs are compared with the actual ones produced by the program. If there is a difference between the expected and actual outputs, then the program has failed the test and will need to be modified so that the actual and expected values match.

The choice of input values is important. A range of values needs to be chosen in each of the following categories.

- **Normal values** are what would normally be expected as an input value.
- **Boundary values** would, in the case of a numeric input, be the highest possible value and the smallest possible value (i.e. the values on the boundary). In the case of a text value they might be a very large number of characters or very few. For example, in a text box where someone's name is to be entered, two extreme values might be 'Ng' and 'Fotherington-Thomas'.
- **Abnormal values** are invalid entries. Examples are 32/10/02 for a date, 205 for someone's age, or a text value where a numeric one is expected.

The test data with the chosen input values and the expected results is *recorded*, usually in some type of table – with an empty column for the actual results of the tests to be recorded once the program has been written.

Dry-run testing

Dry-run testing is used to check the logic of the design. It is particularly appropriate where the logic is complex, such as in nested If statements, or within loops. It involves working through the low-level design documents, such as pseudo-code, using imaginary input values, and keeping track, using a pen and paper, of the values that will be recorded in the variables the design uses.

Chapter summary

This chapter has briefly covered the practical activities listed under the fourth outcome in the specification (validate the completed design specification). A more detailed explanation of this topic can be found in unit 3 on testing.

Create software components using Visual Basic

The chapters in this unit are designed to be an introductory text to Microsoft Visual Basic. The aim is to provide a simplified guide to Visual Basic programming, and this should allow you to develop more advanced programs as your understanding of the subject increases.

Outcomes

◆ Manage the development environment

◆ Use components to create a graphical user interface (GUI)

◆ Create code for a specified software component

◆ Use the debug facilities of the development environment

◆ Test a software component and produce printed output

1 Manage the development environment

1.1 About the Visual Basic language

Visual Basic is a high-level programming language that was developed from an earlier program called Basic. Basic was a DOS-based language, and so its code looked a bit like English. This meant that it was a fairly easy language to learn.

Visual Basic's main advantage over Basic is that it is a *visual language* and requires you to create an interface as a starting point to creating an application. It is also an *event-driven programming language*, which relies on input from the user to define the relative actions and events that will take place. Users can click on objects in a random manner, so these objects have to be programmed individually to be able to respond to the user actions.

A Visual Basic application consists of many forms, each with their own objects and code that can be executed independently, yet still be part of a greater whole that is described as a Visual Basic application.

Programming languages were created essentially as problem-solving tools. These tools are used to define solutions to problems by creating programs based on a user-defined request. As tools, there are hundreds of programming languages, and these can be classified into two main types.

◆ **Procedural languages** specify a sequence of steps that are executed one at a time in response to different conditions and the actions of users. Some examples of procedural languages are Pascal, C++ and Java.

◆ **Event-driven languages** – of which Visual Basic is an example – do not follow a step-by-step logical progression of directions. In fact, the event is triggered by a user action – for example, clicking a particular key or checking a tick box on a form. The event, in this case a key click, causes the program to jump to a pre-written procedure that has been created to handle the specific event or action required.

1.2 The Visual Basic development environment

The development environment is the interface that is built by the programmer to:

◆ create a program

◆ run that program

◆ test the program to ensure that it fulfills the defined requirements.

The interface (see Figure 2.1) is the screen in the program that includes the work area, menus, icons, buttons and various windows.

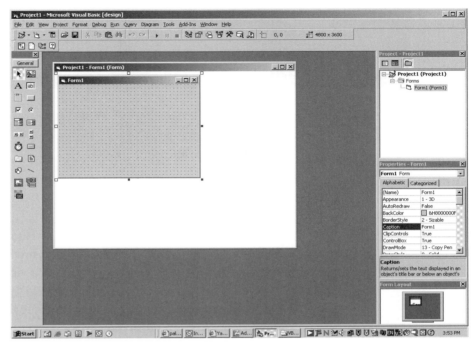

Figure 2.1 The Visual Basic development environment

The Visual Basic development environment contains tools and windows that are used to create Visual Basic programs. There are six main components of the development environment:

◆ menu bar

◆ form window

◆ toolbox

◆ properties window

◆ project explorer window

◆ form layout window.

The tools and windows that are used to create the applications are now examined, to provide you with a much better understanding of the role of each tool.

The menu bar

Visual Basic's menu bar provides a pull-down list of options that provide either commands, more levels of menus, or dialogue boxes that provide information about the user's choices (see Figure 2.2). Many of these menu options have *shortcut keys* which allow the user to make choices without selecting from the menu bar. For example, if you press the Ctrl and C keys, this is the shortcut key combination for the 'Copy' command. As you start out with

Visual Basic, one of the most important sections will be found on the menu bar – that is the 'Help' command which will provide guidance as you develop your programming skills.

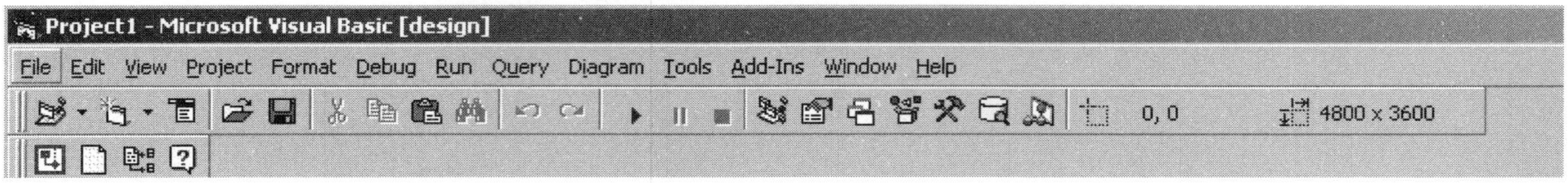

Figure 2.2 The menu bar

The form window

Forms are integral to the development of a Visual Basic program. You use the form window (Figure 2.3) to create the user interface by adding **controls** to forms (see Figure 2.4). Once the controls are included, you can then set or change the control's **properties**. The first form that you create – or *Form1* as it will be known until you change the name – is the default start-up form for your application.

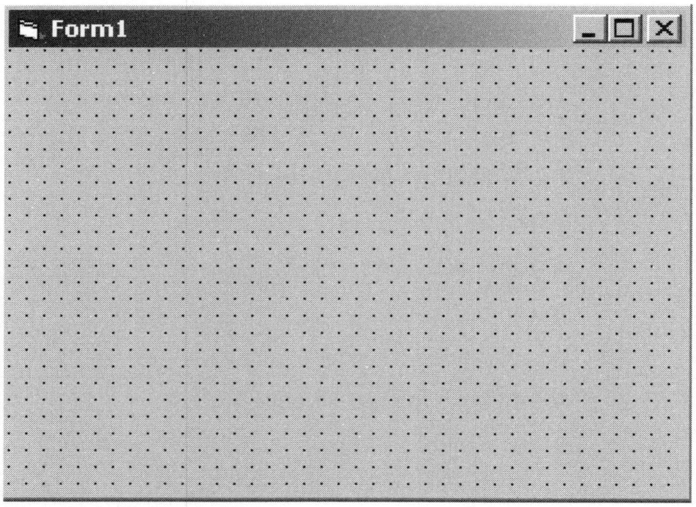

Figure 2.3 The form window

The toolbox

The toolbox consists of special tools called controls which are used to add the elements to the user interface that you are building. Figure 2.4 lists some of the elements that you can add to the user interface.

Figure 2.4 Visual Basic's toolbox

The properties window

To build a Visual Basic application, you place objects on a form. The objects that you place are selected from the toolbox and, once placed on the form, you will then change the **properties** of the object to represent the **attributes** of the objects (see Figure 2.5). A property is, therefore, a description of a feature of the object.

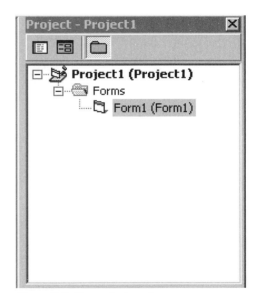

Figure 2.5 *The properties window*

The project explorer

The project explorer window provides you with a list of all the files in the project (see Figure 2.6). You can alter the display of the forms, by expanding or compressing the view to show more or less detail. The project explorer window displays forms, modules or other items such as classes and advanced modules. To select a specific form, double-click on the form in the project explorer window for a more detailed view.

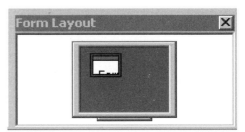

Figure 2.6 *The project explorer*

The form layout window

Whether you have one or more forms in your project, you can control or adjust the placement of the form when your program is running by using the form layout window (see Figure 2.7).

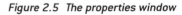

Figure 2.7 *The form layout window*

While you are getting to know Visual Basic, you will meet various terms which you may find confusing. They are there, however, to increase your understanding of the program language and its tools and windows. Table 2.1 provides a list of some of the more common terms and their definitions.

Table 2.1 **Terms and definitions**	
Terminology	**Definition of terminology**
Visual Basic Project	A project consists of one or more forms and other files which together make up the completed project. A project has only one property, its name.
Forms	The windows, through which the user accesses your application, are called forms at the development stage of the project.
Controls	Controls are the objects that are placed on to the form to display information or allow users to perform actions.
Properties	Properties are the characteristics of the objects or controls that are placed on to your form. They define their appearance and behaviour.
Events	Events are actions performed by either the user or the program and recognised by the control because of code that has programmed a response.
Procedure	A procedure contains code that enables events to perform actions on objects.
Methods	These built-in procedures enable an action to be performed on an object. For example list boxes have a Clear method. This empties the list box of items.

1.3 Creating your first application

When creating your first application, there are four major steps that you will follow.

1 *Create the interface:* define the form details, add controls to the form, and define the properties for the controls.

2 *Write the code:* create functions and procedures to control the application, and associate this code with the events of each control.

3 *Debug the program:* examine the lines of code to identify any errors.

4 *Test the program in various environments:* run the program to ensure that it performs as expected.

File types

Visual Basic uses various types of files, depending on what you are creating and saving. In Visual Basic the group of all the files that make up a program is called a **project**. These files may include forms, modules, graphics and ActiveX controls. The main thing to keep in mind about a project is that, as you create your program, each form is saved as an individual file.

The various file types are detailed in Table 2.2.

Table 2.2 *Types of file*	
FRM	The interface you use to create your application
BAS	Module or block of code not attached to a form
FRX	Automatically generated file for all graphic files in your project
OCX	ActiveX controls: additional controls that can be added into your toolbox, whether from Visual Basic or from third-party providers
VBP	Visual Basic project: a collection of files that make your application
EXE	An executable file which is a complete Visual Basic application

Note

When creating your applications and saving them, remember to try to use names that will help you to recognise what the files and projects represent. Meaningful names will act as a prompt to their contents.

Find and replace

The Visual Basic development environment enables you to keep track of your files. It is also possible to search for specific words and strings (which are collections of words) in your projects, to find files that you have lost track of. It even allows you to search for specific words and strings and replace them with different names. These tools are located in the *Edit + Find* command (see Figure 2.8).

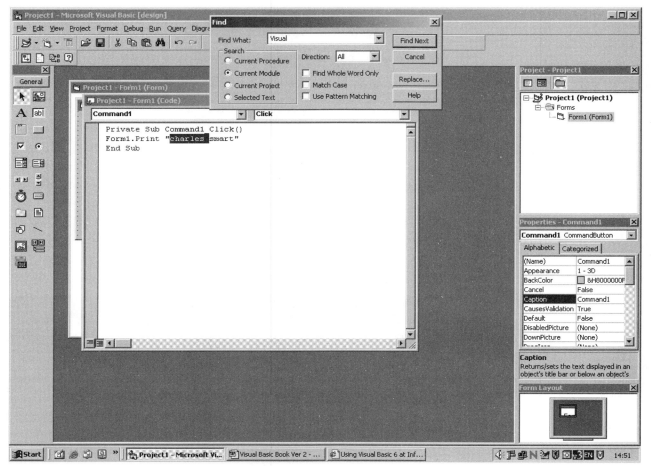

Figure 2.8 Find, Find Next and Replace menu items

PRACTICAL TASK 2.1

Your first application will be a very simple one – it will display your name on a form when the program is run.

1 Create a new folder on your hard disk to store all of your VB files.

2 Start Visual Basic and double-click the *Standard EXE* icon. Name your new project 'Students'.

3 Double-click on the command button in the toolbox. This will place a button on the form.

4 In the properties window, find the property called *Caption* and change the caption on the button from Button1 to 'Name'.

5 Double-click the command button on the form. This will open the code window. This is where you will enter program code to create events and statements.

6 Type the following line of code into the *Click event* of the command button (enter your own name):

    <\f>Form1.Print "*your name*"

7 Your first application is now ready to run, within the development environment. Press F5 to run the program.

Your application will now appear as a separate window in which there appears a single button labelled 'Name'. Click on the button and you will see your name appear in the window you have created. Congratulations – you have just written your first Visual Basic application!

To return to the development environment, click the 'X' button on the form and this will close the running program.

PRACTICAL TASK 2.2

Create a new form and place *two* command buttons on the form. Name one of the buttons 'Name' and the second button 'Postcode'. Enter code to display your name when the Name button is clicked, and your postcode when the Postcode button is clicked.

Chapter summary

◆ Visual Basic is an event-driven language. It does not follow a step-by-step logical progression of directions. Events in the application are triggered by user actions.

◆ A Visual Basic application is built in the VB development environment and is called an interface.

◆ To build an application, controls are selected from the toolbox and placed on to a form which is contained within a project.

◆ Controls – which are also known as objects – have attributes called properties which are features of the object. These can be changed or defined using the properties window.

◆ When the interface has been completed, code will be added to the forms and controls to provide actions to the defined procedures.

2 Use components to create a graphical user interface (GUI)

A Windows application is based on and developed in a window-based environment. These windows at the development level are termed **forms**. A complete application consists of a number of forms, and these forms or windows are used to display images or information, to allow data to be entered by the user, or to provide an interface that allows information to be selected by a user.

At the design stage, you – the creator of the project – will define the boundaries regarding the on-screen behaviour of the form and how the user will interact with it. The **interface** itself must be designed in such a way that the user will be able to access the controls that have been placed on it. This should also allow the user to intuitively navigate through the application without having to experience a long learning curve – which might well lead the person to close the application and find another with a better design.

The design of the interface must suit the users. Ask yourself these questions.

◆ Can the user access the controls that have been placed on the form?

◆ Can the user intuitively navigate through the application?

◆ Will the user experience a daunting learning curve while using the program?

◆ Might the user be tempted to close the application and find another with a better design?

2.1 Creating a form

When you launch the Visual Basic application you are presented with a default form, called Form 1, as in Figure 2.9.

Alongside the default form is the **toolbox** from which you will select the various objects and controls. On the right of the default form, notice the **properties windows** where you will adjust the properties of your controls, and the **project explorer** where the files within your project are displayed – so that you can add or remove files.

The form itself can be treated as a separate entity in terms of naming it and applying actions that will occur when the form is loaded. This will be separate from the actions of the controls and objects that are placed on the form to add the necessary functionality.

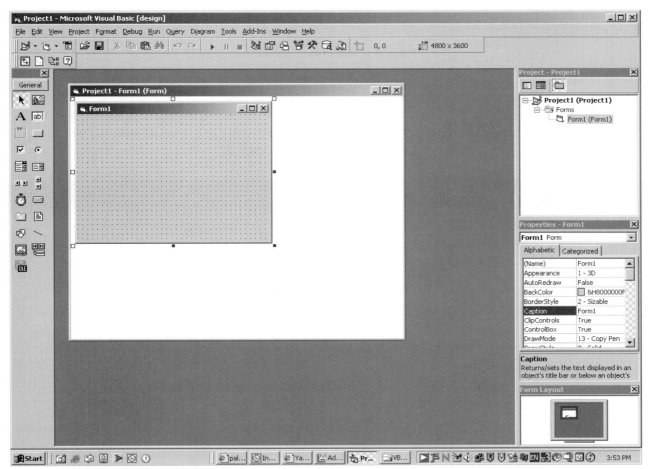

Figure 2.9 The default form

There is a custom that applies to naming forms and form objects. Commence the name using three letters in lower-case (depending on what object is being created) followed by the name of the object in mixed-case letters. For example, a form to receive data from a user might be named 'frmData'. If it was a button it might be named 'btnData'. This permits the type of object to be much more easily identified when reading the program code.

Properties of a form

The form itself will have individual properties that can be set either at design time or when the program is running. These controls affect the appearance of the program window, as well as the behaviour or the actions that occur when the program in run.

The properties themselves will define the size and position of the form window, the colour of the background, and the type, size and appearance of any text which may appear in the window. To bring up the properties window for any form, click on the form and the window will appear. The display will show the name of the property and the default settings of the form window.

Properties can be either single properties that are selected by choosing the appropriate section in the properties window, or they can have more than one option. These options are selected by clicking on items that will appear in drop-down lists. The main form properties that you will probably be changing on a regular basis are shown in Table 2.3.

Table 2.3 *Form properties*

Name:	This is the name of the form as it will appear in the Project explorer window.
Border Style:	This property will specify whether or not the window has a discernible border or the type of border that will be set for the form window. The choices are: **0** – *None:* This selection will create a window without title bar or control buttons. **1** – *Fixed Single:* This property will create a form window with a title bar, and the other buttons that you are used to seeing on a default form window. However, a user will not be able to change the size of the window when using the application. **2** – *Sizable:* This property allows the user to change the size of the form window during use and is the default setting for all new forms. **3** – *Fixed Dialog:* This property creates a form window with a title bar and a control menu button, and no other controls can be placed on the form. It will also prohibit the user from resizing the form during use. **4** – *Fixed ToolWindow* **5** – *Sizable ToolWindow*
Caption:	This property will set the name of the form within the title bar. Select *Caption* in the properties window and enter your chosen name.
Size:	This property allows you set the size of the form window. You can specify the distance of the border from the top and left-hand side of the screen and also the width and height of the form window.
Position:	This property allows you to alter the position of the form by moving it within the form layout window or directly by entering the necessary parameters in the properties window.
Minimise Button:	This property has one of two settings: it is either True or False. If it is set to True, the minimise button will appear on the title bar of the form window. If it is set to False, then the button will not appear on the form window.
Maximise Button:	This property has one of two settings: it is either True or False. If it is set to True, the maximise button will appear on the title bar of the form window. If it is set to False, then the button will not appear on the form window.

Saving the form

When you save a form, the contents of the form will be saved in a separate form file. Select *File + Save* and give the form a sensible name. The file will then be saved with an **extension** that will identify it as a form file – for example, frmNew.frm.

PRACTICAL TASK 2.3

In this activity you will create a new form, name it and change some of the form properties.

1 If Visual Basic is not already running, start it and ensure that you can see the default form, together with the toolbox and the properties window. If you cannot see these, then from the *View* menu select *Project Explorer* and double-click the form icon (see Figure 2.10).

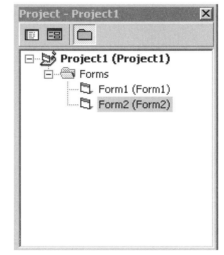

Figure 2.10 *Project explorer showing two forms*

2 If the toolbox is not visible, then from the *View* menu click on the *Toolbox* icon.

3 Click anywhere on the form to select it. Ensure that in the properties window you can see the name of the form in the title bar and under the Name property.

4 Go to the properties window and click on the *Name* item. Change the form name to frmData.

5 Find the *Caption* item within the properties window and change the caption name to 'Data entry'. When you look at the form you will see that the caption of the form is displayed in the title bar of the form (see Figure 2.11).

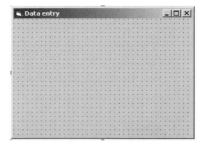

Figure 2.11 Form name in the title bar

6 Finally, save your work to date prior to adding objects to the form. From the *File* menu select *Save Form1 as*, and name it 'Data entry'. When you save the form, Visual Basic will add an **frm extension** to the file name and then display the saved form in the project explorer (see Figure 2.12).

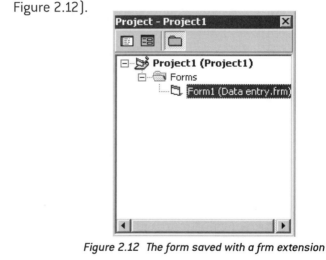

Figure 2.12 The form saved with a frm extension

2.2 Adding forms

You can create an application with more than one form, and you can add new forms to your project as you go along.

PRACTICAL TASK 2.4

To add a new form to your project, do the following.

1 Select *Project* from the menu bar and click on *Add Form*.

2 Click on the *Form* icon and select *Open*. A new form will be displayed with the same property settings as the default form (see Figure 2.10).

The properties for this new form can then be changed in the properties window.

Within the project explorer you will also see an entry for the new form. Remember that when saving these forms using the Save command, only the current form will be saved, so ensure that you click on each individual form before saving it.

Using the project explorer window you can also remove unwanted forms from a project.

PRACTICAL TASK 2.5

In this activity you will open a new form, and change some of the form properties and display your name on the form, when it loads and opens.

1 Launch Visual Basic and start a new project. If Visual Basic is already open, then click on *File + New Project* and select *Standard Exe*.

2 Click on the form window and ensure that the properties window is open and that you can see the default properties for the form.

3 Click on the *Name* property and type in the form name as frmMyName.

4 Click on the *BackColor* property and a palette of colours will be displayed. Select a colour from the palette and return to the form. Ensure that the colour you choose will not be too dark — to enable the standard text colour of black to be visible.

5 Click on the three dots (ellipsis) in the right-hand side of the *Font* property and change the font size to a larger size than that already displayed.

To have your name displayed on the form when it loads, you will need to write a little bit of code. For now, enter this code by following the instructions below.

6 Double-click anywhere on the form and the form window will open. You will be able to see the place where coding will be entered. There will be two lines of code — Private Sub Form_Load( ) and End Sub. It is between these two lines that you will write the code to allow your name to be displayed when the form loads (see Figure 2.11).

7 Type the following two lines of code between the existing two lines, ensuring that you place your name between double quotation marks:

```
frmMyName.Show/
frmMyName.Print"Charles Smart"
```

8 Click on the form name in the project explorer window and you will see your form again.

9 Click the *Start program* button and your program will then run and display your form (see Figure 2.13).

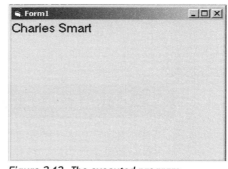

Figure 2.13 The executed program

10 Click on the *Close program* button to stop the execution of the program.

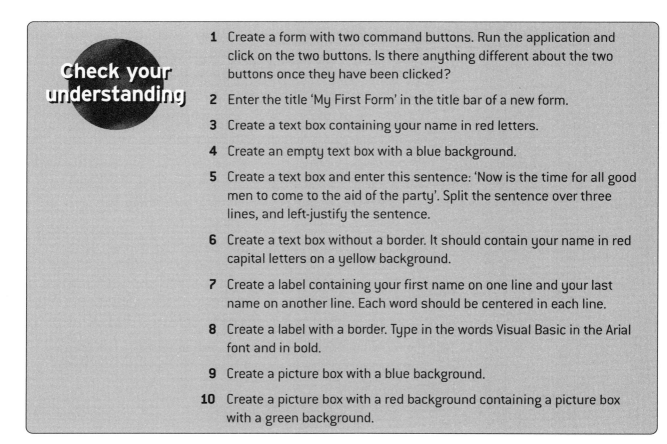

Check your understanding

1 Create a form with two command buttons. Run the application and click on the two buttons. Is there anything different about the two buttons once they have been clicked?

2 Enter the title 'My First Form' in the title bar of a new form.

3 Create a text box containing your name in red letters.

4 Create an empty text box with a blue background.

5 Create a text box and enter this sentence: 'Now is the time for all good men to come to the aid of the party'. Split the sentence over three lines, and left-justify the sentence.

6 Create a text box without a border. It should contain your name in red capital letters on a yellow background.

7 Create a label containing your first name on one line and your last name on another line. Each word should be centered in each line.

8 Create a label with a border. Type in the words Visual Basic in the Arial font and in bold.

9 Create a picture box with a blue background.

10 Create a picture box with a red background containing a picture box with a green background.

2.3 Working with controls

When you created a form and used the form load event to display your name and changed properties, you did not need anything on the form in order to produce a workable program. However, your programs would not have much functionality if all they did was to display forms with limited amounts of events occurring when the form was loaded. For real interactivity you need to add controls to allow users to interface with a program.

When you add controls to a form, you add them according to the design of the program that you are creating. You also try to limit the user's involvement in the process of adding information or interfacing with the form. This is achieved by ordering the controls in the way that you want them to be used. In other words, you must ensure that the interface will work in a manner that is **intuitive** to the user. Make the process of using the program as user-friendly as you possibly can.

The controls that Visual Basic provides are usually more than sufficient for your purposes. You can imagine them as being divided into two types: common or **standard controls**, and more advanced controls. For the activities in this unit you will use mostly the common properties, but later there will be activities that will enable you to use some of the advanced controls.

The standard or common controls are in the toolbox shown in Figure 2.4 on page 54.

2.4 Adding controls to a form

Forms are given functionality by adding controls to create the user interface. The controls will be components on the form. They will be used to either display information or accept input from the user.

Placing a control on a form

There are a number of ways of placing controls on forms. Two ways will be explained here. A third option – using code – will be examined at a later stage.

With a new form, and the toolbox viewable in the form window, you can click the control that you want to place on the form. On the form you then click where you want the upper-left corner of the control to be located, and drag with the mouse to where you want the bottom-right corner of the control to be located. The control will then be created on the form in the location you specified and with the size that you defined.

All controls have a **default size** defined by the program. You can therefore add a control to a form by either dragging it from the toolbox or double-clicking on the control in the toolbox.

PRACTICAL TASK 2.6

1 Click a control you want in the toolbox and drag it to a new form. The control is added to the form in the default size and at the location you have specified.

2 Identify another control you want to add and double-click on that control in the toolbox. The control will be added to the upper-left corner of the form in the default size. Change the location of the control by dragging it, and change its size.

Positioning a control on a form

There are a number of ways of changing the positions of controls on a form.

◆ You can double-click the control on the toolbox and a copy of the control will appear in the centre of your form. If you double-click another control, this one will appear in the centre of your form *on top of the existing control*. The second control can be dragged to a new position.

◆ If you place more than one instance of a certain control on the form, the second and subsequent controls will be numbered consecutively.

◆ You can also click the control on the toolbox once, and then place your cursor on the form and draw a control to an exact size and location.

◆ You can also click on a control and select *Edit + Copy* from the menu bar and create a version of your original control. This copied control will have the same properties as the original control.

PRACTICAL TASK 2.7

1 Click on a control with the mouse and then drag the control to any location on a form.

2 Click on the control and, using the arrow keys on the numeric keypad, move it to a new position.

3 Click on the control and, in the properties window, type a value for the *Location* property to position the control precisely on the form. The first number X is the distance from the left border of the form window; the second number Y is the distance from the upper border of the form window. Both are measured in pixels. Separate the numbers by a comma.

4 Click on the control and drag one of the eight sizing handles that appear, until you are satisfied with the size of the control.

2.5 Naming controls

When a control is added to a form, Visual Basic assigns it a name automatically. However, a control's name is very important, because when you are programming an event for that control you will refer to that name every time you want to do something with it.

The default name provided is not suitable, for the simple reason that with, say, three text boxes on a form they will be automatically named Text1, Text2 and Text3. If you then add two command buttons, they will be automatically named Command1 and Command2. This could become very confusing, especially when you are trying to change their order and remember what each control is supposed to be doing! The advantage of choosing meaningful names is obvious.

PRACTICAL TASK 2.8

1 Add a control to a form and adjust its size as before.

2 Open the properties window and find the *Name* option. Click the control's name in the right column.

3 Delete the default name and add the name you want.

When naming a control object, get into the habit of naming it with a three-letter lower-case prefix that identifies the type of object (in this instance the control) and then use a mixed-case name that will clearly identify the purpose of the object. If you create these names as you add objects to a form, you will avoid having to amend code at a later date to recognise names that have been changed.

For example, if you place a text box on a form to collect information from a user, you could name this control 'txtFirstName' to collect the person's first name. If it were a command button used to clear a form, you could name it 'cmdCancel'.

Table 2.4 displays some of the more common controls that can be placed on a form and gives examples of prefixes that can be incorporated into your programming.

Table 2.4 Common controls

Control	Prefix	Control	Prefix
Label	lbl	PictureBox	pic
Frame	fra	TextBox	txt
CheckBox	chk	CommandButton	cmd
ComboBox	cbo	OptionButton	opt
HscrollBar	hsb	ListBox	lst
Timer	tmr	VscrollBar	vsb
DirListBox	dir	DriveListBox	drv
Shape	shp	FileListBox	fil

2.6 Control properties

Control properties can be set at design time as already described. Alternatively they can be set at run time by means of appropriate code. These properties are shown in Table 2.5.

At design time, changing the properties of controls placed on forms can be achieved in two ways. You can select and change control properties individually, or you can select two or more properties at the same time.

◆ To select an individual control you need simply to click on that control and ensure that you can view the properties window.

◆ To select more than one property, you need to use the mouse to click in a blank area of the form just outside the controls you want to select and, while holding down the mouse button, drag the mouse to cover the controls you want. The selection that you have made will then be outlined with sizing handles (see Figure 2.14).

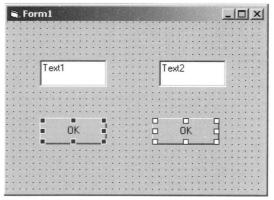

Figure 2.14 Selecting multiple controls

Table 2.5 Common properties of controls

Property	Definition
Appearance	To enable your property to be either seen or used and can be determined by selecting either the Visible or Enabled properties. The **Visible property** will determine whether the control can be seen when the form is run. The **Enabled property** will determine whether the control can be used when the form is run. Normally you will make your applications more user-friendly if your controls are usually visible but not necessarily enabled. This will obviously depend on the functionality of your application. You could use the Enabled property to make a text box read-only, for example. Making a control not visible could be used to require certain information to be entered before making the control visible – for example before saving the entered information.
Caption	This property will enable you to provide a descriptive title that will appear on the face of the control (e.g. on a command button that will be used to shut down an application, the caption could read CLOSE). If you type in an ampersand (&) in front of one of the letters of the caption, then that character will become an access key. In other words the character that is preceded by the & will be underlined. In this way you can select the control by clicking the *Alt key* together with the underlined character.
Colour	The background colour of a control or the colour of either text or graphics contained within the control can be altered by using either the **BackColor** property or the **ForeColor**. You can enter colour values, by either selecting from the palette of colours that is provided or by entering an RGB(red, green, blue) colour number. You can also enter your own colour if you know the hexadecimal numbers that represent the red, green and blue colours.
Fonts	If you have text displayed in your control, you can change its appearance by using this property. When you click on the property within its window, you will see a small button with three dots; clicking on this button will display the Font window. You will be able to set the font type, the font style, the font size and other characteristics of the text. If you make changes to the text, you will see an example of the changes within the sample window in the Font window.
Name	All controls will have a name. This name will be used when referring to the control in a procedure or code segment. Visual Basic will provide a default name for each new control that is added to a form, consisting of the control type and a number (e.g. Label1, Text1 etc.). Change the default name to something more meaningful to enable greater clarity when checking your code.
Size and Position	These properties allow you to determine the size and position of a control on the form. You can set the Width and Height properties to set the size and the Left and Top properties for the position of the control on the form. You can also set the size of controls directly by dragging the sizing handles on the control. However, for more accurate settings, set the properties.
Text	This property allows users to type directly into the control. You have the option to set a default value for this property and this will be displayed when the form is displayed – but will allow the user to overwrite the contents of the text property.

When using the second method, to remove one of the controls from the selection, you can either reselect or click on the control that you want to remove while at the same time hold down the *Shift* key. This technique can also be used to change the selected controls' properties at the same time, and to move groups of controls around on the form in order to change the position of that group.

PRACTICAL TASK 2.9

In this activity you will create a new form, change the properties of the form – including the name and caption properties – and then add controls and change the properties of those controls. Figure 2.15 shows the completed form, which you should refer to as you do this task.

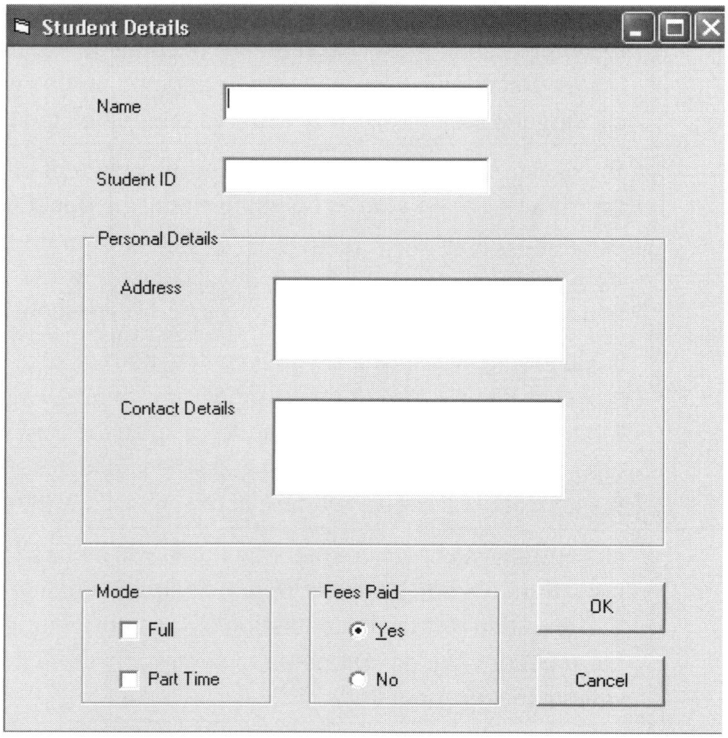

Figure 2.15 Student details form

1 Start a new project.
2 Click on the form window and ensure that the properties window is open and that you can see the default properties for the form. Click on the *Name* property and type in the form name as 'frmStudent'. Click on the *Caption* property and enter 'Student Details' as the property setting.

3 Click on the *Label* icon on the toolbox and draw a label on the form. Change its caption to 'Name'.

4 Click on the *Text box* icon on the toolbox and draw a text box next to the Name label. Change its *Name* property to 'txtName' and change its *Text* property to blank by deleting the text that was entered by default.

5 Click on the *Label icon* on the toolbox and draw a label on the form. Change its caption to 'Student ID'.

6 Click on the *Text box icon* on the toolbox and draw a text box next to the Student ID label. Change its *Name* property to 'txtStudentID' and change its *Text* property to blank by deleting the text that was entered by default.

7 Click on *Frame* on the toolbox and draw a frame on the form. Resize it to make it large enough to contain a label and a text box – and create these two elements (refer to Figure 2.15 for guidance). Change the frame properties to: name = 'fraPersonal' and caption = 'Personal Details'. Change the label properties to: name = 'lblStreet', caption = 'Street' and alignment = 'Street1 – Right Justify'. Change the text box properties to: name = 'txtStreet', caption = <blank>, and multiline = True.

8 Again click on *Frame* on the toolbox and draw another frame on the form, ensuring that this frame is large enough to contain two check boxes. Change the frame properties to: name = 'fraType' and caption = 'Mode'. Change the first check box's properties to: name = 'chkFull' and caption = 'Full'. Change the second check box's properties to: name = 'chkPart' and caption = 'Part Time'.

9 Again click on *Frame* on the toolbox and draw another frame on the form, ensuring that this frame is large enough to contain two radio buttons. Change the frame properties to: name = 'fraFees' and caption = 'Fees Paid'. Change the first radio button's properties to: name = 'optYes', caption = '&Yes' and value = True. Change the second radio button's properties to: name = 'optNo', caption = 'No' and value = False.

10 Add a command button to the form. Change its properties to: name = 'cmdOK' and caption = 'OK'.

11 Add another command button to the form. Change its properties to: name = 'cmdCancel' and caption = 'Cancel'.

12 Save the form, and then press F5 to run the application.

2.7 Common dialog control box

Windows-based applications need to load files or save files possibly on disk. This can lead to you writing a large amount of code. Fortunately, Visual Basic simplifies the process by using a common dialog control.

When you place a common dialog box on a form it will not be visible. This means that you will not be able to resize it or change its appearance. Your runtime code will have to display the common dialog box when necessary, and the appearance of the box will depend on what your code specifies at that time.

PRACTICAL TASK 2.10

This is how to create a picture viewer to enable your application to display various types of image files.

1 Place a picture box, a button and a common dialog control on a form. If the common dialog icon is not shown on the toolbox, select *Project + Components* from the menu bar and scroll down the list until you see the Microsoft Common Dialog Control 6.0 (SP 3). Tick the box next to the control and then click on OK. The control will then appear on the toolbox. Click it and drag it to your form.

2 Open the form's *Load event* and add the following two lines of code:

```
CommonDialog1.Filter = _
"Pictures (*.bmp, *.ico, *.wmf) | *.bmp, *.ico, *.wmf"
```

Then add the following three lines of code to the button's *Click event*:

```
CommonDialog1.ShowOpen
Set Picture1.Picture = _
LoadPicture(CommonDialog1.filename)
```

Test the application by running it. Find a bitmap file from the directory displayed.

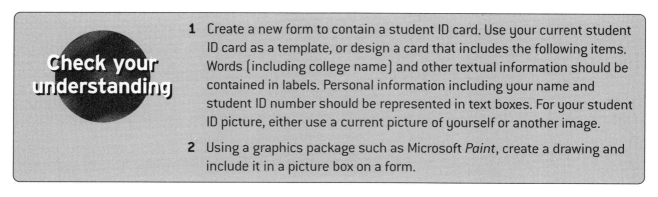

Check your understanding

1 Create a new form to contain a student ID card. Use your current student ID card as a template, or design a card that includes the following items. Words (including college name) and other textual information should be contained in labels. Personal information including your name and student ID number should be represented in text boxes. For your student ID picture, either use a current picture of yourself or another image.

2 Using a graphics package such as Microsoft *Paint*, create a drawing and include it in a picture box on a form.

Chapter summary

◆ Visual Basic allows you to create Windows-based applications. It does this by using forms to create windows that allow users to access and interface with applications.

◆ Visual Basic provides a default form with default properties – including a title bar, minimise and maximise buttons, a control menu box and a close button. The form controls allow you to amend the design of the form.

◆ A Visual Basic form can be configured by changing the form properties to perform actions and change the appearance of the form according to the design and purpose of the form.

◆ The forms that you create in Visual Basic can be tracked using the project explorer window to identify by name the forms that you have created as part of your application. The names of Visual Basic forms should be prefixed by the three letters 'frm' followed by the actual form name.

◆ To set the form title and display it in the title bar, select the caption option in the properties window and enter the appropriate name.

◆ When you save a form, its contents will be saved in a separate form file. The file will be saved with an 'frm' extension that will identify it as a saved form file.

◆ If the application you are creating requires more than one window, you can add new windows by adding new forms to the project at the design stage of the process.

◆ Controls are added to forms according to the design of the application and to ensure that the interface between the user and the application makes this process as user-friendly as possible.

◆ The standard controls provided are usually sufficient for the purpose of creating most types of application. These controls can be augmented with more advanced controls as your applications become more specialised.

◆ All of the controls provided have default properties which can be altered or amended to represent application functionality.

◆ Once controls are placed on a form they can be selected individually or as a group.

3 Create code for a specified software component

You have seen that Visual Basic programs consist of forms with objects placed on them. These objects are then programmed to respond to either user input or other functions.

The types of object that can be placed on a Visual Basic form are quite varied. They can range from objects that enable the user to click, drag or enter information into a text box. It is also possible to move through the objects on a form in any order that the user likes. This functionality forces the programmer to avoid restricting the user to following a pre-determined path through the program.

So, whatever the user does it will be a direct result of the design of the form and the objects that are placed on it. The programmer must create a robust design that will allow the user to feel comfortable using the program. If the programmer finds it necessary to limit the user's involvement in the program, then buttons can be 'greyed out' (made non-functional).

This is the Visual Basic approach to programming using an event-led approach that allows the program to respond to the user's actions. This approach leads us nicely into the next chapter of this unit — the programming of objects using coding techniques.

The user interface is the link between your application and the end user. A well-designed interface makes it easy for the user to learn how to use your application. Conversely, a poorly designed interface will lead to user problems and frustration. A little preparation will go a long way to helping you create a viable and effective application that is simple to use and understand.

3.1 Approaches to coding

When coding your events and objects, bear in mind that good presentation of the code will enable any subsequent editing or error correction to be simplified. To this end, when you are writing code make good use of two simple techniques:

◆ **indentation**

◆ **comments.**

Even though it is not really necessary to indent code as you write it, it is still good practice. If you use *a consistent indentation policy*, it will improve the readability of the code and make examination or analysis of it much simpler. The following piece of code illustrates how effective indentation can be:

```
Private Sub Form_Load()
Dim Score As Integer
Score = InputBox("Enter a score from 0 to 100")
   If score >= 85 Then
      MsgBox "Excellent"
   ElseIf Score >= 65 Then
      MsgBox "Good work!"
   Else
      MsgBox "You need to work harder!"
   End If
End Sub
```

A **comment** is a message or remark that you put inside a program's code to clarify it and to aid future maintenance. Visual Basic will ignore all comments because they are for people looking at the program code. Users do not see comments because they do not see the program code.

Programmers add comments to their code for the following reasons:

◆ to describe in the general section the overall goal of the program

◆ to describe at the top of every procedure the particular goal of that procedure

◆ to explain tricky or difficult statements so that others who modify the program later can understand the lines of code without having to decipher cryptic code.

Even if you simply write programs for yourself, still add comments! Weeks or months later you will have forgotten the exact details of the program, and comments that you interspersed throughout the code will help you to find code that you might need to amend. Try to add these comments as you write the code. Their free-form nature enables you to add comments whenever and wherever needed.

Visual Basic supports two types of comment:

◆ comments that begin with the **Rem** statement

◆ comments that begin with the apostrophe (').

What does it mean?

*When a line of code begins with the **Rem** statement, anything that follows on that line of code will be completely ignored when the program is executed. When the program is displayed or printed, the comments will be displayed or printed. Rem statements and any text following an apostrophe will be displayed in a different colour.*

The Rem statement is more limiting than the apostrophe and is not as easy to use. Nevertheless, you will come across programs that use Rem statements, so you should learn how it works. This is the format of the Rem statement:

```
Rem The remark's text
```

You can put anything you want in place of 'The remark's text'. The following are examples of comments:

```
Rem Programmer: C Smart, 30 June 2004


Rem This program supports the check-in and check-out
Rem process for the dry-cleaning business.


Rem This event procedure executes when the user
Rem clicks on the Exit command button. When pressed,
Rem this event procedure closes the program's data
Rem files, prints an exception report, and terminates
Rem the application.
```

The first of these lines consists of a one-line comment that tells the programmer's name and the date the program was last modified. If someone else must modify the program later, that person can possibly track down the original programmer if needed to ask questions about the code.

The second comment describes the overall program's goal by starting with a high-level description of the program's purpose. The third comment might appear at the top of a command button's click event procedure.

As you can see, you can add one or more lines of comment depending on the amount of description needed at that point in the program. Visual Basic ignores all lines that begin with Rem.

What happens if you use apostrophes in place of the Rem statement in the previous comments? The following rewritten comments demonstrate that they are even more effective because the word 'Rem' doesn't get in the way of each comment's text:

```
' This program supports the check-in and check-out
' process for the dry-cleaning business.
' This event procedure executes when the user
' clicks on the Exit command button. When pressed,
' this event procedure closes the program's data
' files, prints an exception report, and terminates
' the application.
```

The comments do not have to go at the beginning of event procedures. You can place comments between lines of code, as done here:

```
Dim intRec As Integer
Rem Step through each customer record
For intRec = 1 To intNumCusts
' Test for a high balance
```

```
        If custBal(intRec) > 5000 Then
        Call PayReq
        End If
    Next intRec
```

You can place apostrophe comments at the end of Visual Basic statements. By placing a comment to the right of certain lines of code, you can clarify the purpose of the code. Consider how the following code section uses a comment to explain a specific line of code:

```
    a = 3.14159 * r ^ r        ' Calculate a circle's area
```

By reading comments, you can understand the code's purpose without taking the time to interpret the Visual Basic code. However, ensure that your comments are informative – do not comment just for the sake of it. The following comment is unnecessary as the code is self-explanatory:

```
    Dim Sales As Single        ' Define a variable named Sales
```

3.2 Why coding is needed

It is possible to create applications or programs that simply require the placement of objects on a form and the changing of object properties. However, in order to create useful applications you have to add code to create relationships between objects or controls and to be able to perform calculations. It would not be possible to add a control to a form that would allow a user to perform salary calculations – code is needed to perform the relevant calculations. The code itself that you write is a detailed set of instructions that will tell the program what functions to perform that will respond to user input.

Much of the code in a Visual Basic application consists of small **event procedures** that respond to various events. Typically the controls on a form trigger the events when a user interacts with the program by selecting these controls. An event is what happens when a user clicks a button, or double-clicks an object. An application can have a large number of events that can be triggered by the user. You, the programmer, choose the events that you want to be responded to and then add the code to tell Visual Basic what to do.

3.3 Writing event procedures

Code for event procedures is entered through the code window, as shown in Figure 2.16.

To access the code window, double-click on any control. The code associated with that object can then be entered into the window. Underneath the title bar of the window on the left-hand side you can see the type of object you are currently working on – Form. On the right-hand side of the window you can see the event that you are writing code for – Load. The code that you write is

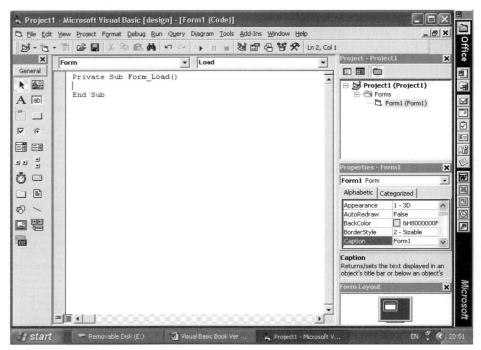

Figure 2.16 Visual Basic code window

called an **event procedure**. The procedure's name consists of the name of the object (in the above example it is the form) followed by an underscore and then the name of the event (in the above case it is the Load event). The code will be entered between the **Private Sub** statement and the **End Sub** statement.

When code is connected to a specific form, it is called a **form module**. Within the form module will appear the event procedures for that form. You will also find other code here that is not directly connected to events – such as calculations and routines for sorting data. All applications will consist of at least one form and will therefore have at least one form module. This is created in Visual Basic by adding a new form module to every form that you add to a project.

In the bottom-left corner of the code window there are two more buttons: Full Module View and Procedure View.

◆ **Full Module View** will show the code associated with that form module in a continuous list with a horizontal line separating each code procedure.

◆ **Procedure View** will show the code for the current event that is being viewed.

As well as form modules, an application can contain **standard modules**. A standard module contains code but has no forms or controls associated with it. The code that is entered in a standard module will be used within several applications. For example, you may write code to calculate a salesman's commission using different calculations relating to the value of total sales. You would create the standard module and then add it to applications that can use the module. This saves you having to type the same piece of code in different applications.

3.4 Types of data

The data that will be entered into an application is not the same as the code that is written to control the event procedures. Those procedures will only process the data that is entered.

There are three main categories of data that you will be using:

◆ numeric
◆ string
◆ special.

Numeric data is – as its name implies – mainly numbers. **String data** consists of a series of zero or more characters that will be treated as a single entity, such as a person's last name. **Special data** consists of other data type categories, such as dates or True and False values.

Table 2.6 shows a complete list of the data types that are supported by Visual Basic.

Table 2.6 *Visual Basic data types*			
Data type	**Description**	**Values**	**Bytes**
Integer	Whole numbers	−32,768 to + 32,767	2
Long	Whole numbers	−/+ 2147,483,648	4
Single	Decimal numbers	Very small to very large	4
Double	Floating-point numbers	Up to 16 significant digits	8
String	One or more characters	Text values	1 each
Date	Dates and times	Dates and times	8
Currency	Monetary values	Exact number of decimal places	8
Boolean	True or False values	True or False	2
Variant	Any type of value	Any value	16+1 each

3.5 Variables

Computer programs require data to be stored in temporary locations while applications are being executed. If, for example, you wish to store information that has been entered in text boxes by a user, then this data has to be stored somewhere until the program is ready to use it. The data is actually kept or stored in an area of the computer's memory, and this area is called a variable. Each variable is given a name, called an **identifier**. When a variable name is first identified and used within a program, Visual Basic will create the temporary storage needed and assign to it a value that is dependent on the type of data to be stored.

Default values

If the variable is a numeric variable then the default value will be zero. Otherwise the default value assigned will depend on the type of variable: null string for a string variable, or False for a variable with Boolean values.

*A **Boolean** value is one that is either True or False.*

The process of creating a variable requires that it first has to be declared within the program (to be described later). Then the variable will be assigned a value that can be retrieved as the program runs or changed whenever it is necessary, according to the program code.

Naming variables

There are certain rules that have to be followed if you want to avoid problems within your programs.

You should use names that will make sense to you later, and which represent the type of data that is going to be stored within them. For example, if you are creating a variable to store birth dates then it could be 'BirthDate'. The rule of thumb, therefore, is to choose names that are meaningful to the data stored within them.

Here are the rules for naming variables:

1 Variable names can consist of letters, numbers or the underscore character (_) and can be up to 255 characters long.

2 Variable names must start with a letter.

3 Variable names cannot contain spaces or any symbols.

4 Variable names can have upper- or lower-case letters.

5 Variable names must not have the same names as the Visual Basic **keywords**. These are names that have special meaning within Visual Basic, such as And or Command.

Declaring variables

Once you have decided on the name and type of variable to use, the next step is to declare the variable. This is the process of specifying the name and the variable type. If you do not specify a data type when declaring a variable, its default data type will be that of a **variant**.

If more that one variable is declared on the same line of code, you must ensure that you separate each type with a comma, and the data type must be provided for each variable name.

Dim and As

When declaring variables you must make use of the Visual Basic keywords, **Dim** and **As**.

The following code extract declares variables of different data types:

```
Dim Number As Integer
Dim Name As String
Dim DateofBirth As Date
Dim Choice As Boolean
```

These individual variable declarations could have been written on the same line, like this:

```
Dim Number As Integer, Name As String, DateofBirth As Date,
                                          Choice As Boolean
```

When creating applications it is a good idea to get into the habit of always declaring variables *before you commence programming*. Visual Basic will allow you to use variables that you have not declared, but this is highly likely to create problems as you develop your application.

It is possible that the use of upper or lower case, or similar names, could lead to confusion, so it is much more efficient to declare your variables first. To ensure that you do declare your variables, you can set the program to require variable declaration at the start. There are two ways of doing this.

◆ The first way is to write the phrase 'Option Explicit' before declaring a variable, like this:

```
Option Explicit
Dim Item as Integer
```

◆ The second way is to click on *Tools* in the menu bar and select *Options*. Click the check box *Require Variable Declaration*. This will force Visual Basic to automatically put the phrase 'Option Explicit' in the code window.

Before you go any further, go to the Tools *menu and change the option to require all variables to be declared by ticking the* Require Variable Declaration *box.*

Assigning values to variables

Having declared your variables, you are now ready to assign values. The values that you will assign will obviously relate to the type of data that the variable can store.

To assign a value to a variable after declaring it, use the following code extract:

```
Option Explicit
Dim Item as Integer
Item = 50
```

This example declares a variable called *Item* as an *Integer* data type.

The declaration **Integer** *means that the variable will store whole numbers.*

The process of creating a variable requires that it first has to be declared within the program. Then the variable will be assigned a value that can be retrieved as the program runs or changed whenever it is necessary, according to the program code.

The line 'Item = 50' will place the value 50 into the variable *Item*. Now, wherever you refer to that variable in your program, the value 50 will be substituted.

Scope of variables

There will be times when you will want to define variables to cover specific parts of the program or all parts of the program. This means that you need to understand the concept of scope as it relates to programming.

Scope is an important concept. Here we are interested in two levels of scope as it applies to Visual Basic.

◆ **Local scope**. Variables that are declared at the start of a procedure are available only within that procedure. They are therefore not available for use by the rest of the application.

◆ **Global scope**. Variables declared at the *form level* are available to all procedures on that form. They are therefore not restricted to one particular procedure.

Declaring constants

A **constant** is a value that you do not want to change – you will use it within your application as a fixed value. For example, when creating an application to calculate value-added tax (VAT) on various items, you would declare the percentage rate of tax in a constant variable. This avoids the need to declare the tax rate whenever it is needed in the program. If the tax rate changes at a later date, it is necessary only to change the declaration in one location in the code.

A constant variable is declared using the **Const** keyword. This is the format for the assignment statement:

```
Variable Name = Expression
```

The code extract for the example would be as follows, assuming a VAT rate of 17.5 per cent:

```
Const VatRate As Single = 17.50%
```

To store a value for the current exchange rate of the pound sterling against the euro, you would do it this way:

```
sngConvert = 1.44
```

Note that the data type of the expression must match the data type of the variable to which you are assigning it. If you mismatch data types, Visual Basic will produce an error. For example, this assignment would not work:

```
sngConvert = "One pound forty four pence"
```

the reason being that 'sngConvert' is a variable of the data type single, while the phrase 'One pound forty four pence' is a text string.

3.6 Using operators

One of the advantages of using variables is that they make it possible to perform calculations on data that is entered either at the design stage of the project or later by the user. The calculations are performed using operators.

Table 2.7 lists the **arithmetical operators** that you will need to know at this stage. It also sets out the order in which the operations will be carried out in situations where several operators appear together – their **order of precedence**.

Table 2.8 explains the meanings of these arithmetical operators and gives examples of their use.

Table 2.7 *Arithmetical operators*

Arithmetical operator	Representation	Order of precedence
Exponentiation	^	1
Negation	–	2
Division	/	3
Multiplication	*	3
Integer division	\	4
Modulus	Mod	5
Addition	+	6
Subtraction	–	6

Note

Division and multiplication, and addition and subtraction, have equal precedence. They are carried out working from left to right.

Table 2.8 *Definitions of arithmetical operators*

- The *exponential operator.* The exponential operator (^) is used to raise a number to an exponent – for example, raising 2 to the power of 3.

- The *negation operator.* The – sign is used to indicate the negative value of an expression.

- The *division operator.* The / operator is used to find the result of dividing one quantity by another.

- The *multiplication operator.* The * operator is used to find the product of two numbers.

- The *integer division operator.* The \ operator is used for division, and returns an integer result. For example, in the expression 5 \ 2 the result would be 2.

- The *mod operator.* The mod operator is used to find the remainder part of a division. For example, in the expression 50 Mod 6 the answer would be 2.

- The *addition operator.* The + operator is used to find the sum of two numbers.

- The *subtraction operator.* The – sign is be used to subtract one number from another.

PRACTICAL TASK 2.11

Perform the calculations on the following sums and complete the table with the correct answers.

Operator	Name	Sum	Result
+	Addition	10 + 5	
−	Subtraction	10 − 5	
−	Negation	−10	
*	Multiplication	10 * 5	
/	Division	10 / 5	
\	Integer division	10 \ 3	
∧	Exponentiation	10 ∧ 2	
Mod	Modulus	10 mod 3	

When using arithmetical operators, remember that inserting round brackets (parentheses) in an expression will override the natural order of precedence. Any items inside parentheses are calculated first. Ensure that you use parentheses always in pairs (it is a common mistake to forget the closing bracket). If you place parentheses inside parentheses – or in other words, **nest** them – the calculations will start with the innermost parentheses and work outwards. Here is an example:

$$10 + (2 * (24 / 8 + 5)) / 2$$
$$= 10 + (2 * 8) / 2$$
$$= 10 + 16 / 2$$
$$= 18$$

PRACTICAL TASK 2.12

Examine the following list of items. Identify variable or constant names, and data types. Write out the variable declarations.

First name   Annual salary
Last name   Income tax rate
Date of birth   National Insurance no.
Age   Smoker? (Y/N)

When you have decided on variable or constant names and data types, assign relevant values to them.

There are two more types of operator you need to know about:

◆ **Relational operators**: <, >, <>, <=, >= are introduced on page 88.

◆ **Logical operators:** And, Or, Not are introduced on page 92.

CASE STUDY

Heart rates

The British Medical Association has issued advice about optimum heart rates that should be maintained when performing physical activities. Your training heart rate – the optimum rate at which your heart should beat so as to maximise aerobic benefits – is calculated using a formula that they have created. The formula is:

$$0.7 * (220 - a) + 0.3 * h$$

where a is your age and h is your resting heart rate (determined to be your pulse when you awake in the morning).

◆ Create a program that will request a person's age and resting heart rate, calculate his or her optimum training heart rate, and display the result. Use this program to calculate your personal training heart rate. Remember to choose sensible names for the variables and to present your code clearly.

Check your understanding

1 What two characteristics does Visual Basic need to declare a valid variable?

2 What keywords are necessary for Visual Basic to recognise what you are typing as a variable declaration?

3 What phrase would you include in code to force Visual Basic to require variables to be declared before they are used?

4 What does the 'scope' of a variable relate to, and what are the two main types of scope?

5 Define the term 'constant' as it applies in Visual Basic, and provide an example.

6 What are the eight arithmetic operators, in order of precedence?

7 How does one declare two or more variables on the same line? Provide an example, using *three* variables of *two* different data types.

3.7 Comparison operators

Comparison (or **relational**) operators compare data, and are used in program constructs for selection so that decisions based on the comparison results can be made at run time.

Comparison operators produce results that are either True or False. For example, if a comparison operator returns False when comparing whether a salesman's total sales for a period exceeded a pre-determined level, then the calculation of his salary will be without a performance bonus for exceeding the sales figure.

Table 2.9 describes Visual Basic's six comparison operators. The comparison operators can be used to compare numbers against numbers, or any kind of string against another string. In fact, comparison operators compare either variables, literals, control values, or combinations of these data sources.

Table 2.9 **Comparison operators**	
Operator	**Description**
>	The **greater than operator** compares whether one value is greater than another.
<	The **less than operator** compares whether one value is less than another.
=	The **equal to operator** compares whether values on both sides of the sign are equal to each other.
>=	The **greater than or equal to operator** compares whether one value is greater than or equal to another.
<=	The **less than or equal to operator** compares whether one value is less than or equal to another.
<>	The **not equal to operator** compares whether a value is not equal to another value.

You must understand how to use the True or False result. Table 2.10 illustrates how the various operators can produce values that are either True or False.

Table 2.10 **Using comparison operators**	
Relation	**Result**
380 > 375	True
375 < 333	False
41 < 50	True
99 <= 100	True
"O'Neill" < "o'neill"	True
100 >= 100	True
0 <= 0	True
1 <> 2	True
2 >= 3	False

Take extra care that the expressions on each side of a comparison operator conform to the same data type, or at least compatible data types. In other words, you cannot compare a string with a numeric data type. If you try to do that, you will get a **type mismatch error**. You can compare any numeric data type against any other numeric data type – most of the time. In other words, you can test whether a single value is less than or greater than an integer value.

Comparison operators can compare values for equality, inequality and differences in size or nature. On their own these operators would not have much utility, but they can be used to compare data by using **selection constructs**.

Selection constructs

Selection means that either one or more lines of code within an application may execute depending on whether a defined condition is True or False. The simple examples we have looked at so far have started at the first line of code and worked down in a linear fashion until the last line of code has been executed. This is an idealised situation – procedures are not all like that. There will be times when choices have to be made; and, as a result of those choices, statements will be executed only if a particular condition is True. An example is the use of an error message to warn the user that a particular value has not been met.

Visual Basic has two selection constructs:

◆ **If**

◆ **Select Case**

The 'If' statement can be sub-divided into a further two sub-categories:

◆ **If Then**

◆ **If Then...Else**

The 'If' statement

The 'If' statement uses the comparison operators introduced earlier to test data values. It then performs one of two possible actions, depending on the result of the comparison that it used to test data. It will then either execute or not execute one or more lines of code, depending on the results of the comparison.

So, the 'If' statement allows your program to become decision-based and execute only those parts of the program that need to be executed. If a comparison test is True, the body of the statement executes. Code takes the following form:

```
If (comparison test) Then
    one or more Visual Basic statements
End If
```

The 'End If' statement lets Visual Basic know where the body of the 'If' statement ends.

Here is an example. Suppose you have created an application that calculates commissions due to salespeople. This requires a user to enter the total sales figure into a control called 'txtSalesVal'. The following code extract would calculate the commission due based on the input sales figure:

```
If (txtSalesVal.Text > 17500.00) Then
    sngCommission = txtSalesVal.Text * 0.12
End If
```

If you have not assigned a value to a variable, then Visual Basic stores 0. Thus the variable sngCommission will have a value of 0 assigned to it before the 'If' statement executes. Once the code has executed, the 'If' statement changes the sngCommission variable only if the value of the txtSalesVal.Text property is more than 17500.00. Therefore the code actually says that if the value of sales is more than 17500 then commission can be calculated. If the value of sales entered is less than 17500 then no commission will be calculated.

You can have more than one statement within the code following an 'If' statement. This is known as a **block of code**. In the following example the statement will calculate commission, cost of sales and a minimum re-order amount based on the txtSalesVal text box entry:

```
If (txtSalesVal.Text > 17500.00) Then
    sngCommission = txtSalesVal.Text * 0.12
    curCostOfSales = txtSalesVal.Text * 0.35
    curReorderCost = txtSalesVal.Text * 0.40
End If
```

The three statements within the body will execute only if the condition txtSalesVal.Text > 17500.00 is True.

If you then add another assignment statement immediately after 'End If', that statement will not be part of the 'If' statement, so the True or False result of the condition will not affect it. In the next example the bonus calculation will execute as it is not dependent on the value of sales:

```
If (txtSalesVal.Text > 5000.00) Then
    sngCommission = txtSales.Text * 0.12
    curCostOfSales = txtSalesVal.Text * 0.35
    curReorderCost = txtSalesVal.Text * 0.40
End If
sngBonus = 0.08 * txtSales.Text
```

Remember that the 'If' statement executes code that is based on the comparison test evaluating to True.

The 'If...Else' statement

'Else' is an optional part of the 'If' statement. 'Else' specifies the code that executes if the comparison test is False. Here is the complete format of the 'If...Else' statement:

```
If (comparison test) Then
     one or more Visual Basic statements
Else
     one or more Visual Basic statements
End If
```

The 'If...Else' statement is sometimes called a **mutually exclusive statement**. This means that one set of code or the other executes, but not both. The statement contains two sets of code – that is, two parts of one or more Visual Basic statements – and only one set executes, depending on the result of the 'If' statement.

Suppose that a salesperson receives a bonus if sales are above £7500, or suffers a pay cut if sales are below £7500. The 'If...Else' statement shown below contains the code necessary to reward or penalise the salesperson. The 'If' part computes the bonus. The 'Else' part subtracts the penalty from the salesperson's pay, which is stored in the variable named 'curPayAmt', if the sales quota is not met. Here is the code:

```
If (txtSales.Text > 7500.00) Then
     sngBonus = 0.05 * txtSales.Text
     curPayAmt = curPayAmt + sngBonus
Else
     curPayAmt = curPayAmt - 25.00
End If
curTaxes = curPayAmt * 0.42
```

The fifth line subtracts £25 from the value stored in curPayAmt and then assigns that result back to curPayAmt. In effect, it lowers the value of curPayAmt by 25.

Logical operators

Visual Basic supports three additional operators – And, Or and Not – that look more like commands than operators. They are called logical operators. Logical operators let you combine two or more comparison tests into a single compound comparison. Table 2.11 describes the logical operators, which work just like their spoken counterparts.

The And and Or logical operators let you combine more than one comparison test in a single 'If' statement. The Not operator produces a comparison test with a negative result. As using the Not operator can produce difficult comparison tests you should use it cautiously. You can often turn a Not condition around by using a 'not equal to' operator.

Table 2.11 *Logical operators*		
Operator	**Usage**	**Description**
And	If (A > B) And (C < D)	Produces True if both sides of the And are true. Therefore, A must be greater than B *and* C must be less than D. Otherwise, the expression produces a False result.
Or	If (A > B) Or (C < D)	Produces True if either side of the Or is true. Therefore, A must be greater than B *or* C must be less than D. If both sides of the Or are False, the entire expression produces a False result.
Not	If Not(strAns = "Yes")	Produces the opposite True or False result. Therefore, if strAns holds "Yes", the Not turns the True result to False.

If your code performs an assignment, prints a message, or displays a label if two or more conditions are true, the logical operators make the combined condition easy to code.

For example, suppose you want to provide a bonus to a salesperson if sales total more than £5000 and if he or she sells more than 10,000 units of a particular product. You would normally have to embed an 'If' statement in the body of another 'If' statement, like this:

```
If (sngSales > 5000.00) Then
    If (intUnitsSold > 10000) Then
        sngBonus = 50.00
    End If
End If
```

However, if you use an And operator, it is easier to read and to change later if you need to update the program:

```
If (sngSales > 5000.00) And (intUnitsSold > 10000) Then
    sngBonus = 50.00
End If
```

Select Case

When just one or two comparison tests are to be made then you can easily use an 'If' statement. However, when you need to test against more than two conditions then an 'If' statement becomes more difficult to use. The logical way would be to nest the 'If...Else' statements, but that has the disadvantage of making your code quite complicated to maintain.

Instead you can use a construct that Visual Basic calls 'Select Case', which handles multiple-choice conditions much better. This is the format of the Select Case statement:

```
Select Case expression
    Case value
        one or more Visual Basic statements
    Case value
        one or more Visual Basic statements
    Case value
        one or more Visual Basic statements
    Case Else
        one or more Visual Basic statements
End Select
```

Select Case is an ideal substitute for long, nested 'If...Else' statements where several choices are possible. You set up your Visual Basic program to execute one set of Visual Basic statements from a list of statements inside the Select Case construct, according to a data value.

Select Case can have two or more 'Case *value*' statements. The code that executes then depends on which value matches the required expression. If none of the values match, then the 'Case Else' part of the code executes, if you use this part of the construct. Otherwise, nothing happens and control continues with the statement that follows End Select.

For example, the following code contains a Select Case construct that will classify student grades into categories. Using the Select Case construct analyses the results into a more manageable format:

```
Select Case intGrade
    Case 1: lblTitle.Caption = "Pass"
    Case 2: lblTitle.Caption = "Merit"
    Case 3: lblTitle.Caption = "Distinction"
    Case 4: lblTitle.Caption = "Fail"
    Case 5: lblTitle.Caption = "Referral"
    Case Else: lblTitle.Caption = "Absent"
End Select
```

As you can see, using the Select Case construct rather than an 'If...Else' statement produces code that is much simpler to read and easier to maintain.

The body of each Case can consist of more than one statement, just as the body of an 'If' or 'If...Else' can consist of more than one statement. Visual Basic executes all the statements for any given Case match until the next Case is reached. Once Visual Basic executes a matching Case value, it skips the remaining Case statements and continues with the code that follows the 'End Select' statement.

Check your understanding

Your friend Myra has had problems explaining to her children how to identify the number of days in the months of the year. She has asked you to write a program to help resolve this issue.

Create a program that will request from a user a month of the year, perhaps by means of a text box input or from a drop-down list. The program should then display the number of days in that month when a button is clicked (label the button 'Number of days').

If the user enters 'February', then query whether or not the year is a leap year. Display the answer as either 28 days or 29 days, according to the user's response.

3.8 Working with loops

A **loop** is a section of code that can be executed more than once in an application. Instructions are written to tell the computer when and how often to perform the actions. This allows you to write simpler programs that would otherwise require many lines of code.

Loops can be used to change the properties of a program's controls, and to perform a set of tasks for as long as a certain condition exists, or to skip a set of tasks until a certain condition is met.

Types of loop

There are two main types of structure that can be used to repeat lines of code:

◆ **For...Next** loop
◆ **Do...** loop.

Table 2.12 shows in what circumstances you would use these loops.

Table 2.12 *Circumstances to use which loop*	
Condition	**Use**
You know how many times you will repeat the instructions in advance	For...Next loop
You need the loop to execute at least once	Bottom test Do... loop
You do not need the loop to execute at least once	Top test Do... loop

For...Next loops

This type of loop is used when you know how many times you would like the code to be repeated. It uses a **counter** to control the number of repetitions made. The syntax is:

```
For counter = start value To end value Step increment
    some instructions
Next counter
```

This is an example of a procedure:

```
Private Sub ShowSquares()
Rem This program displays a group of numbers with their squares
    Print "Number", "Square"
    For Number = 0 To 6
        Square = Number * Number
        Print Number, Square
    Next Number
    Print "End of table"
End Sub
```

In this procedure, the counter is 'Number' which is increased (incremented) by 1 each time it goes through the loop. When the variable *Number* becomes 7, the program resumes its execution on the line after the 'Next Number' statement. The result would look like this at runtime:

Number	Square
0	0
1	1
2	4
3	9
4	16
5	25
6	36

End of table

If you include a 'Step' instruction at the end of the 'For' instruction you can alter the way the counter is increased. You can even set the counter to decrease if desired. Look at the following procedure with the 'Step' instruction:

```
Private Sub ShowSquares()
Rem This program displays a group of numbers with their squares
    Print "Number", "Square"
    For Number = 0 To 6 Step 2
        Square = Number * Number
        Print Number, Square
    Next Number
    Print "End of table"
End Sub
```

The result will now look like this:

Number	Square
0	0
2	4
4	16
6	36

End of table

Instead of having actual values that the loop goes From and To, you can use pre-defined variables. Here are some examples:

```
For Class = 1 To NumPupils
For WageIncrease = Min To Max Step Rise
```

Occasionally you may want to exit a 'For' loop when certain criteria have been met. To do this, you use the 'Exit For' instruction. Here is an example:

```
For Counter = 1 To 500
    If EmployeeName(Counter) = "" Then
    Exit For
        ' This exits the loop before its natural conclusion
    Else
    Print EmployeeName(Counter)
    End If
Next Counter
```

Do... loops

There are many ways in which to structure a Do... loop. Each way will affect the way the loop operates. The structures can be broadly divided into:

◆ top-test structures

◆ bottom-test structures.

Here are some examples:

```
Do While expression
    some instructions
Loop
```

and

```
Do Until expression
    some instructions
Loop
```

The 'While' statement will execute the code if the condition is True, but will cease the loop when the expression becomes False. The 'Until' statement will execute the code when the condition is False, but cease when the condition becomes True. These two types of Do... loop are called top-test structures.

The next two examples of Do... loops are called bottom-test structures:

```
Do
    some instructions
Loop While expression
```

and

```
Do
    some instructions
Loop Until expression
```

The advantage of these two structures is that the code will be executed at least once regardless of whether the condition is met or not.

Note

A Do... loop can be exited in mid-flow. To do this, place an 'Exit Do' instruction in your code.

In the 'Do While' loop, the set of statements in the loop are executed repeatedly as long as the test condition evaluates to True at the start of each iteration:

```
Do While test condition
    statements
Loop
```

In the next example the code prints a countdown from 10 to 1:

```
Dim Count As Integer
Count = 10
Do While Count > 0
    msgbox str(count)
    Count = Count - 1
Loop
```

In contrast, in the 'Do Until' loop, the set of statements in the loop are executed repeatedly as long as the test condition evaluates to False at the start of each iteration:

```
Do Until test condition
    statements
Loop
```

In the next example the code prints a countdown from 10 to 1:

```
Dim Count As Integer
Count = 10
Do Until Count = 0
    msgbox str(count)
    Count = Count - 1
Loop
```

PRACTICAL TASK 2.13

1   Create a new form and place a command button on it. Name the
    button 'cmdPress' and set its caption to 'Please enter a password'.

2   Double-click on the command button to open the code window, and
    enter the following code in the button's click event:

```
Dim Password As String
Dim EnterPassword As String
Dim Tries As String
Password = "password"
Tries = 0
Do
   Tries = Tries + 1
   EnterPassword = InputBox("Please Enter a password.
                    This is try " & _ "number" & Tries)
      If EnterPassword = Password Then
    MsgBox("Your password is correct")
   Else
      MsgBox("This is an incorrect password")
   End If
   Loop Until (Tries = 3) Or (EnterPassword = Password)
```

3   Run the program.

N.B. The line of code beginning Enter Password should be entered as one
line and not split over two.

Check your understanding

Create a program that will convert temperatures from Celsius to Fahrenheit
and display the results in a table. The entries in the table will cover the
range from −40 degrees to +40 degrees Celsius, in increments of 5
degrees. The formula to convert Celsius to Fahrenheit is:

$$F = (9 / 5) * C + 32$$

3.9 Procedures

A procedure is a block of Visual Basic statements enclosed by a **declaration
statement** and an **End** statement. All Visual Basic code is written within
procedures.

A procedure is invoked from some other place in the code. When it is finished
executing, it returns control to the code that invoked it; this code is known as
the **calling code**. The calling code is a statement, or an expression within a
statement, that specifies the procedure by name and transfers control to it.

Why use procedures?

Visual Basic starts from a different viewpoint from that of procedural programs, such as Java. At any time there will be a variety of objects or controls on the form. These will consist of buttons, menus, text boxes, etc. The user will then click an object, type in text, or drag on any object and will not be constrained to a particular sequence of actions. This event-led environment requires a new approach to programming. The programmer must create a program that reacts to the user and what he or she does.

For every object on the form, there are a number of possible events, some initiated by the user, some arising as a result of events occurring in the system. The code to respond to these events is contained within Visual Basic procedures.

For example, if you have placed a command button on the form, then the command button's event would include the button being clicked by a user. You therefore write code for the *Click* event, which is a Visual Basic procedure.

So, after you have created the user interface, you have to make decisions on what events are to be handled and then create the appropriate procedures.

Procedures and structured code

Every line of code (other than comments) in your application must be inside a procedure.

Procedures are useful for performing repeated or shared tasks, such as frequently used calculations, text and control manipulation, and database operations. You can call a procedure from many different places in your code, so you can use procedures as building blocks for your application.

Using procedures to structure your code provides you with several advantages.

◆ They allow you to break your programs into discrete logical units. You can debug separate units more easily than you can an entire program without procedures.

◆ You can use procedures developed for one program in other programs, often with little or no modification.

If you subdivide large procedures into smaller ones, your application will be more readable.

Types of procedures

Visual Basic uses several types of procedure.

◆ **Sub procedures** perform actions but do not return a value to the calling code.

◆ **Event-handling procedures** are Sub procedures that execute in response to an event triggered by a user action or by an occurrence of that event in a program.

◆ **Function procedures** return a value to the calling code.

◆ **Property procedures** return and assign values of properties on objects or modules during runtime.

Creating a procedure

You create procedures in the **code window**. To display the code window, you can either click on the View Code button in the project explorer window, or double-click on a control or on a blank part of a form. The code window has two list boxes below the title bar – the **Object box** and the **Procedure box** (see Figure 2.17).

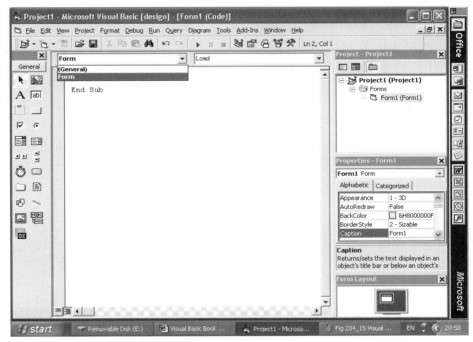

Figure 2.17 The code window showing list boxes

◆ The Object box is on the left side of the window. This shows the current object, whether it be a form or a control.

◆ The Procedure box is on the right side of the window. This shows the event that is being coded (Load in the screen shot).

You can select a new object and event whenever you like. When you do select one, the procedure code for that object and event will be displayed.

Every procedure must have a unique name within the form. The name will consist of the object name, an underscore (_) and the event name. For example, cmdMemberNo_Click details the object name which is a command button called Member No and the event which is a Click event. The procedure would be written in the following format:

```
Private Sub object_event()
    statements
End Sub
```

Static procedures and variables

A variable can be declared within a procedure. This is known as a **local variable**. Local variables are allocated memory when the procedure is currently being executed, and then de-allocated memory when the procedure terminates. Programming languages are designed in this way to save memory use outside of the procedures. Local variables are often not needed, and thus you can just do away with these.

There will be instances when you want to keep a variable throughout the program's execution. This can be done by either declaring the variable outside of procedures or by making them static. **Static variables** are allocated and initialized once the form is loaded. You declare a static variable by preceding the variable declaration with the keyword Static, like this:

```
Static Dim x As Integer
```

If you need to make all local variables static, you just need to create a static procedure, like this:

```
Private Static Sub MyProcedure()        ' static procedure
    Dim x, y, z As Integer
    ...
End Sub
```

In this example, x, y and z are static variables – regardless of whether variables are explicitly declared static.

PRACTICAL TASK 2.14

1 Create a form similar to the one in Figure 2.18.

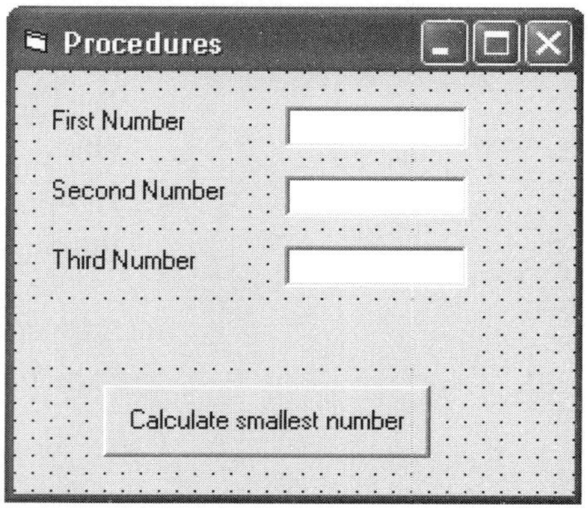

Figure 2.18 Using static variables

2 Change the property settings of the controls to the following:

Control	Property	Settings
Form	Caption	Procedures
Label 1	Caption	First Number
Label 2	Caption	Second Number
Label 3	Caption	Third Number
Text box 1	Name	txtNum1
Text box 2	Name	txtNum2
Text box 3	Name	txtNum3
Text box 1	Text	Blank
Text box 2	Text	Blank
Text box 3	Text	Blank
Label 4	Name	lblOutput
Label 4	Caption	<blank>
Command button	Name	cmdCalculate
Command button	Caption	Calculate Number

3 Write the following code in the click event procedure of the command button:

```
Private Sub cmdCalculate_Click()
Dim first As Integer, second As Integer, third As Integer
    first = Val(txtNum1.Text)
    second = Val(txtNum2.Text)
    third = Val(txtNum3.Text)

' Call the 'get minimum' function and pass first, second, third
    smallest = MinimumAmount(first, second, third)
    lblOutput.Caption = "Smallest value is " & Str(smallest)
End Sub
```

4 Select *General* from the Object box in the code window and type in the following code:

```
Private Function MinimumAmount(min_val As Integer, y As
                            Integer, z As Integer) As Integer
If (y < min_val) Then
    min_val = y
End If
If (z < min_val) Then
    min_val = z
End If
MinimumAmount = min_val
End Function
```

5 Run the program.

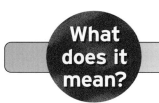

Check your understanding

Create a program that requires a user to enter his or her name as an input value and then displays the name, followed by the number of letters in the name. The output will require you to create a Sub procedure called 'Name Length', and to call it from within your program.

3.10 Functions

The programming language you have learned so far – variable declaration, assignments, and operator usage – has focused on programming *statements*. This section introduces another concept called a function.

Visual Basic supplies several built-in functions (often called **intrinsic functions**) that do work for you. Many functions perform common mathematical tasks such as computing a square-root. Other functions manipulate string data, such as converting text inside a string to upper-case or lower-case letters. Other functions, such as those to be explained here, perform input and output.

What does it mean?

*A **function** is a routine that accepts zero, one or more arguments and returns a single result based on the argument list (see Figure 2.19).*

Figure 2.19 *A function accepts arguments and returns a single value*

What does it mean?

*An **argument** is a value you pass to a function so the function has data to work with.*

The most important thing to remember is that a function always returns a single value.

A function's job is to save you time. For example, if you need to compute the square-root of a user's entered value, you could write the assignments and expressions to compute the square-root. The square-root, however, is such a common routine that the code has already been written and stored as an intrinsic function. Now, if you want the square-root of a value, you will pass the value as a single argument to the square-root function, which will return the result.

In this and subsequent examples, your application will need to display messages and ask questions of the user. The application needs to receive the user's response from the questions. Now, although the label and text box controls work well for giving and receiving user information, such controls do not lend themselves to messages and questions that the program displays during execution – such as error messages and warning boxes.

For example, suppose you want to know whether the user has prepared the printer for printing. To prepare a printer, the user has to turn on the printer, make sure paper is there, and ensure that the online light is on. Your program should not attempt to print a report until the user has performed these actions, or an error will occur. Therefore, when the user initiates a report for printing, your application can gather the data and then ask the user whether the printer is ready. If the user responds affirmatively, you can start the report's output. The form's controls simply do not provide such interaction.

You will learn how to display message boxes and input boxes that provide input and output during runtime.

Message boxes and input boxes

A **message box** is a dialogue you display to give the user some information. An **input box** is a dialogue you display to ask the user one or more questions.

Because users don't always know what is expected of them, a message box can be made to pop up when the user enters a bad value, for example. The message box can then explain that the user needs to enter certain information in a certain format. If the user enters an invalid code, your program could display an error message like the one shown in Figure 2.20.

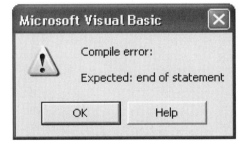

Figure 2.20 Example of a message box

The text box controls discussed earlier are useful for getting values from the user. Other controls that you'll learn about later accept input from the user's keyboard or mouse. Nevertheless, Visual Basic's controls are not enough to handle all the input that your program will need.

Input boxes can be used when the user must respond to certain kinds of questions. Text boxes and other controls are fine for getting fixed input from the user, such as data values on which the program will perform computations. Input boxes are also fine for asking the user questions that arise only under certain conditions. Input boxes always give the user a place to respond with an answer. In Figure 2.21, for example, the input box is asking the user for a title that will go at the top of a printed report listing.

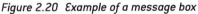

Figure 2.21 Input boxes gather information from the user

The MsgBox() function

Always assign a MsgBox( ) function to an integer variable. The variable will hold the returned value, and that value will indicate the button the user clicked (message boxes can display multiple buttons such as OK and Cancel).

The assignment statement shows the format of the MsgBox( ) function:

*an*IntVariable = MsgBox(strMsg [, [int*Type*] [, str*Title*]]])

◆ **strMsg** is a string (either a variable or a string constant enclosed in quotation double marks) and forms the text of the message displayed in the message box.

◆ **int***Type* is an optional numeric value or expression that describes the options you want in the message box. Tables 2.13, 2.14 and 2.15 contain all the possible values you can use for the type of message box you want displayed. Visual Basic will *not* display an icon if you do not specify an intType value. If you want to use a value from two or more of the tables, you add the values together. Although you can use the integer value, if you use the built-in Visual Basic named '**literal**', you will more easily understand the message box's style if you ever have to change the message box in the future.

◆ **str***Title* is an optional string that represents the text in the message box's title bar. If you omit str*Title*, Visual Basic uses the project's name for the message box's title bar.

The options that you select, using the int*Type* value in the MsgBox( ) function, determine whether the message box displays an icon and controls the **modality** of the message box. The modality determines whether a message box is application-specific or system-specific.

◆ If the message box is application-specific, the user must respond to the message box before the user can do anything else in the application.

◆ If the message box is system-specific, the user must respond to the message box before doing anything else on the system.

Table 2.13 Buttons displayed in the message box

Name	Value	Display
vbOKOnly	0	The OK button
vbOKCancel	1	The OK and Cancel buttons
vbAbortRetryIgnore	2	The Abort, Retry and Ignore buttons
vbYesNoCancel	3	The Yes, No and Cancel buttons
vbYesNo	4	The Yes and No buttons
vbRetryCancel	5	The Retry and Cancel buttons

Table 2.14 Icons displayed in the message box

Name	Value	Display
vbCritical	16	Critical message
vbQuestion	32	Warning query
vbExclamation	48	Warning message
vbInformation	64	Information message
vbSystemModal	4096	SystemModal dialogue box that needs to be acknowledged before proceeding

Table 2.15 The default button in the message box

Name	Value	Display
vbDefaultButton	0	Button 1 is the default button
vbDefaultButton2	256	Button 2 is the default button
vbDefaultButton3	512	Button 3 is the default button

Modality also determines how the system handles a dialogue box. The modality often causes confusion in programming.

◆ If you don't specify a **system modal** int*Type* value of 4096 (or if you don't use the named literal vbSystemModal to specify the system's modal mode), Visual Basic assumes that you want an application-modal message box. The user's application will not continue until the user closes the message box. However, the user can switch to another Windows program by pressing *Alt + Tab* or by switching to another program using the application's control menu.

◆ If you do specify that the message box is system modal, the user will not be able to switch to another Windows program until the user responds to the message box, because the message box will have full control of the system.

For this reason, reserve the system modal message boxes for serious error messages that you want the user to read and respond to before continuing the program.

Remember that the MsgBox() values such as vbQuestion and vbYesNoCancel are not variables but are named literals that Visual Basic has defined to correspond with matching integer values. vbQuestion and vbYesNoCancel produce both a question mark icon and the three buttons. A title also appears due to the third value inside the MsgBox() function (see Figure 2.22).

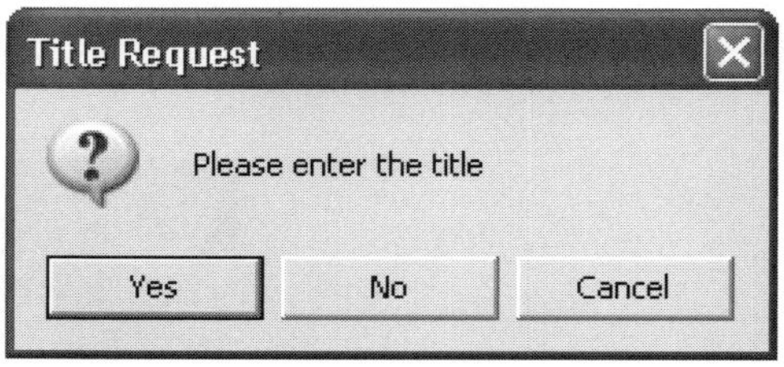

Figure 2.22 **Message boxes support several command buttons**

The return values of MsgBox()

MsgBox() functions are assigned to variables so that the program knows which button the user presses. Suppose that the user presses the Yes button in Figure 2.22. The program could then print the report. If, however, the user presses the No button, the program could describe what the user needed to do to get ready for the report. If the user presses the Cancel button, the program would know that the user does not want the report at all. Table 2.16 lists the seven possible MsgBox() return values. You can test either for the integer or the **named constant**, i.e. the **literal return value**.

Table 2.16 *MsgBox() return values*

Named constant	Value	Description
vbOK	1	The user clicked the OK button.
vbCancel	2	The user clicked the Cancel button.
vbAbort	3	The user clicked the Abort button.
vbRetry	4	The user clicked the Retry button.
vbIgnore	5	The user clicked the Ignore button.
vbYes	6	The user clicked the Yes button.
vbNo	7	The user clicked the No button.

Visual Basic's code window Help

Can you remember the named literals in the tables that we have looked at so far? How can you remember that the named literal value to display three buttons – Yes, No and Cancel – is the vbYesNoCancel named literal?

Visual Basic supplies you with ample help. As soon as the code window editor recognises that you are entering a function, the editor displays pop-up help that displays the function's format. An example is shown in Figure 2.23.

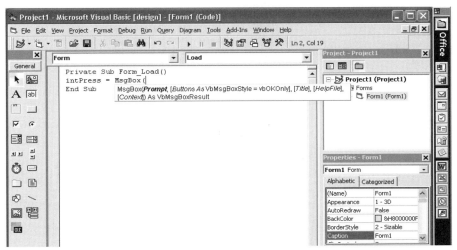

Figure 2.23 Visual Basic helps you with a function's correct format

Visual Basic gives you help also with the function's named literals. When you reach any function argument that requires one of the named literals, a drop-down list box is displayed (like the one in Figure 2.24), from which you can

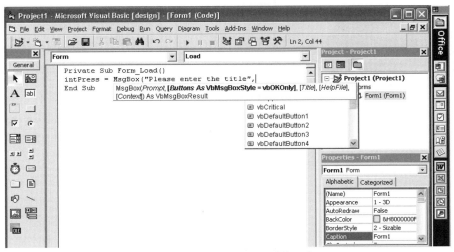

Figure 2.24 Visual Basic displays the function's named literals

select a named literal. To accept the selected named literal, press *Enter* and type a comma, or press the *Spacebar* to continue with the program.

The format and argument list box pop-up help appears throughout Visual Basic. As you learn additional Visual Basic statements, you'll see the pop-up code window help more often.

The InputBox() function

The InputBox() function is easy to use because it acts very much like the MsgBox() function. The InputBox() function receives answers that are more complete than the MsgBox() function can get. Whereas MsgBox() returns one of seven values that indicate the user's command button press (see Table 2.16), the InputBox() function returns a string data value that holds the answer typed by the user.

Here is the format of the InputBox() function:

str*Variable* = InputBox(str*Prompt* [, [str*Title*] [, str*Default*] [, int*Xpos*, int*Ypos*]]])

◆ **str***Prompt* works a lot like the strMsg value in a MsgBox() function. The user sees str*Prompt* inside the input box displayed on the screen.

◆ **str***Title* is the title inside the input box's title bar.

◆ **str***Default* is a default string value that Visual Basic displays for a default answer. The user can accept the default answer or change the default answer.

◆ **int***Xpos* and **int***Ypos* positions indicate the exact location where you want the input box to appear on the form. The int*Xpos* value holds the number of twips from the left edge of the Form window to the left edge of the input box. The int*Ypos* value holds the number of twips from the top edge of the form window to the top edge of the input box. If you omit these values, Visual Basic centres the message box on the form.

There are 1440 twips (twentieth of a point) to an inch, and approximately 567 twips to a centimetre.

Input boxes always contain OK and Cancel command buttons. If the user clicks OK (or presses Enter, which selects OK by default), the answer in the input box is sent to the variable being assigned the returned value. If the user clicks Cancel, a null string ("") returns from the InputBox() function.

The following statement displays an input box that asks the user for a company name. The user either enters a response to the prompt or clicks the Cancel command button to indicate that no answer is coming.

```
strCompName = InputBox("What is the name of the company?",
    "Company Request", "XYZ Ltd")
```

You can offer a default answer that the user can accept or change in the 'strDefault' argument. The input box function returns the answer to the string variable to which you assign the function. Figure 2.25 contains the message box displayed from this InputBox() function.

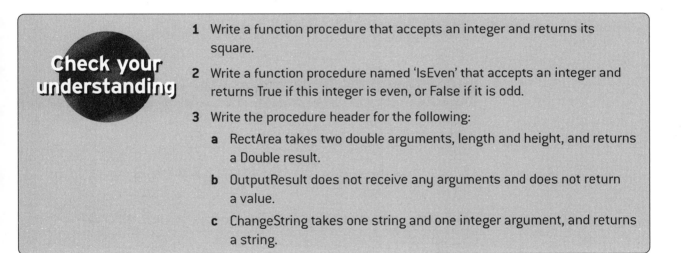

Figure 2.25 Asking the user a question and obtaining the answer with InputBox()

1 Write a function procedure that accepts an integer and returns its square.

2 Write a function procedure named 'IsEven' that accepts an integer and returns True if this integer is even, or False if it is odd.

3 Write the procedure header for the following:

   a RectArea takes two double arguments, length and height, and returns a Double result.

   b OutputResult does not receive any arguments and does not return a value.

   c ChangeString takes one string and one integer argument, and returns a string.

3.11 Properties, methods and events

In Visual Basic, properties describe objects or controls. Methods will then cause an object or control to do something. Events are what happens when an object does something.

Every object, such as a form or control, has a set of **properties** that describe it. Although this set is not identical for all objects, some properties such as those listed in Table 2.17 are common to most controls. You can see every property for a given control by looking at the properties window in the development environment.

Table 2.17 Common properties of Visual Basic controls

Property	Description
Left	The position of the left side of a control with respect to its container
Top	The position of the top of a control with respect to its container
Height	A control's height
Width	A control's width
Name	The string value used to refer to a control
Enabled	The Boolean (True/False) value that determines whether users can manipulate the control
Visible	The Boolean (True/False) value that determines whether users can see the control

Methods are blocks of code designed into a control that tell the control how to do things – such as move to another location on a form. For example, consider a telephone. It has a property of colour and method of ring. The ring is something that the telephone does. Just as with properties, not all controls have the same methods, although some common methods do exist, as shown in Table 2.18.

Table 2.18 Common methods of Visual Basic controls

Method	Use
Move	Changes an object's position in response to a code request
Drag	Handles the execution of a drag-and-drop operation by the user
SetFocus	Gives focus to the object specified in the method call
ZOrder	Determines the order in which multiple objects appear on-screen

Events are what happens in and around your program. For example, when a user clicks a button, many events occur: the mouse button is pressed, the CommandButton in your program is clicked, and then the mouse button is released. These three actions correspond to the MouseDown event, the Click event, and the MouseUp event. During this process, the GotFocus event for the CommandButton and the LostFocus event for whichever object previously held the focus also occur.

Be aware that not all controls have the same events, but some events are shared by many controls (see Table 2.19). These events occur as a result of some specific user action, such as moving the mouse, pressing a key on the keyboard, or clicking a text box. These types of events are user-initiated events and are what you will write code for most often.

Table 2.19 *Common events of Visual Basic controls*

Event	Occurrence
Change	The user modifies text in a combo box or text box.
Click	The user clicks the primary mouse button on an object.
DblClick	The user double-clicks the primary mouse button on an object.
DragDrop	The user drags an object to another location.
DragOver	The user drags an object over another control.
GotFocus	An object receives focus.
KeyDown	The user presses a keyboard key while an object has focus.
KeyPress	The user presses and releases a keyboard key while an object has focus.
KeyUp	The user releases a keyboard key while an object has focus.
LostFocus	An object loses focus.
MouseDown	The user presses any mouse button while the mouse pointer is over an object.
MouseMove	The user moves the mouse pointer over an object.
MouseUp	The user releases any mouse button while the mouse pointer is over an object.

PRACTICAL TASK 2.15

This activity will use the input box function to collect and calculate total sales for a salesperson.

1 Start a new project, and open its code window by clicking the *View Code* button in the project explorer.

2 Ensure that *General* is selected in the Object list box at the top of the screen, and then enter the following code:

```
Option Explicit
Dim TotalSales As Integer
Dim TotalReturns As Integer
Dim Sales As Integer
```

3 Select *Form* in the Object list box and enter the following code:

```
Form1.Show
TotalSales = InputBox("Enter your total sales")
TotalReturns = InputBox("Enter your total returns")
Sales = TotalSales - TotalReturns
Print "Total Sales are ", Sales
```

4 Run the program.

PRACTICAL TASK 2.16

This activity will use the message box function to collect information about a user's age and then inform the person whether he or she can retire yet.

1 Create a new form and then double-click on the form to show the form code window.

2 In the Load event, enter the following code:

```
Option Explicit
Dim Age As Integer
Age = InputBox("Enter your age")
    If Age >= 65 Then
        MsgBox "You can retire."
    ElseIf Age >= 40 Then
        MsgBox "You can think about retirement."
    Else
        MsgBox "Don't even think about retirement!"
    End If
```

3 Run the program.

Check your understanding — Create a program that will ask the user to enter personal details into an input box and then display the details in a message box.

3.12 Menu controls

When creating an application, remember that it is important for the users to be able to **navigate** around your application. To do this effectively they need a **menu** so they will know what items are on offer for selection. Once they become more familiar with the application, they will also learn various shortcut keys to facilitate navigation.

Almost all Windows-based programs contain common menu commands. Visual Basic is no exception. Many of the Visual Basic pull-down menus contain the same commands as other programs from Microsoft. If you group your file-related commands on the menu bar's File option, your users will immediately feel comfortable with your application.

Your application will also require some menu options that no other application uses. While your application may not be as complex or advanced as other programs, try to adopt as many common principles as you can so that your users can adapt quickly to your application's interface.

Menu Editor

A **menu** is a control object just like a command button or a text box. Once you add a menu bar to an application, the menu bar and its options are all controls that you can manage from the properties window.

Adding menus to your applications requires only that you master the Menu Editor. Most menu items require that you specify a caption and name property, as well as indenting the item properly under its menu bar command. Optionally, a menu item might contain a shortcut keystroke or a checkmark next to the item.

Menu Editor lets you quickly and easily place menu bar items into your application by selecting command buttons and entering a few property values. Menu Editor contains menu description tools that let you create the application's menu bar, menu commands, and shortcut access keys to all of your applications.

Menu Editor is, in fact, a dialogue box that you access from the Form window by selecting *Tools + Menu Editor* from Visual Basic's own menu bar. Figure 2.26 shows the dialogue box.

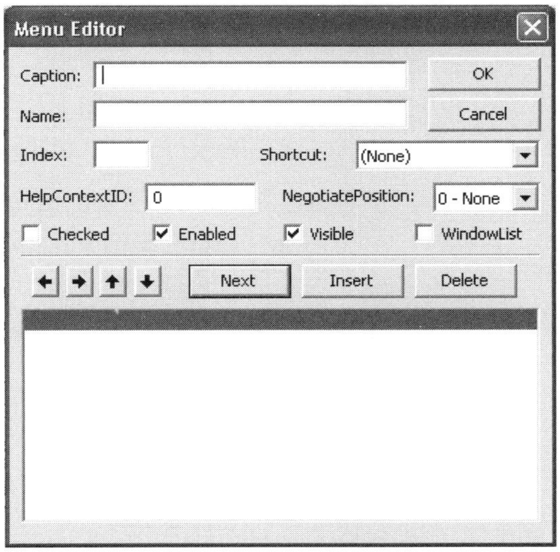

Figure 2.26 Creating a menu with Menu Editor

When the user selects a menu command, Visual Basic generates an event, just as it generates an event when the user clicks a command button. The only event that menu items support is the *Click( ) event*. Therefore, whether the user selects a menu option with a mouse or with a keyboard, that selection triggers a Click( ) event.

Menu Editor lets you add a menu bar, pull-down menu commands, separator bars (bars that help group menu options), sub-menus (menus that appear from other menu options), checked items and shortcut access keystrokes.

While Menu Editor creates your menu, you still need to write event procedures for each menu option to link menu commands to actions taken by your application.

Creating a menu bar

A menu bar is one of the easiest parts of the menu system to add to your application. This section walks you through the steps necessary to add a menu bar. Subsequent sections show you how to add pull-down menu options to each of the menu bar commands.

PRACTICAL TASK 2.17

Perform the following steps to add a menu bar to your project.

1 Press *Ctrl + E* to display Menu Editor. Each menu bar command requires a caption (specified by the Caption property) and a name (specified by the Name property). The other Menu Editor items are optional.

2 At the Caption prompt, type '&File'. The ampersand, as with the other controls' Caption properties, indicates an **accelerator keystroke** of *Alt + F* for the File menu item. As you type the Caption value, notice that Visual Basic adds the caption in Menu Editor's lower section. Menu Editor's lower half displays the menu bar and the pull-down options as you add them to the menu. Menu Editor's top half contains a description of individual items in the menu.

3 Press *Tab* to move the focus to the Name text box, and type 'mnuFile'. The application will refer to the File menu bar item by the name 'mnuFile' as needed. The three-letter prefix indicates that the mnuFile object is a menu item and not some other kind of control. Your Menu Editor's window should now look something like the one in Figure 2.27.

Don't press Enter or click the OK button to close Menu Editor just yet, because in Practical task 2.18 you will have to add the additional menu bar options before closing the Menu Editor's window.

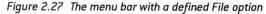

Figure 2.27 The menu bar with a defined File option

The additional Menu Editor properties — such as the Enabled property that determines whether the menu item is greyed out and unavailable for certain procedures, as well as a Visible property, which determines when the user can see the menu bar command — are not needed for every option. You'll rarely change these extra property values from their default values for menu bar commands.

The only accelerator keystroke available for menu bar options is the underlined Alt *+ keystroke that occurs as the result of the Caption property's underlined letter. Do not attempt to select* Ctrl *+ keystroke from the shortcut drop-down list box for the menu bar options.* Ctrl *+ keystroke shortcut combinations are available only for pull-down menu options.*

Naming menu options

You should follow a standard naming convention when naming menu options.

The event procedures within any Visual Basic application reference menu options by their menu option names. Preface all menu items, both menu bar and pull-down menu items, with the **mnu prefix** so that you can easily distinguish them. Therefore, the *File + Exit* item would be named 'mnuFileExit', *View + Normal* would be named 'mnuViewNormal', and so on. The names then clearly describe the menu items that they represent. If a sub-menu appears, append its item name to the parent's name — for example, 'mnuViewNormalFull'.

PRACTICAL TASK 2.18

Follow these steps to complete the creation of a menu bar:

1 Click the Menu Editor's *Next* command button to inform Visual Basic that you want to add the next item. The lower window's highlight bar drops down to the next line in preparation for the next menu item. The buttons right above the lower window control the addition, insertion and deletion of menu items from the menu you are building.

2 Type '&Edit' at the Caption text box and press *Tab*. Name this second menu bar item 'mnuEdit'. Click the *Next* command button to prepare Menu Editor for the next menu bar item.

3 Type '&View' and press *Tab* to move the focus to the Name text box. Type 'mnuView' and select *Next* to prepare for the final menu item.

4 Type '&Help' and press *Tab* to move the focus to the Help text box. Type 'mnuHelp'. Your screen should now look like the one in Figure 2.28.

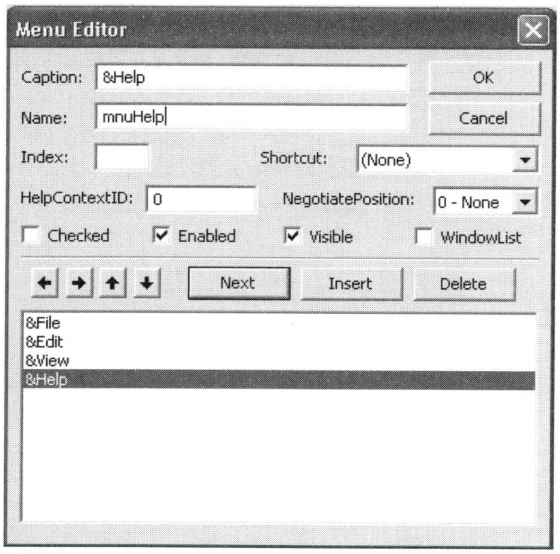

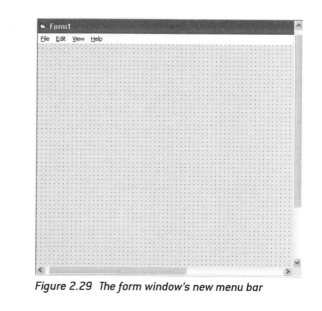

Figure 2.28 Complete menu bar with four options

5 Close Menu Editor by pressing *Enter* or clicking the OK command button. Immediately, Visual Basic displays the new menu bar across the top of the application's form window, as shown in Figure 2.29.

Figure 2.29 The form window's new menu bar

Adding pull-down menu options

Obviously, the menu you created in Practical task 2.18 is incomplete. The menu bar exists, but no options pull down from the menu bar. You are now ready to add the individual pull-down options to the menu. This section explains how to complete the File pull-down menu.

Each menu bar command opens a pull-down menu that consists of a series of options, separator bars, access keystrokes and sub-menus. Menu Editor's four arrow command buttons let you indent the pull-down menu commands from their matching menu bar commands to show which items go with which menu bar commands.

Note that you did not have to complete the menu bar before completing each pull-down menu. You could have added the File option to the menu bar and then completed the File option's pull-down menu before adding the View option to the menu bar. The order in which you add menu items doesn't matter at all. It is where you place them and how you indent them that determines the order in which the menu items appear.

The File pull-down menu will need to contain the following items:

◆ the *New* command
◆ the *Open* command, with a shortcut access keystroke of Ctrl + O
◆ the *Close* command
◆ a separator bar
◆ the *Exit* command.

After you have added these sub-menu items, you can hook up the menu commands to Click( ) event procedures that you write, as explained in the next section.

Adding pull-down items requires that you follow the same steps you followed when you added the menu bar items. The difference is that Menu Editor options that the previous section ignored, such as the Shortcut option, become more important because you will apply some of these options to the pull-down menu items. Table 2.20 explains the remaining Menu Editor properties (see also Figure 2.30).

In Menu Editor, the left and right arrow command buttons indicate which items go with which menu bar option. In other words, if four items in the lower window are indented to the right and appear directly beneath the File menu bar item, those four indented items will appear on File's pull-down menu. The left arrow removes an indentation level and the right arrow adds an indentation level. The up- and down-arrow keys move menu items up and down the list of menu items, rearranging the order if you need to do so.

Table 2.20 *Menu Editor's further properties*

Property	Description
Checked	This indicates whether a menu item has a checkmark next to it. Generally, you will add checkmarks to menu options that perform on or off actions, such as a View menu that contains a highlighted command. The checkmark appears when you, at design time or through code, set the menu item's Checked property to True. The checkmark goes away (indicating that the item is no longer active or selected) when you set the Checked property to False.
HelpContextID	This is a code that matches a help file description if and when you add help files to your application.
Index	If you create a menu control array rather than name individual menu items separately, this Index property specifies the menu item's subscript within the control array.
Shortcut	This is a drop-down list of Ctrl + keystroke access keys that you can add to any pull-down menu item.
Window List	This specifies whether the menu item applies to an advanced application's MDI (multiple-document interface) document. The menus that you create for this unit do not require the use of MDI features.

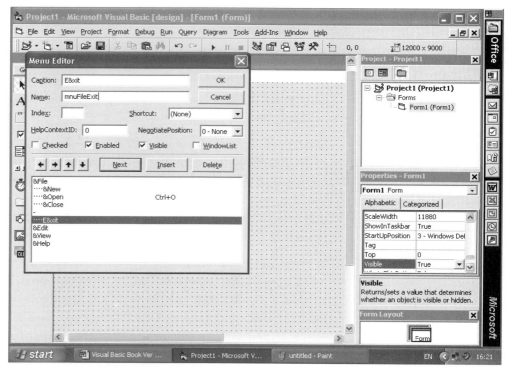

Figure 2.30 Menu Editor's remaining properties

PRACTICAL TASK 2.19

Follow these steps to create the File pull-down menu bar's sub-menu.

1 Move the lower window's highlight line to the *&Edit* menu bar item. Click the *Insert* command button. You always insert *before* an item.

2 Click the right-arrow command button. Visual Basic adds four dots (similar to an ellipsis, ...), showing that the newly inserted item will be indented under the File option.

3 Move the focus to the caption prompt and type '&New'.

4 Press *Tab* to move the focus to the name prompt and type 'mnuFileNew'.

5 Click *Next* and then *Insert*, and press the right arrow command button to insert another item beneath the New item. Your Menu Editor should look like the one in Figure 2.31. Note that the File menu bar option now has a pull-down menu; you know this because of the indentation of the &New option right below &File.

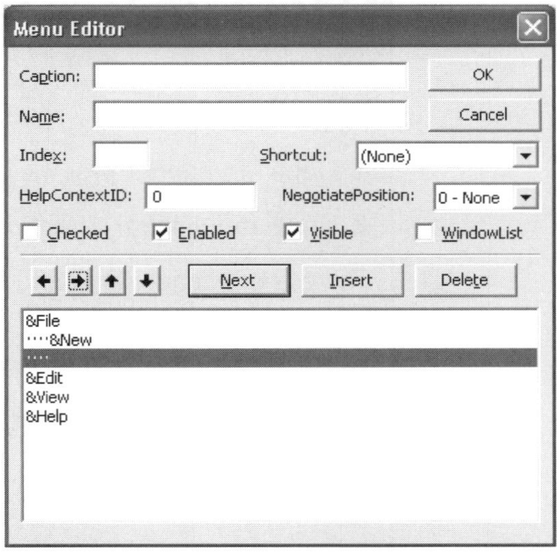

Figure 2.31 The File pull-down menu is gaining additional options

6 Move the focus to the caption prompt and type '&Open'. Press *Tab* and enter the Name property value 'mnuFileOpen'. Rather than add the next item, click the Shortcut drop-down list and select *Ctrl + O* from the list. When the user now displays the File pull-down menu, Ctrl + O will appear as the shortcut key next to the *File + Open* menu item.

7 Click *Next*, then *Insert*, and then the right arrow command button to make room for the next item. Add the 'Exit' caption with the Name property 'mnuFileExit'. Click *Next* again and then *Insert* to insert another item beneath the Close item.

You can now add a **separator bar**. Separator bars divide individual pull-down menus into separate sections. Although several options appear on most Windows applications' File pull-down menus, these options do not all perform the same kinds of task. Some options relate to files, some relate to printing, and the Exit command always appears on the File menu as well. The separator bars help to distinguish these groups of different items from each other on the pull-down menus.

All separator bars have the same Caption property, which is nothing more than a hyphen (-). You must give every separator bar a different name. Usually, the name of the separator bars on the File menu are mnuFileBar1, mnuFileBar2, and so on. Some programmers prefer to name the first separator bar Sep1, the second Sep2, and so on, no matter which menu the separator bar appears on.

You must add the separator bars on an indented menu level so that they indent properly beneath their pull-down menus.

PRACTICAL TASK 2.20

Follow these steps to add the single separator bar for the File pull-down menu.

1 Type - (a hyphen) for the Caption property and press *Tab*.

2 Type 'mnuFileBar1' for the Name property.

There is one more item to add – the Exit item. You now know how to add the Exit option to the File menu. After adding Exit, your Menu Editor should look like the one shown in Figure 2.32.

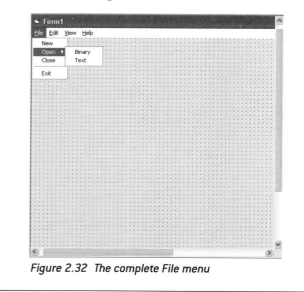

Figure 2.32 The complete File menu

Menu extras

You do not have to complete all the menu bar options. You already know how to add routine options. This section looks at adding additional menu elements.

To practice adding a **checked object**, add one checked item to the View pull-down menu bar item. Add an indented option that uses 'Highlighted' for the Caption property and 'mnuViewHighlighted' for the Name property. Click the *Checked* check box. The *View + Highlighted* option will initially be checked when the user displays the View pull-down menu. Your code can check and uncheck the item by changing the mnuViewHighlighted object's Checked property to True or False.

If you want to add a sub-menu from a pull-down menu item, add an additional level of indentation. For example, to add a two-option sub-menu off the *File + Open* option that gives the user an additional choice of Binary or Text (binary and text are two possible kinds of files), insert a place for the first item right beneath Open and click the right-arrow command button to add a second ellipsis. Type '&Binary' for the Caption property and 'mnuFileOpenBinary' for the Name property. Insert an additional item beneath that, indented at the same level, and type '&Text' for the Caption property and 'mnuFileOpenText' for the Name property.

Your menu has a slight bug now! Go back to the &Open menu option and set the shortcut keystroke back to None. You cannot add a shortcut keystroke to a sub-menu's parent option.

Now that the menu is completed to this stage, click the OK command button. When Menu Editor disappears, you will see the application's form window with the menu bar across the top of the screen. Open the *File* menu and then select *Open* to see the sub-menu. Observe the right arrow next to Open, which indicates that an additional sub-menu will appear for that option.

Connecting menus to event procedures

With your menu built, you need to tie each menu command to your application. To respond to menu selections, you need to write Click() event procedures for Visual Basic to execute when the user selects a menu command.

Visual Basic generates a click event when the user selects a menu command. The name of the menu command, combined with Click(), provides the name of the event procedure. Therefore, the *File + Exit* menu item named 'mnuFileExit' will generate the execution of the event procedure named 'mnuFileExit_Click()'.

Adding the mnuFileExit_Click() event procedure requires only that you select that menu command during the program's development. At the form window, click the File menu bar command. Visual Basic displays the form window's File pull-down menu. Even though you are not running the program but are working on the program from the form window, the File menu shows you what happens when the user selects *File* at runtime.

Click the *Exit* item on the File pull-down menu. As soon as you click Exit, Visual Basic opens the code window to a new event procedure named 'mnuFileExit_Click()', as shown in Figure 2.33.

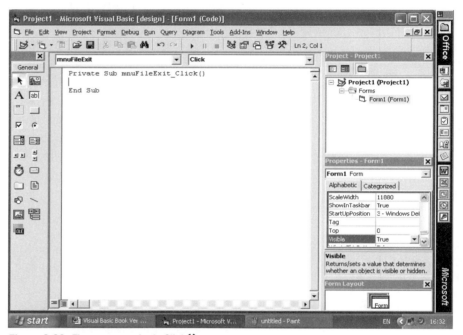

Figure 2.33 The menu option's Click() event procedure

This event procedure is simple to code. When the user selects *File + Exit*, you want the application to terminate. Therefore, insert an 'Unload Me' and an 'End' statement to the body of the mnuFileExit_Click() procedure and close the procedure by double-clicking its control button. As you can see, adding event procedures requires little more than clicking the menu item and adding the body of the procedure that appears.

Although the application is far from complete, you can run the application to see how the menu looks and to test the *File + Exit* option.

If any menu command duplicates the functionality of other controls, such as command buttons, do not copy the command button's code into the body of the menu event procedure. Instead, simply execute that command button's event procedure from the menu item's event procedure.

Check your understanding

Create a new project with the following menu bar items: Reading, Writing, Communicating. Then create a sub-menu under Reading with the following options: Text Books, Novels, Comics, Newspapers. Create a Communicating sub-menu with the following options: Verbal, Non-verbal, Overt, Covert, Body Language.

Chapter summary

Forms

◆ Visual Basic allows you to create Windows-based applications by using a form to create windows that allow users to access and interface the application.

◆ It provides a default form with default properties, including a title bar, minimise and maximise buttons, a control menu box and a close button. The form controls will then allow you to amend the design of the form.

◆ A form can be configured by changing the form properties to perform actions and change the appearance of the form according to the design and purpose of the form.

◆ The forms that you create can be tracked using the project explorer window. The names of forms should be prefixed by the three letters 'frm', followed by the actual form name.

◆ To set the form title and display it in the title bar, select the Caption option in the properties window and enter the appropriate name.

◆ When you save a form, its contents are saved in a separate form file with the frm extension.

◆ If the application you are creating requires more than one window, you can add new windows by adding new forms to the project at the design stage.

Controls

◆ In order to add functionality, you add controls to a form to allow the user to interface with the application. Controls are added according to the design of the application and to ensure that the interface between the user and the application makes this process as user-friendly as possible.

◆ The standard controls provided within Visual Basic are usually sufficient for the purpose of creating most types of applications. These controls can be augmented with more advanced controls as applications become more specialised.

- All of the controls provided by Visual Basic have default properties which can be altered or amended to represent application functionality.

- Controls can be added to forms in two ways. They can be added by clicking a control on the toolbox and drawing the control on the form. Alternatively they can be added by double-clicking the control icon on the toolbox, which causes a control to be placed on the form, and then dragging the control to its desired position on the form.

- Once controls are placed on a form they can be selected individually or as a group. To select an individual control, click once on the control. To select a group or collection of controls, use the mouse to highlight them.

Interface and coding

- Code in a Visual Basic application consists of small event procedures that respond to various events. When coding event procedures, this code is entered in the code window.

- There are three main categories of data: numeric, string and special.

- A variable is an area of computer memory used to store data in a temporary location if the data is required within your application.

- Variables can be categorised into two types: numeric and string.

- To declare a variable, use the following syntax:

    Dim *identifier* As *data type*

- When working with variables, always enter the phrase 'Option Explicit' to force you to declare variables before starting your application.

- When creating variables, use names that are realistic. Try to name them to represent the types of data that will be held within them.

- Variables must be of a certain data type that corresponds to the data that will be held within them.

- Arithmetic operators have an order of precedence. The order of these operators can be changed only by using brackets.

- A constant holds a value that will not change during the time the program is running.

- If you need to join two or more strings together (called concatenation), use the ampersand (&).

Comparison operators

- Visual Basic's comparison operators produce results that are either True or False. There are six comparison operators.

◆ Comparison operators are used to write programs that make runtime decisions based on the comparison results.

◆ Visual Basic has selection constructs, including the 'If' and the 'If Then...Else' constructs. The 'If' statement provides the logic that enables applications to analyse data and then make decisions based on that analysis. The 'If Then...Else' statement executes code based on the comparison's False condition.

◆ Visual Basic supports three logical operators: And, Or and Not. These operators let you combine more than one comparison test in a single 'If' statement.

◆ Visual Basic also provides support for a 'Select Case' statement. Select Case statements are used when you need to test against more than two conditions.

Loops

◆ A loop is a section of code that will repeat.

◆ The two main types of structure are the 'For...Next' loop and the 'Do... loop'. A 'For...Next' loop is used when you know how many times you want the code to be repeated. A 'Do... loop' is used when you want the loop body to be executed at least once.

Procedures

◆ A procedure is a block of statements enclosed by a declaration statement and an End statement. All Visual Basic code is written within procedures.

◆ Procedures are created in the code window. This is displayed by either double-clicking on a control or a blank part of a form, or by clicking on *View Code* in the project explorer window.

◆ Procedures are useful for performing repeated or shared tasks.

◆ Structuring code with procedures provides benefits to the programmer.

◆ Variables declared within procedures are known as local variables.

◆ To make a local variable static, you create a static procedure.

Functions

◆ Visual Basic functions perform input and output tasks.

◆ Visual Basic has several built-in functions, called intrinsic functions.

◆ A function is a routine that accepts zero, one or more arguments and returns a single result based on the argument list.

◆ The purpose of using functions is to save time when writing programs.

◆ You use message boxes and input boxes when you need to ask questions or display messages and advice to the user.

◆ Visual Basic provides you with help when entering functions.

Properties, methods and events

◆ Visual Basic properties describe objects or controls. Every object, such as a form or control, has a set of properties that describe it.

◆ Methods are blocks of code designed into a control that tells that control how to do things.

◆ Events are what happens within and around your program.

Menus

◆ To add menus to your application you use Menu Editor.

◆ A menu is a control object just like a command button or a text box.

◆ When naming menu options you should follow a standard naming convention.

◆ Once you have built your menu you need to tie each menu command to your application by writing click event procedures.

4 Use the debug facilities of the development environment

A code error that causes a program to stop running is commonly termed a **bug**. If your program has bugs, you will have to analyse the code you have written in order to identify and correct the errors. This process is called **debugging**. Visual Basic provides many debugging tools.

A Visual Basic program can be in one of three modes depending on what you the programmer are doing.

◆ The program is in **design mode** mode when you are developing the application. This will be indicated in the title bar with the word 'design' noted.

◆ The program will be in **runtime mode** mode when the application is being run. Again this mode will be indicated in the title bar of the program.

◆ The program will be in **break mode** mode when the program is halted to use the debugger. When you are in break mode you can look at the code to examine values and compare expected outcomes. This is explained later.

4.1 Types of error

You will typically encounter three types of error:

◆ runtime errors

◆ syntax errors

◆ logic errors.

Runtime errors

Runtime errors occur when your program is running. If Visual Basic finds a statement that is impossible to carry out it will generate an error message (see Figure 2.34).

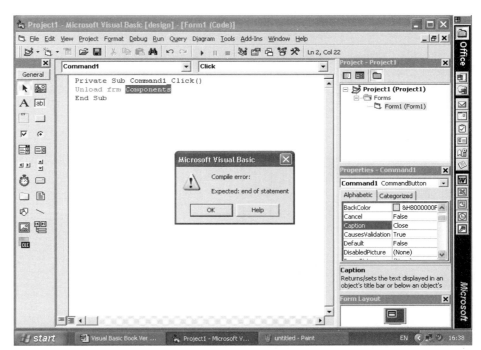

Figure 2.34 Error dialogue box

Visual Basic supplies you with the error type number together with a message. When you see the message there are several options available to you.

◆ You can change the line of code that created the problem, and then select *Run + Continue* to continue executing the program.

◆ You can radically alter the structure of the program, and then restart it by selecting *Run + Continue*.

◆ You can close the program by selecting *Run + End*.

◆ You can select *Help* to receive guidance from Visual Basic.

Syntax errors

Syntax errors result from incorrectly structured code or a mistake in the grammar of Visual Basic. Examples are the misspelling of keywords, having a 'Do' statement without a corresponding 'Loop' statement, or having an opening quote for a string but no closing quote. These types of error are the easiest to identify because Visual Basic finds them for you! The Options dialogue box selected from the Tools menu allows you to set Visual Basic to turn on the automatic detection of syntax errors (see Figure 2.35).

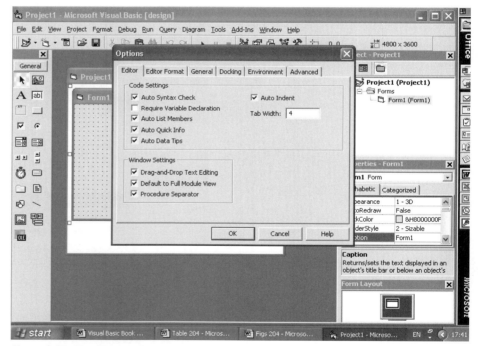

Figure 2.35 The Options dialogue box

What does it mean? *Syntax is the set of rules that state how words and phrases must be used when creating programs. For example, a grammatical error – including missed punctuation – will produce an error message explaining that the instruction was not executed because of a syntax error.*

Logic errors

Logic errors occur when your code does not execute in the way you expected. Logic errors are the most difficult errors to locate, especially as the program does not produce an error message. That is because the program is using the correct syntax and is not performing invalid operations, even though it is not giving the expected result. The only way forward is to go through your code very methodically. By analysing your results carefully, you should be able to find the problem.

4.2 Using the debugging tools

Visual Basic's debugging facilities provide you with the means to search your program's runtime details *while stepping through your code one line at a time*. In this way you can examine variables and try new values as you move through the code. You could, therefore, perform all your debugging and consequent testing from within the Visual Basic development environment.

When Visual Basic encounters a code error it displays the Error dialogue box. If you select the *Debug* button, the code window is displayed with the line that caused the problem highlighted (see Figure 2.36). *Be aware that the program has not stopped running* – it has been suspended temporarily. If the error is not serious, you can make corrections and continue with the running of the program.

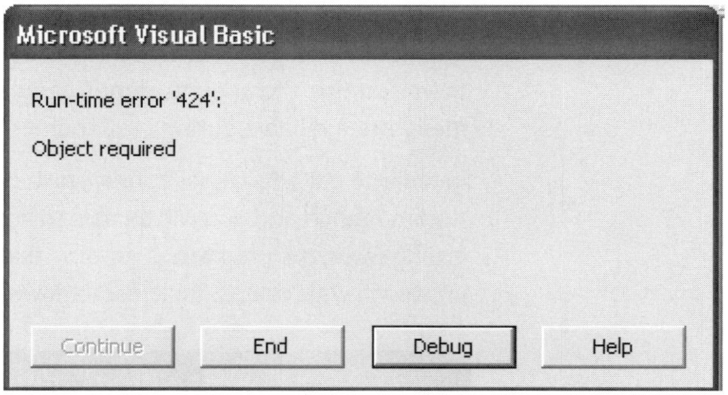

Figure 2.36 Debug code window

The Debug toolbar and menu have various options which allow you to step through the code. Ensure that the Debug toolbar is visible by selecting it in the *View + Toolbars* menu. When your program is running you can pause it by pressing the *Break* button on the toolbar (see Figure 2.37).

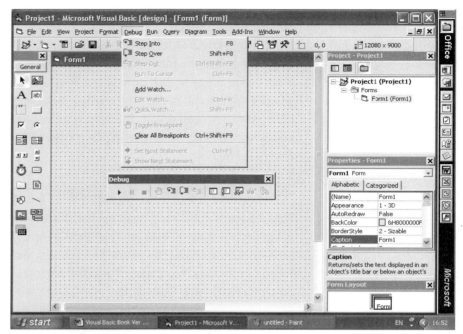

Figure 2.37 Debugging toolbar and menu

Setting breakpoints

You can force Visual Basic to stop the execution of the program at a particular point in the program by setting a **breakpoint**. You can set as many breakpoints as you like. When the program stops at a breakpoint you can then examine the code to identify any problems. The options from the Debug menu are available during breakpoint stops.

In order to set a breakpoint, first start the program. This will put Visual Basic in runtime mode and you will be able to access the break mode. This is because it is only when the program is running that the controls and other events will be initialised with values. Table 2.21 shows how to enter the break mode.

Table 2.21 Entering break mode
Press the *Ctrl* and *Break* buttons simultaneously during the program's execution at the place where you want to stop it.
During the execution of the program, select *Run + Break* from the menu bar.
Click the *Break* button on the Debug toolbar.
When designing the program or during a break mode, set your own breakpoint at the location where you would like the program to halt.
Visual Basic will enter the break mode if a runtime error occurs.

Note

When you are finished with your breakpoints you can cancel them. Cancel individual breakpoints by pressing the F9 key. *To cancel all the breakpoints in one action, select* Clear All Breakpoints *from the Debug menu.*

Stepping through code

When a program has stopped because it has met either a breakpoint or a coding error, the line of code that was to be executed next will be highlighted. To step through the rest of the code one line at a time, you have the following options.

◆ Press the *F8 key* or select *Step Into* from the Debug menu. This will allow you to execute the line. If the line contains a procedure or a function, then that procedure or function will be displayed and you will be able to step through it one line at a time. This is know as **single-stepping**.

◆ Alternatively, press the *Shift + F8 keys* simultaneously or select *Step Over* from the Debug menu. This will allow you to execute the line and any procedures or functions. The next line in the current procedure will then be highlighted.

◆ A third option is to move the cursor to another point in your program and press *Control + F8* or select *Run To Cursor* from the Debug menu.

On completion of single-stepping you can then continue running the program, or stop it by selecting the *Run* command.

Watching variables

A **watch** gives you the opportunity to observe the value of a variable as the program is running. As you step through the code, the value of the variable or expression will be displayed in the Watch window. In order to add a watch, you must use the Debug menu.

Having stopped a program during its execution, you can inspect the values of the variables or expressions in the program. If you locate the cursor on a variable name, the current value of that variable will appear below the name. In order to see how the value changes as the program progresses, either select a variable name or highlight an expression within the code. Select *Add Watch* from the Debug menu. Once you have confirmed that you have the right variable or expression, the Debug window will be displayed. This will show the current value of the selected variable or expression. You can then continue selecting variables by using *Add Watch*. You can now single-step through the program and see the values of variables and how they are affected by the code. This obviously makes it much easier to identify coding problems.

The Immediate window

When using breakpoints you can request to view the **Immediate window**. This is a special window in which it is possible to directly enter Visual Basic commands and then view and change variables and control values during the execution of your program.

To display variables and controls you need to apply the *Print* method. When you use the Print method, Visual Basic sends the output to the Immediate window. If you use the Immediate window you will find that it recognises some simple Visual Basic commands and methods. You will be able also to use assignment statements within the window.

To print to the Immediate window you have to enter a Debug object before the name of the Print method. For example, the following code excerpt executed from within an application's code prints the value of two variables with appropriate titles in the Immediate window:

```
Debug.Print "Number: "; intNumberVal, "Volume: "; intVolumeVal
```

Remember to always preface the Print method with the Debug object. If you forget to use the object, the program will print the output on the form itself.

PRACTICAL TASK 2.21

1 Load a program into Visual Basic.

2 Open the code window using the *F7 key*.

3 Locate a line of code within your program and then click the mouse button at a point in the line.

4 Select *Debug + Toggle Breakpoint*. Visual Basic will change the colour of the line of code to indicate that a breakpoint will take place during execution of the program.

5 Close the code window and then run the program.

When Visual Basic reaches a breakpoint it will enter the break mode.

Check your understanding

Load up a program of your choice and then go through each line and set a number of breakpoints within the code. Run the program and then step through the program a line at a time.

4.3 Error handling

If you write applications that contain invalid entries, you will find that they crash unceremoniously. You can inspect the code and try to find its errors, but this involves time to find and time to fix. Users tend to become frustrated when an application fails to function as expected without adequate warning or explanation. It is therefore extremely important that you consider how your application will handle and report errors. Designing and implementing an effective error handling strategy can aid development and reduce costs while maintaining trust in your applications.

If you do not create an effective policy to handle errors in your code, Visual Basic will handle them for you. It will do this by displaying a message box before terminating your application without warning.

Error handling strategy

If you implement an effective error handling strategy, it will ensure that errors are detected as and when they appear, and your applications will not terminate abruptly without explanation or warning. Apart from this benefit, there are better reasons why you should decide on a proper error handling policy. Error messages will:

- offer the user a meaningful description of an error
- advise the user of the possible impact of an error
- give the user advice that may remedy a problem and avoid unnecessary support calls
- give the user advice on how to proceed
- specify the source code error location so that it can quickly be determined.

Visual Basic error handling

To be sure that all errors are handled properly, error handlers must be registered. To register an error handler there are three statements that can be used:

- On Error GoTo <*label*>
- On Error Resume Next
- On Error GoTo 0

The **On Error GoTo** <*label*> statement directs program execution to restart at the specified *label* if an error occurs. The error handling code is normally placed at the end of a procedure to improve the readability of the source code. If this is the case, then you must ensure that the running program code does not proceed into your error handling code.

The **On Error Resume Next** statement directs the program execution to restart at the statement that follows the statement responsible for the error. If the error occurs in a nested procedure with no active error handler, then the next statement will actually be that of the active error handler and not the statement following the statement responsible for the error.

The **On Error GoTo 0** statement removes any active error handler for the current procedure, which then directs errors back to the last registered error handler – which now becomes the active error handler.

To avoid letting Visual Basic handle errors with its default error handler, it is necessary to code **error traps** and to handle errors directly within your application. If you adopt a rule that all procedures must contain an error handler, this will ensure that all errors are intercepted immediately. This attitude will leave very little room for mistakes when you are producing code. If you create an error handling policy, then this approach leads to a **log trace** showing the exact origin of each error – which is helpful during debugging and testing.

Adopt a policy of having a single error trap per procedure. This will keep error handling simple and readable. Always end the error handler with a 'Resume', 'Resume Next', 'Resume <*label*>', 'Exit Sub/Function/Property', 'End Sub/Function/Property' or 'Err.Raise' statement.

PRACTICAL TASK 2.22

1 Create a new form and enter two text boxes and three labels. Change the Text property of each text box to <blank> and change the Caption property of each label to the following: label 1 = 'Number 1' and label 2 = 'Number 2'.

2 Add a command button to the form and change its caption to 'Calculate'.

3 Add the following code to the Click event of the command button:

```
Dim sum As Integer
On Error GoTo ErrorHandler
sum = Val(Text1.Text) * Val(Text2.Text)
Label3.Caption = "The answer is: " + _
Trim(Str$(sum))
Exit Sub

ErrorHandler:
If Err.Number = 6 Then
   Label3.Caption = "The result is too big"
   Else
   Label3.Caption = "Error" + Err.Description
End If
Exit Sub
```

4 Enter the number 259 into text box 1 and enter the number 438 into text box 2.

5 Click on the Calculate button. Instead of a vague message you will get a proper error message.

Check your understanding

Identify the types of errors that can occur in your programs and explain what they are and why they happen. Explain how you would deal with each of the errors. How do you register an error handler?

Chapter summary

Bugs and debugging

- Coding errors are known as bugs, and in order to resolve them you use a process called debugging.

- The three main types of error are runtime, logical and syntax.

- Breakpoints are used to analyse programs with coding errors.

- Code can be stepped through a line at a time to evaluate errors.

- Watching variables are used to inspect the values of variables and expressions.

- The Immediate window can be used to display variables and controls using the Print method.

Error handling

- If you do not create an effective error handling policy then your applications will not run properly.

- If you do not take deliberate steps to trap and handle errors, then Visual Basic's default error handling facility will take over.

- Implementing an error handling strategy identifies errors as they occur and provides meaningful descriptions of those errors.

- Error handlers must first of all be registered in Visual Basic.

- Ensure that all of your procedures contain an error handler.

5 Test a software component and produce printed output

When you have successfully built a complete application, the next step is to test it. Testing is used to ensure that the application conforms exactly to the design specifications that have been agreed with the client. Testing is also used to identify any errors that may be apparent when the application is running and to correct these. It may not be possible to identify every single error that might appear in the program, because some may not appear until the program has been run in a variety of situations.

Note *The subject of testing will not be covered comprehensively in this chapter. Refer to unit 3 for more information.*

Table 2.22 lists types of error. Obviously these errors will be resolved during the testing phase and should not hamper the final compilation of the program. Do bear in mind that you are almost certain to put code errors or bugs into your programs at first. The idea is to reduce the number of errors by testing continually.

Table 2.22 *Types of errors*

Type of error	Description
Syntax errors	Errors that appear while you write your code Visual Basic checks your code as you type and prompts you if there is a mistake, such as misspelling a word or using a language element improperly. They are the most common type of errors; however, you can correct them in the development environment as soon as they are indicated. Using the Option Explicit statement is one means of avoiding syntax errors. It forces the programmer to declare, in advance, all the variables to be used in the application.
Logical errors	Errors that appear when the application is running These often take the form of unexpected results or values in response to user actions. A mistyped key or other event may cause your application to stop working. These errors are normally the hardest type to resolve as it is not always easy to discover where they originate.
Runtime errors	Errors that occur during the execution of your application There are two types. One comes from the misuse of a method or other function that will trigger an error that Visual Basic recognises. The second type happens when your application performs an unexpected action. This type of error does not generate an error that is recognised automatically.

5.1 How to test

There are several general approaches to testing.

◆ *Test as you go.* As you build your application, run the program at regular intervals to ensure that (a) the screen creates the application pages in line with your expectations; (b) the expected values are returned by the program; and (c) the code is doing what you expect of it.

◆ *Use another developer.* If you have the opportunity, ask another developer to test your code by building and running the program and viewing the code that you have written. The fact that you know that somebody else will be examining your code will ensure a little more attention. It also helps to let somebody else examine your code, because they may identify code errors that you are finding difficult to track down.

◆ *Step through your code*. You can examine your code line by line by stepping through the code.

◆ *Create test data*. Try to either create data or have data to hand that you can use to test your program as you build it. It is easier to have created test data before you begin coding.

◆ *Involve the users.* If it is possible, ask the users to test your application. This obviously will depend on what position you have reached in your build. But if you can allow them to test your progress, their feedback may help you to identify potential problems in your code or design.

5.2 Creating a testing plan

Your testing plan should start with a description of the program to be tested together with the objectives of the test. The plan will include the following information:

1 a diagram or chart for the application, showing the relationships between the forms contained within the application and the form objects, and identifying the necessary outcomes of the program

2 a description of how the tests will be performed

3 a listing of the test data that will be made available

4 any parts of the program that you will not be testing, with valid reasons for exclusion

5 a test schedule showing the main milestones of the project

6 a list of possible tests including a reference to the item to be tested

7 the expected results

8 observations that describe how these test results provide evidence that form and control properties comply with the specification.

5.3 Create an executable file

Once you have created an application that you are satisfied fulfils the design criteria and specification, and has been thoroughly debugged and tested, then you are ready to distribute your application to other users. You will accomplish this by **compiling** your application.

The process of compiling will translate your application together with all of its projects into an **executable file** (with extension .exe). This file will then be capable of being loaded and run on other computers (that is, outside the Visual Basic development environment).

You should compile your application to ensure the following.

1 Your application loads quickly and runs smoothly from the Start menu's *Run* command.

2 The application is secure. Remember that once a program is compiled it is more difficult to change the code than when it was uncompiled source code.

Check your understanding

Start an application that you have built completely. Select *File + Make* and select a location from the *Make Project* dialogue box that appears. Click *OK*, and Visual Basic will compile the program. Exit Visual Basic and run the program from the Start menu's *Run* command.

Chapter summary

◆ Once you have built a complete application and are ready to distribute it, you must ensure that it is thoroughly tested.

◆ Define a testing plan and identify what approaches you are going to use to complete the tests.

◆ Once testing has been completed and you are satisfied with your application, you are ready to distribute it to other users.

◆ The process of compiling your application creates an executable file. This can be run on another computer using the Start menu and the *Run* command.

Test software components

Testing software to make sure that it does what it is supposed to do is just as important as writing the programs. This unit covers the testing of programs so that the developer is confident that it is as correct as it can be.

This unit also covers IT health and safety issues.

Outcomes

◆ Prepare for testing

◆ Record the results of tests

◆ Analyse test results

◆ Identify health and safety requirements

1 Prepare for testing

This chapter shows how to identify – from a given specification – what tests are required to carry out functional testing. From this, it explains how to prepare a test plan and how to prepare test data.

The unit specification often refers to a 'tester' and a 'developer or programmer'. In the business world, and more likely in a large company, these may be two separate people. They may even be in different parts of the company. However, as a student, you are likely to be testing your own programs. This means that you should separate in your mind these two roles: your role as a program tester and your role as a programmer.

There are a number of ways in which developers can tackle the testing of their programs.

- **White box testing** is logical testing. This depends on knowing the structure or logic of the program code that is used in the software.
- **Black box testing** is functional testing. This is carried out without any knowledge of the layout of the code used in the program.
- **Top-down testing** checks first that the high-level program modules work. Only then is the detail tested.
- **Bottom-up testing** checks first that the low-level program modules work on their own. After this, the low-level modules are linked together at a high level. The program is then tested as a whole.

1.1 White box testing

In the student world, almost all of the initial testing will be white box testing. It is the most common form of testing used by any program developer writing any type of program. It should be used where the developer and tester are the same person. It is also the right way to do it for all but the very largest of programs.

The aim of white box testing is to go through all of the possible paths and lines of code in a program. This is only ever fully done in fairly simple programs. In the business world, it is good professional practice to write **error handling code** for unusual conditions. These are situations that should never occur or occur only very infrequently. However, it is usually very difficult to set up those error conditions. It is therefore not reasonable to test them. It is a balance of cost of testing against the risk of a coding error.

The first step for testing is to write a **test plan**. How to do this is explained in section 1.5. The structures of the test plans for both white and black box testing (see section 1.2) are similar, but the aims of each type of test are different.

1 It starts with simple **valid transactions**.

2 There then follow more complex valid transactions and **error transactions**.

3 Finally, there are one or two valid transactions.

White box testing usually starts with the simplest possible valid functions or transactions. These are passed through the main parts of the program. The aim of this is to answer these questions.

◆ Do the high-level links from one module to another work?

◆ Do the main parts of the program do what they are supposed to do?

◆ Does the program start correctly?

◆ Does the program end as it should?

The developer then tests more complex – but still valid – functions. This is to cover:

◆ valid processing in the less frequently used parts of the program

◆ the more complicated parts of the program.

This is often the most difficult part of the program to debug (see page 179). Errors here may occur only from time to time rather than on a consistent basis.

The final tests are with **error conditions** and with invalid functions and transactions. These check that the error handling routines work in the way that they should. These are left until last because the developer wants the error handler to be called correctly in the code.

The last one or two tests or transactions in any set of test data should always be valid transactions. Programs usually set error flags when they find an invalid transaction. A common programming mistake is not to reset the error flag once the error transaction ends. The error flag should always return to its initial value to show 'no error'. If this is not done, then it can have the effect of rejecting every transaction that follows. A final valid transaction or two makes sure that this has not happened

Program coverage routines

Some development environments have program coverage routines. With this option switched on, it records and then reports on how many times the program ran each part of the code. This gives a report for the developer.

◆ How well did this set of program tests cover the program?

◆ Which sections of code never ran?

◆ Which sections ran repeatedly?

Figure 3.1 shows diagrammatically how program coverage routines can be represented. The left-hand structure chart shows good test coverage – the same amount of testing for each module and each part of a module. The right-hand chart shows poor test coverage – the modules have had different amounts of testing, and the testing within a module is patchy.

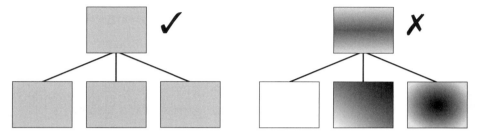

Figure 3.1 Schematic representation of the testing coverage of modules

In the business world, technical management can also use a review of the program coverage report. This report can give them confidence (or not!) on how well and how thoroughly the tester has tested a program.

Check your understanding

1 Note one or more ways in which you could check, before your tests start, that your tests plan to cover all paths through your program.

2 Find out whether your development environment has a program coverage routine. If it has, list how you switch it on and switch it off.

1.2 Black box testing

Black box testing generally happens in the later stages of testing. However, it is also used in these special cases.

◆ The tester is not the same person as the developer.

◆ Several programs are being tested together as part of a system.

◆ The internal program structure is complex.

◆ The internal program structure is unknown. An example of this is where the program or system uses an application development package.

In black box testing, the tester either does not know (or pretends not to know and does not use this knowledge) about the structure of the program. Instead, the tester treats the program as a 'black box' – in other words, its contents are hidden. The tester can see the inputs, and can see the outputs, but cannot see what goes on inside the box – what it is that turns the inputs into the outputs.

The structure of the test plan for black box testing is similar to that for white box testing.

1   It starts with simple valid transactions.

2   There then follow more complex valid transactions and error transactions.

3   Finally, there are one or two valid transactions.

The sequence of the complex and valid transactions varies from white box testing, though. The big difference between black box and white box testing is that in black box testing:

◆   the test cases are created from the *user's* point of view

◆   the emphasis is on testing *what* the program does.

In white box testing:

◆   the test cases are from the *tester's* point of view

◆   the emphasis is on testing *how* the program works.

What does this mean for a black box test?

1   Test cases that the programmer might not have expected may well occur. Black box testing makes sure that the program can handle these unexpected events.

2   A test may cover the same path through a program many times.

3   It is quite probable that more parts of the program will remain untested than for white box testing.

PRACTICAL TASK 3.1

1   For a simple program that you have already designed or written, write a set of white box tests to cover all of its program paths.

2   Write a set of black box tests to cover all of its functions.

3   List those parts of the program that the black box test does not cover. Explain why this is.

4   List those parts of the program that the black box test covers repeatedly. Explain why this is.

Check your understanding

1   When would you use white box testing?

2   When would you use black box testing?

3   What are the advantages of white box testing?

4   What are the advantages of black box testing?

1.3 Top-down and bottom-up testing

◆ **Top-down testing** checks first that the high-level modules fit together. Only then does it plug in the lower-level modules.

◆ **Bottom-up testing** checks first that low-level modules work on their own. After this it links them together into the rest of the program.

The tester uses top-down or bottom-up testing when the program or system under test is too large or complex for the straightforward white and black box testing.

Top-down testing

For top-down testing, a **test harness** lets the developer plug in dummy modules in place of any missing lower-level modules. When the program reaches that point when it is running, it hands over control to the dummy module. Usually, this dummy module just returns typical values from the lower-level module. It does not do any of the lower-level module processing.

*A **test harness** is a software testing aid that helps developers to do top-down and bottom-up testing. This aid either provides the missing parts of the program or lets the developer plug in a dummy.*

Another way of doing top-down testing is to use the **breakpoint** facility of the development environment. The breakpoint stops the program running at the point at which it is about to enter the missing lower-level module. The tester can then check that the input variables to the missing module have the expected values.

*A **breakpoint** is a location in a program under test where the program stops running normally and control is given back to the developer. The developer can look at the values of variables, change these values, or go to another point in the program.*

If the variables do have the right values, then the tester can set the output variables for the missing module. These are set to what the lower-level module would have calculated. The tester then starts the program running again.

If the input variables to the missing module did not contain the right values, then the tester halts this test and raises an **error log** (see page 171). This is to record this as an error for the developer to fix.

Bottom-up testing

Bottom-up testing is the opposite of top-down testing. It is typically used to test calculation modules before the rest of the program is written. The tester also uses bottom-up testing for a module where a program can call that module from many places.

A test harness may be used with a simple looping program to replace the higher-level modules, as shown in Figure 3.2.

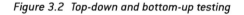

Top-down testing
• Program code
• Program code
▸ Dummy code for call to missing routine
• Program code
• Program code
▸ Dummy code for call to another missing routine
• Program code
• Program code
Bottom-up testing
• Test harness replaces missing code
• Call to low-level module
▸ Program code under test
• Test harness replaces missing code
• Another call to low-level module
▸ More program code under test
• Test harness replaces missing code

Figure 3.2 Top-down and bottom-up testing

The real lower-level or calculation module is linked in to the test harness. The test-harness test program might just supply a set of input values to the lower-level module. It then also prints or displays the values returned from the lower-level module.

The developer may also use the breakpoint facility of the development environment for bottom-up testing.

1 The tester sets breakpoints at the entry to and exit from the module under test.

2 On entry, the tester sets the input variables to the values that the rest of the program would have set.

3 The tester restarts the program.

4 The module is then tested.

5 When the module hits the breakpoint at its end, the tester checks that the output variables are the expected values. If they are, then the test is a success. If they are not, then an error log is raised.

6 The tester then does the next test with a different set of input variables.

CASE STUDY

Café Theresa

Café Theresa is a chain of coffee shops. It is developing a stock ordering system for its stores. Each store manager orders a stock of food and drink each day for delivery the next day. The new computer system will advise the manager on how much of each product to order. The store managers want to have the right amount of stock. They want enough stock so that they do not turn their customers away through not having the product that is wanted. However, they want to keep their costs low by not throwing away food when it passes its sell-by date. The amount of each product that they sell varies a lot from day to day.

◆ Ice-cream sells well on hot days, and hot soups sell well on cold days.

◆ Premium products sell well during Monday to Friday lunch breaks of local business people.

◆ There is a peak in sales on Saturday afternoons and mid-week evenings when the local football team is playing in the nearby stadium, particularly when they win or play popular opponents.

◆ Croissants sell well in the mornings, while cakes sell better in the afternoons.

A team of three developers is working on the build phase of this project. Lynne has been assigned the roles of project leader and main tester. Her job is to make sure that the system meets the company's business need. She is also testing that the programs do what they are supposed to do.

Jane has the role of senior programmer. Her programs:

◆ manage the input from the screens in the stores

◆ retrieve information from the database

◆ produce displays and reports for the stores.

Kevin is an employee of a specialist software house. He and his software house have a lot of experience in stock control calculations. Lynne employs Kevin just to write the calculation modules. These work out how much of each product to order. This depends on past usage and current and future circumstances.

Lynne decides on this testing strategy for the project:

◆ Jane will use white box testing for her own input and output programs.

◆ Lynne and Jane will use top-down testing for the processing programs.

◆ Kevin will use bottom-up testing for the stock control calculations.

◆ Lynne will use black box testing to test that the complete suite of programs fit together.

1 Why use white box testing for the input and output programs?

2 Why use top-down testing for the processing programs?

3 Why use bottom-up testing for the stock control calculations?

4 Why use black box testing for the complete suite?

5 Do you agree with Lynne's choices? If you do, then justify them. If you do not, then give your reasons.

1.4 The purpose of testing

Testing makes sure that a program really does what it is supposed to do. More broadly, the overall purpose of testing is to make sure that a computer program or system meets the needs of the intended users. For many programs, the purpose of testing is to show that the program:

◆ meets the specification

◆ conforms to site standards

◆ is in line with good programming practice.

This section describes the different forms of testing. In reality, the tester may need to work at a number of different levels for a large complex business system. The programs developed and tested in this course are likely to require just one level of testing.

CASE STUDY

Café Theresa

Café Theresa's development standards say that all batch programs should end with a standard report. This report should give:

◆ the name of the program run

◆ the date and time of the run.

In addition, for each transaction type, the report should give:

◆ how many transactions were input

◆ how many were processed successfully

◆ how many were rejected.

A standard module from their program library produces this report.

1 Why should the tester test for the production of this report?

2 What might be the causes of this being wrong or missing?

In a complex IT environment, there are at least five levels of testing:

◆ **module testing**

◆ **unit** or **program testing**

◆ **system testing**

◆ **customer** or **user testing**

◆ **beta testing.**

Module testing

This checks that just one module, sub-routine, sub-program or part of a program does what it should. The module specification is what the tester compares the module to. The programmer who writes a module usually produces his or her own module test data. Module testing is usually white box testing. The tester makes sure that all the main paths of the module or program run successfully.

Unit or program testing

This is the next step up from module testing. It checks that all the modules of a program fit together correctly. Its purpose is to confirm that the program works in line with the program specification.

1 All the input modules validate and pass data correctly to the processing modules.

2 The processing modules perform their calculation functions according to the specification.

3 The output modules correctly write to the screen, printer, database or other output device.

The team leader or programmer with overall responsibility for the program will usually write the unit test data. This level and later levels of testing are usually black box tested.

System testing

The aim of a system test is to make sure that a suite of programs, such as a payroll or accounting package, meets the computer design specification. This is the final level of testing done by the IT team.

1 It checks that output from one program forms an acceptable input to the next program.

2 It checks that updates to all databases are in line with each other or consistent.

At a large IT site, there may be a **testing quality group** who write the system test data. At smaller sites, the systems analyst or programming team leader may write the system test data.

Customer or user testing

The IT department or the supplier hands over a new or changed system to the customer or user for control-led user testing. This is before the system is used in a real situation. It means putting a copy of real data through the system. The customer or user tester makes sure that the system processes the data in line with the rules of the business.

1 For software developed in-house, user testing checks that the IT department have understood and met the company's business needs.

2 For bought-in software, user testing checks that this company has set up the software correctly for its use. It also confirms that the company has

made the changes in its business processes that are necessary for it to use the new software correctly.

Before using a new system, there is usually a period of **parallel running**. This can be seen as a form of testing, but often it is more about making sure that any changes to the business processes work. The new system takes the place of the old system only when the results from the new are at least as good as from the old system.

What does it mean?

Parallel running is where both the old and new systems are run together 'in parallel'. The tester compares the results from both systems.

It is good practice to have a **cutover** plan. This says what steps the site needs to go through to move from the old system to the new system. This might have:

◆ development staff on site or on call to fix things quickly if they go wrong

◆ extra checking of inputs and outputs until everyone is confident that the new system is working

◆ a management review and escalation process to manage things if they start to go wrong.

What does it mean?

*When a new system is first run for real, or put into production running, this is called **cutover**.*

It is good practice also to have a **contingency** plan in place. This is a plan that will only be put into practice if things go wrong, usually only in a big way. If things have gone badly wrong, sometimes the only thing to do is to **fall back**.

What does it mean?

Fall back means to go back to the system, program or program version that ran successfully before the changes were made.

Beta testing

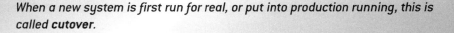

For mass-market PC software, beta testing is the process in which the software vendor runs a controlled programme of testing by potential customers. Volunteer users can download a new application and test it for errors before it is generally released to the market.

Go out and try!

Look on the Internet for a software vendor's beta testing programme.

1   List what the vendor gives to the user.

2   What is the user to give back to the vendor?

3   Who do you think has the better deal from this? Give your reasons.

1.5 Test plan essential features

There are test plans for each level of testing. The first step in developing a test plan is to work out your **test strategy**. For this, the developer needs to answer these questions:

1 What, in general terms, am I trying to test?

2 What tests do I need to do to test that part of the program is working as specified?

3 What shall I use as input test data, both valid and invalid?

4 What output will come from each of the input test cases?

To provide a structure to a test plan, it is best to write down the answers to those questions. This is the test strategy. It often forms the introduction to the test plan. The test plan then consists of a set of test plan sheets, one for each test. An example of a blank test plan is shown in Figure 3.3.

The tester fills in each field in the test plan as shown in Table 3.1.

PRACTICAL TASK 3.2

For this exercise, you should work in pairs. Take a simple program that one of you has developed earlier.

1 On your own, write a test plan introduction. This should answer the four questions given in the topic.

2 On your own, write a test plan. You should complete a set of test plan forms.

3 Compare your test plan introduction with your colleague's.

4 If any of your and your colleague's answers are different, list the different answers and give explanations.

5 Compare your test plan forms with your colleague's.

6 If any of your and your colleague's forms are very different, list the different answers and give explanations.

7 Explain any relationship, or not, between your answers to question 4 and your answers to question 6.

TEST PLAN				
System name: Program name: Module name:			Version no: Tester name:	Page no:
Test no.	Date	Purpose/Type of test	Input/Filename	Expected output/Filename

Figure 3.3 A blank test plan

Table 3.1 ***Fields in a test plan***		
Field name	**Description**	**Examples**
System name	General description of the project – usually bulk-copied	Café Theresa stock control
Program and module names	The piece of code or system that this test plan covers – usually bulk-copied	Stock-control calculation module
Tester name	The person who prepared the test plan – usually bulk-copied	Sara Student
Version number	The date the test plan was prepared (not the date it was run) – usually bulk-copied	17/9/2004
Test number	Sequential number for this test plan	003
Purpose	What this particular input is testing for	Is month number valid (value too large)?
Type of test	Whether or not this input is valid	No
Input	The precise conditions to be tested	Valid day and year, month number >12
Input values	The input values	Date 01/13/2005; other input fields with valid values
Expected output	The expected result of the transaction	Transaction should be rejected with a meaningful error message stating 'Month invalid: it is >12' There should have been no change to the database.

1.6 Approaches to the design of test data

There are three approaches to the design of test data:

◆ the computing approach
◆ the business approach
◆ the data approach.

The **computing approach** looks in turn at each of the computing functions of a program or system. These are input, processing and output. The test data first checks all of the input functions. It then goes through all the processing functions. The last part of the tests checks all of the output functions. The developer often uses this way of doing things to test a set of batch programs.

In contrast, the **business approach** tests each of the business functions in turn. 'Business' here does not mean that the tester can use this for commercial programs only. As an example, this is how a tester might test a multi-function calculator program using the business approach. First, the tester might test on their own each of these functions: Add, Subtract, Multiply, Divide. After this, the tester might test the more complex mathematical or scientific calculator functions. Finally, the tester might test linking a set of calculator functions together.

The **data approach** is the least common. It first tests all the transactions or functions that read or update a particular table or file. It follows this by testing transactions for the next table or file. The tester often uses this approach if the developer has used a data-driven way of writing a computer system to design the program.

1.7 Choosing data values for testing

It is important to design test data to confirm that a program works in the right way under both normal and exceptional circumstances. To do this, the tester writes test data with three types of value: valid, invalid and boundary.

Valid and invalid test data

Valid test data should run normally through the program. It should produce the right answers that the tester expects. For the first programs that a developer writes, it is most unlikely that this happens on the early test runs. However, as the developer takes out bugs from the program the tester finds that:

◆ fewer valid transactions are rejected
◆ more and more of the expected valid transactions run correctly all the way through the program
◆ there is correct updating of the database or files
◆ the program returns the right output to the user.

The tester looks to make sure that the program throws out **invalid test data** when the program checks if it is valid. With their first few programs, developers are often pleased when early test runs do reject a lot of their invalid test cases. However, it is important to make sure that the program rejects these test cases for the correct reason. If the program's error messages are not very helpful, then this is very difficult to check. An example of a poor error message is 'Invalid input: please re-submit'. The message 'Month invalid: greater than 12' makes it much clearer what is wrong – the error is that the input has failed the test that the month number must be in the range 1 to 12.

Sometimes, invalid data runs all the way through a program or system because it is wrongly taken as valid. This often has strange results. The tester and developer should check these carefully. This might hide a much bigger problem with the program logic.

Boundary conditions

The initial efforts of the tester are to make sure the program is correctly processing clearly valid transactions and rejecting for the correct reason obviously invalid transactions. Then it is time for the tester to check that **boundary conditions** work properly. In programming terms, what the tester is seeking to do is to make sure that the developer has coded all **relational operators** correctly. For more information on relational operators, see page 12.

- Has the developer written 'less than' instead of 'less than or equal to'?
- Has the developer written 'greater than or equal to' instead of just 'greater than'?
- Does the program go round a loop once too often?
- Does the program go round a loop once too few times?

The tester tests for each boundary condition and writes two types of test cases. There is a valid test case that uses the last correct value. This forms a pair with an invalid test case that uses the first wrong value.

Here is an example of testing a date. If the program has a month input, then the tester checks that month 12 is accepted as valid. He or she also checks that month 13 is rejected as invalid. There is something wrong with the program if the two test cases are then both accepted or both rejected.

A subtler test is needed to check for day numbers. Clearly, a day number of 0 or 32 is always invalid. A day number of 1 or 28 or any number in between is always valid. Numbers 29 and 30 are always valid in all months except February. Finally, in some months 31 is valid and in some months 31 is invalid. So, there must be correct code in the program to test for day number based on month number. To cater for February, there should also be code that tests the year number to see whether 29 February is a valid date (in a leap year).

Check your understanding

Explain why 'Invalid input: please re-submit' is a poor error message from the point of view of (a) the user, (b) the developer, and (c) the tester.

PRACTICAL TASK 3.3

1 Write in structured English, or as a flowchart or code, a day validation routine to check whether the day number input is valid depending on the month number input. This should allow 29 February as a valid date.

2 Produce a list of boundary test cases of day numbers and month numbers.

3 Test a colleague's answer to question 1 by taking your boundary test cases and desk checking his or her day validation routine.

4 Write in structured English, or as a flowchart or code, a February day validation routine to check whether the day number input is valid depending on the month number and year number input.

5 Produce a list of boundary test cases of day numbers, month numbers and year numbers.

6 Test a colleague's answer to question 4 by taking your boundary test cases and desk checking his or her February day validation routine.

1.8 Recovery testing

The testing that has been covered so far is for what the developers have written to meet the user's business needs. This assumes that supporting hardware, systems software and site operating procedures work exactly as they should, for all of the time. Unfortunately, this happy state of affairs does not yet exist. It is unlikely to exist in the future. **Recovery testing** is done to make sure that data can be recovered after a hardware or software failure.

Hardware at a basic level is now very reliable. There is now a very high mean time between failure (MTBF) rate of all units. However, the growth in reliability of individual units is about the same as the growth in the total number of units. This growth is needed to manage the size and complexity of today's business. Large IT sites have grown from tens of mainframes or servers that they had around 1990, to tens of thousands of networked smaller servers today. The system designs must allow for some small part of the overall computer network to fail without collapsing the rest.

Operating system software reliability has also improved. This has not been at the same rate as hardware. Here, the trend has been to automated system recovery and speed of return. This has led to higher system availability, rather than a lot fewer system failures.

System failures

Even with automated operating environments, there are still operating problems at a site that can cause a system failure. The power supply might fail, or the state of the computer network causes a server to stop or hang. An air-conditioning problem can cause a system shutdown as it is too hot or too cold. An operator might just switch off or power off a processor or a disk unit.

The test plan and the operating procedures for an overall system should therefore include making sure that data can be recovered after a hardware or software failure. For a complex system, where the individual transactions and their timing cannot easily be reproduced, this would typically involve these tasks:

1   Take a fixed or frozen copy of the data, say every week or month.

2   Record or log every change that the user or system makes to the data. This means the system writes to a journal file or log database a 'before' image. This is what a data block looked like before any data change. It also writes an 'after' image. This is what the data block looked like after the change.

3   Record or log every update transaction. The system links these transactions with the changes made to the database. This is also done through the journal.

4   Merge regularly the changes in the journal file. This is because, often, the same record is changed over and over again.

If the operating system fails, then it is necessary to roll back any changes that are in progress or only partially completed. This is so that the database following this roll back is in a consistent state.

CASE STUDY

Café Theresa

Café Theresa's sales database records from the till each item sold to customers. It also records in a different place the total value of each customer's order for all items sold. If the computer system fails while updating sales records, then it must either have recorded all of a customer order or none of it. It would not be acceptable to have different answers for daily sales for a store by adding up the values from individual order lines and by adding up the order totals.

1   What do you think Café Theresa's management would think of the computer system if it gave different answers for daily store sales? Give your reasons for this.

2   List ways in which you might design the system so that it always gave a consistent answer even if there had been a system failure during update.

To provide more system availability and protection if it is the hardware that fails and a disk is damaged, sometimes a site has **mirrored disks**.

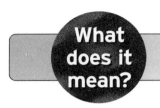

Mirrored disks are where there are two, or more, identical copies of the contents of a disk.

For a disk failure with mirrored disks, this is what happens:

Disk 1 fails.
Computer operations carry on using disk 2.
Disk 1 is repaired or replaced.
All the data on disk 2 is copied on to disk 1.
Disk 1 is brought back into operation.

If disks are *not* mirrored, then this happens:

Disk 1 fails.
Computer operations stop.
Disk 1 is repaired or replaced.
The frozen data is copied on to disk 1.
New data is added to disk 1.
Disk 1 is brought back into operation.
Computer operations start again.

This more complex process is needed so that the disk ends up with the current data with no data loss.

Database management systems

Operating systems and database management systems (DBMSs) such as Oracle often have recovery features as part of the way they work. However, it is important to know the principles of what they are doing. The developer explains the recovery needs to the DBMS expert. The expert sets up the DBMS so that these needs should be met. The tester must test to make sure that the setup has actually met these needs.

For a simple system, often all that has to be done is to put the files into read-only mode once a day. This is usually overnight. All the files are then copied or a **backup** is taken. The daily transactions are often logged. To recover from a failure, the backup is used. This restores the files to where they were the previous night. If needed, the daily transactions are reapplied from the log or journal.

*A **backup** is a copy taken of some or all of the files in a system for recovery purposes. It may be a full backup where the copy is taken of all the files in the system. More usually, it is a partial backup or incremental backup – this is just those files or parts of files that have changed since the previous full backup was made.*

Disaster recovery

The most dramatic form of recovery is disaster recovery. For their most business-critical applications, a company may have a second backup site in some other part of the country. This might be the site that their developers usually use. In the event of a disaster, this development use stops or is greatly restricted. The company may also have a recovery agreement with another disaster recovery site. This is the main business for disaster recovery IT companies. Their business model is that disaster will not strike many of their customer's sites at the same time.

These are the disaster recovery steps. Each day, the first site sends a backup copy of the critical data to the recovery or second site. Sometimes, the first site captures and sends the daily transactions as well. Then disaster strikes the first site. At the recovery site, personnel copy the backups on to the database, and possibly apply the daily transactions too. They switch the network to the second site, restart and operate the systems.

That is an idealised description of the process. There are three major concerns for a disaster recovery or standby site:

◆ What if it does not work when it is needed?

◆ How much does it cost to have the computing power unused or doing lower priority work?

◆ How can the second site be kept to the same technical standard as the primary site?

Mirrored sites are a solution to this. Here, the two sites share computing power and share and often copy databases. If one site fails, then the other site can still process the workload. The amount of computer power is less. Some functions and data may not be available, but the application keeps running.

Go out and try!

1 Search the Internet for PC software that supports recovery.

2 Select one or more of these software products and list what they do.

3 Explain how you would use each of these products to provide the parts of a disaster recovery system for a PC-based system.

1.9 Performance testing

Performance testing is making sure that the program or system meets the response time and availability needs of the user.

In many cases, the program specification does not state explicitly these response time and availability needs. In this case, the developer uses professional judgement on what the user will accept and at what cost.

For a large or complex system, or when it is necessary to meet a specific business need, the performance requirements are explicitly stated. This is often in some detail. The contract between the supplier and the user may also state or refer to the performance needs. Often, there are financial penalties if performance needs are not met.

The users will have an idea of what response times to expect from similar programs they have run in the past. The tester should make sure that the program is not a lot slower than this. Table 3.2 gives examples of what acceptable performance might mean to a user.

Table 3.2 **What is acceptable performance?**

Type of software	Speed	Testing notes
Graphics, especially games	Fast enough that movements appear smooth, not jerky	Test on an adequate computer, not the most powerful available development computer.
Desktop software	Immediate for character display, scrolling and response to input events	A few seconds is OK to 'think' or 'do' something that the user sees as a large amount of work. Examples of this are: • searching through a large database of many thousands of records • recalculating a large complex spreadsheet or other calculation • redrawing a large complex diagram.
Transaction processing	Two or three seconds is acceptable for a display or update transaction	A little longer is OK to search for a long list of records from a very large database and display all those records. Here a good way to do this with a fast response time is to just return the first screen or the first 100 records that meet what the user asks for. A PF key press or one button click sets off another transaction that returns the next screen or the next 100 records.
System utilities	As short a time as possible while still doing the utility function	Whether on a server or a desktop, running system utilities often hits the use of that computer. They may even stop any useful work while the utility runs.

CASE STUDY

System utilities

A server vendor gave away free system utilities with their servers. The company put very little developer time into writing these utilities. They ran very slowly. The vendor saw writing of this necessary software as an overhead to their main business of selling servers.

Later, the vendor changed their marketing policy. They began to sell these utilities at a nominal price. When the sales force tried to sell them, there was no interest from any of the potential buyers, so the sales people asked existing customers what was wrong with the utilities.

None of their customers actually used them, even though they had been free. Instead, they had paid a lot of money to competing software companies for equivalent utilities that ran much faster, were easier to use and had more features.

1 Discuss this case study with others in your group.

2 What lessons can be learned from this?

3 What options does the server vendor now have?

4 Which of these options would you choose? Justify your choice.

In doing performance testing, the tester should try to use full volumes of data. If this is not possible, then the tester should scale the results to what will happen for the maximum expected volume of data.

CASE STUDY

Defrag utility

A defragmentation utility for a desktop computer was designed when the standard disk storage was 2 gigabytes. For a partly full disk, following regular defragmentation, it ran in less than an hour. This was acceptable for most users. Technology quickly moved on, and for a 20-gigabyte computer it takes 13 hours for this utility to complete. So this utility, while it still works correctly, is not suitable for use on today's desktop computers.

1 Find out and write notes to explain what defragmentation involves.

2 How long would you regard as a reasonable maximum run time for this utility? Justify your answer.

3 In what ways could the PC user overcome this problem?

4 Find out and list what each of these ways would cost.

Batch programs

With batch programs, the performance aim is to keep as small as possible the amount of server resource that a program uses. This is because the shared server is heavily used in a many-user site. The aim may also be to meet elapsed clock time needs.

Many businesses do a lot of computer processing overnight. For example, the business need might be that the processing cannot start until their call centre closes at 2200 hours. The warehouse may need the output from the system at 0200 hours. This is so that the warehouse staff can pick the stock and ship the stock to the store for 0800 hours. Another need might be to email or fax sales reports for the previous day to managers around the country by 0700 in the morning.

CASE STUDY

Café Theresa

Café Theresa invested heavily in a new system to change the way one of the head office departments worked. It had a dedicated server which was the most powerful that could be bought of that type. The user department was very happy with the testing on a sample of data. The tests showed that the new system met its functional needs completely.

The department started parallel running. The new system even showed up faults in the old system that had been there for years. However, as more and more data moved across to the new system, the run times slowed. At last, it took nearly 24 hours each day to run the daily batch processing. If they hit a problem that delayed the runs for 6 hours, it took a week to get back up to date.

This could not go on, so this is what Café Theresa had to do.

◆ Stop taking on more data.
◆ Delay putting the system fully live for a long time.
◆ Rewrite much of the system to run more quickly.
◆ Drop some functions they had already built as they just took too long to run.

So, failing to performance test turned what should have been a great success into a near disaster.

1 Discuss why the system went wrong and how the problem could be prevented.

2 List a set of performance needs for this system.

3 How would you set about testing these needs?

4 What could you do when you found the system did not meet them?

Performance testing should be thought about at the time the system is being specified. The systems analyst should ask the user about response time or clock time needs, beyond the good practice described earlier in this section. Here are some examples of what the user might say.

◆ One set of functions is done across the Internet. The company's customers will be waiting for a response and there will be Internet delays to consider.

◆ The company's customer service agents do a second set of functions. This is either face-to-face to the customer or with the customer on the phone.

◆ A third set of functions is online to the company's staff. There is a staff productivity benefit if these run quickly.

◆ Other functions can run in the background. They can run at lower priority. They can accept a delay when the system is busy.

The designer should take these performance needs into account when designing the computer system. Note that the designer should not deliberately slow down lower-priority transactions. However, the designer may decide, for example, to move slow-running but infrequently wanted functions into separate transactions. The user then enjoys fast responses for most of the time. The user knows when there is going to be a slow response.

The tester should pick up those transactions that perform badly in the same way as identifying others that do not conform to good programming practice. The tester should raise an error log. The developer then reviews what is causing the delay.

Sometimes, it is straightforward to see what is going wrong. For example, the program might read every record in a file to find the one it wants. It would be faster to go through an index directly to the record. To code this might be more complex, and the index might not exist for anything else, so the developer will need to consider whether it is worthwhile to create and maintain an index for this program to use.

At other times, it is just not clear what is causing the delay in response time. There may be a more experienced senior programmer who has more technical knowledge and experience who can look for the cause.

Response-time analysis software

Response-time analysis software reports on which modules and which statements within those modules demand the most computing power. Both testers and developers use this software, though in different ways. These analysers also exist for databases. They can help the developer find which database calls take the most time and use the most system resources. Some sites also produce guides showing best practice. This helps the developer in terms of the balance between:

◆ speed of writing

◆ ease of understanding and maintenance

◆ performance.

Benchmarking is measuring how fast something works in relation to some standard. This is done when there is a need to meet tough response times or run times for a system. Computer hardware and software makers also run benchmarks, to show how much faster their new hardware or software is. This comparison can be with their own older products. More often they compare their new product (always favourably!) with the older products of their competitors.

The tester takes into account any specific performance needs stated in the specification when drawing up a **performance test plan**. Recording software is used to measure for each transaction the response time and the amount of system resources used.

A **thread** of transactions is a set of transactions that run one after another. Single-thread is when just one of these sets is run on its own. Each transaction runs on an empty machine without other transactions running. When one transaction finishes, the next transaction starts. This might run immediately. More usually, it is after a delay to simulate user thinking time. Multi-thread is when several of these sets are run at the same time.

An illustration of this is running in a relay race. When a relay team is practising on its own or running just against the stopwatch, then the one team on the race track is like a computer running in single-thread mode. When several teams are competing in a relay race, then the racetrack is like a multi-thread computer.

Testing should first be carried out using just one set (or stream or thread) of transactions running in single-thread mode. The tests are then repeated in multi-thread mode. Many streams of transactions run at the same time, usually with slightly different test values.

When the machine is fully loaded, increasing the number of threads that are running does not increase the number of transactions processed per minute. Sometimes, it even decreases. This is because the system has to spend more time managing the queues of transactions awaiting running. This is the capacity of that machine for that transaction mix.

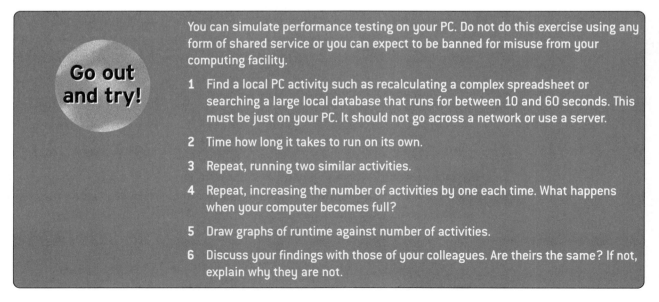

Go out and try!

You can simulate performance testing on your PC. Do not do this exercise using any form of shared service or you can expect to be banned for misuse from your computing facility.

1 Find a local PC activity such as recalculating a complex spreadsheet or searching a large local database that runs for between 10 and 60 seconds. This must be just on your PC. It should not go across a network or use a server.

2 Time how long it takes to run on its own.

3 Repeat, running two similar activities.

4 Repeat, increasing the number of activities by one each time. What happens when your computer becomes full?

5 Draw graphs of runtime against number of activities.

6 Discuss your findings with those of your colleagues. Are theirs the same? If not, explain why they are not.

1.10 Test-data generation software

For the simplest of programs, the test stream consists of the tester sitting at a PC or terminal. He or she enters each transaction in turn from the test plan. For each, the tester notes down or copies and pastes the responses. There are several disadvantages to this:

(a) mistakes in entry of the transaction

(b) missing transactions

(c) mistakes in recording the response to a transaction

(d) the very time-consuming need to repeat many times a long transaction stream.

Software to generate test data

This is used to simplify, speed up and reduce the errors in the test process. It also often has features to help to create large volumes of data for performance tests.

What this software does is to simulate the user sending a stream of transactions to a system. It then captures the stream of replies that come back from the system. This is how it works.

1 From the test plan, the tester enters into the software the data that he or she would have entered online into the program under test. This is done field by field.

2 The software records the data for this transaction on to its database.

3 The tester then repeats this for each transaction input and response that he or she wants to test.

4 At the end of this process, the software has on its database the complete test plan.

This is in the format and sequence that the program under test expects. The tester can now check that no mistakes have been made in entry of the transactions. If they have, it is easy to correct just the field or transaction that is wrong. Thus, the software removes disadvantages (a) and (b) above.

Testing harnesses

Many test-data generators work with a testing harness. This software takes the generated test data and runs the transactions with this as input. This is instead of the tester having to enter manually all of the transactions. The harness captures the responses of the program to the inputs. It writes these to its database and associates them with the inputs.

The tester now reviews the output from the test. He or she compares it to what is on the test plan. Where there are differences, the tester raises a **test**

error log. This tells the developer what should have happened and what actually happened. The developer uses this to look into and fix the bug – described further on page 180.

It is helpful for the developer if the tester raises only one test error log per problem rather than one per transaction. For example, if all 20 test cases for transaction 32 failed to run, then the tester should raise only one log form for this. This shows how the software removes disadvantage (c) above.

When the developer has looked into the bugs raised on the first test run and believes that most of them have been fixed, the tester runs the test again. In this way, the software removes disadvantage (d) above.

The tester concentrates on those test cases that failed on the previous run. He or she checks that the test cases now produce the correct action and response.

- If a test case does work, then the tester signs off the error log for that error as it is now fixed. Note that it does not always produce the correct action; the first bug may have hidden a second bug! Here, the tester will raise another error log for the developer.
- If the developer has not properly fixed the first bug, then the tester does not sign it off. The tester sends the original error log back to the developer for the bug to be fixed properly.

Test output comparison

Some test software has an **output comparison** feature. This checks the full output results of one test run with the output results of a previous test run. It then indicates which outputs were the same as previously and which outputs changed, and lists the changed outputs. This is most useful when the tester is near the end of testing, when he or she is confident that most transactions work.

The tester splits the work into four classes:

- *No change and correct last time.* There is no need to check, because it still works.
- *No change and wrong last time.* The developer still has not fixed this problem, though he or she may have made an attempt to do so.
- *Changed and correct last time.* The developer has introduced an error into what was a working transaction, so the tester needs to raise a new error log.
- *Changed and wrong last time.* The developer may have fixed this error. The tester needs to look at this in detail. He or she must make sure that it is now doing what the test plan expected.

This output comparison feature is also useful in **regression testing**. This involves testing that things still work as they used to, when minor changes are made to an already working system. There is more information on this in section 3.6.

Test-data creation

There are additional features in the software to help in creating the content of the test data. More features help to copy and change this for many sets of data.

◆ Constant values can be set into specified fields.

◆ Fields can have a constant value, often 1, added to them or taken away from them between one transaction and the next.

◆ Bulk changes can be made to one set of inputs to form another set of inputs.

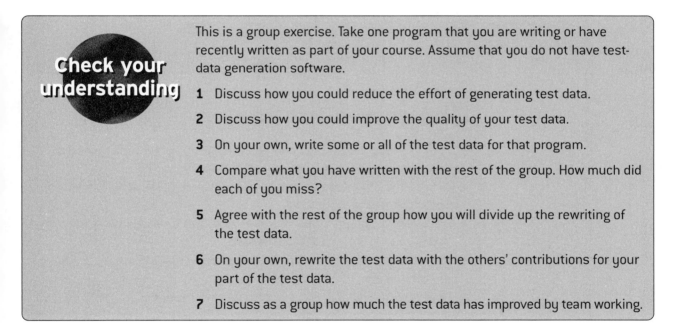

Check your understanding

This is a group exercise. Take one program that you are writing or have recently written as part of your course. Assume that you do not have test-data generation software.

1 Discuss how you could reduce the effort of generating test data.

2 Discuss how you could improve the quality of your test data.

3 On your own, write some or all of the test data for that program.

4 Compare what you have written with the rest of the group. How much did each of you miss?

5 Agree with the rest of the group how you will divide up the rewriting of the test data.

6 On your own, rewrite the test data with the others' contributions for your part of the test data.

7 Discuss as a group how much the test data has improved by team working.

1.11 Quality control

Most sites have quality control procedures. These put into practice, for that site, the principles described earlier in this unit. To comply with them, a standardised and rigorous approach to testing is required.

Testing is about checking that the program meets both the specification and the business need. It is also about recording that the tester has gone through these checks. With those records, both the tester and colleagues can be confident that the program has been tested. They can know how much the program has been tested.

Check your understanding

In a progress report, a tester states that 'testing is now 90 per cent complete'. That is a rather vague statement! The team leader asks the tester to define what is meant by 90 per cent, and to prove it. For each of the meanings below, state what proof you could give.

1 Ninety per cent of entries in the test plan are written.
2 Ninety per cent of the test plan inputs and outputs are written.
3 Ninety per cent of the test cases are generated.
4 Ninety per cent of transactions have had at least one test run.
5 Ninety per cent of the test plan transactions either work correctly or have an error logged.
6 Ninety per cent of the error logs have been returned.
7 Ninety per cent of the test plan transactions work correctly.
8 For the 10 per cent of test plan transactions that still do not work, 90 per cent of the error logs have been returned.

Which measure do you think is of most value, and why?

Chapter summary

- Four types of testing have been considered: white box, black box, and top-down and bottom-up testing.
- Five forms of testing have been considered: module, unit, system, customer and beta testing.
- Recovery testing is done to make sure that data can be retrieved after a hardware or software failure.
- Performance testing makes sure that the program meets the needs of the users.
- Software is available to help with testing routines.

2 Record the results of tests

This chapter shows how to use a test plan to carry out a series of tests. It then describes how to record the results of those tests in a test log. It explains how to provide evidence of testing. Examples of this are printed output, screen shots and file output.

- The **test plan** is the input to your testing. It says what makes up the input to each of your tests. It then says what you expect to happen as a result of these tests.

- The **test log** is the record of what actually happened on each of the tests.

If a program performs just one simple function then it is easy enough to keep trying to run the program until it does that. However, in the real world, even the simplest program does many things. It is therefore important to record what happens on each test. This is so that the developer knows which parts of the program still have errors that need to be fixed. The developer also needs to know which parts of the program already do what he or she expects. Finally, especially if there are deadlines to meet, it is important to know what parts of the program have yet to be tested effectively.

2.1 Test log essential features

A simple test log is shown in Figure 3.4. Some of the information that the developer enters on this is repeated from the test plan (Figure 3.3 on page 153). Table 3.3 explains the purpose of each field in detail.

Table 3.3 *Fields in a simple test log*

Field name	Description	Examples
System name	Brief title of the project (sometimes just the project code or initials) – usually bulk-copied	Café Theresa stock control
Program name	The larger piece of code that this test plan covers – usually bulk-copied	Stock-control calculation program
Module name	The detailed piece of code that this test plan covers – usually bulk-copied	Stock-control minimum-order-quantity calculation module
Version number	Either the version number of the program that is under test or the version number of the relevant test plan – usually bulk-copied	004
Tester name	The person who completed the test log (not necessarily the same person who created the test plan) – usually bulk-copied	Sarah Coder
Test number	Cross-reference to the test number on the test plan (a sequential number for that test plan)	003
Date	The date this test run took place (not the test plan date, which is when the test plan was prepared)	30/9/2004
Actual output and/or filename	The actual result of the test transaction or program run and/or the filename where the results of this test were written	The transaction was rejected with the error message 'Month invalid: it is >12' There was no change to the database.
Comments on discrepancies	A record of discrepancies between actual results and expected results (the differences between what should have happened and what actually happened)	The month should have been accepted as valid. The transaction should have updated the database.

TEST LOG				
System name: Program name: Module name:			Version no: Tester name:	Page no:
Test no.	Date	Actual output/Filename	Comments on discrepancies	

Figure 3.4 A blank test log

PRACTICAL TASK 3.4

For this activity you should work in pairs. First choose a simple program that one of you has recently written.

1 Working on your own, fill in one page of a test plan and one page of a simple test log. Compare your results with your partner's.

2 As a pair, list which parts of your forms you have completed the same and which parts are different. Give your reasons for this.

2.2 Cross-referencing tests

One very important piece of information in testing is the **test number**. This number acts as the cross-reference between the various documents:

◆ the test plan

◆ the test logs that record the runs

◆ test output that is either printed output, screen shots or the output file or files.

For each test, the tester works out and records on the test plan what is the right input and the expected output. He or she assigns a test number to each test case – usually the next number in a sequence. If a program has many different functions, then more than one set of numbers may be used. The tests for credit transactions may be numbered C1, C2, C3, etc., while the tests for debit transactions may be D1, D2, D3, etc. In the same way, if there are several testers then Jane may use test numbers J1, J2, J3, etc. while Kevin uses K1, K2, K3, etc.

In the business world, the number of test cases may run into thousands. However, in the student world, the number will be in tens or at most in the low hundreds. For example, for a small three-module program:

◆ test cases 1 to 20 test module 1

◆ test cases 21 to 40 test module 2

◆ test cases 41 to 60 test module 3

◆ test cases 61 to 100 test the complete program.

For most programs, there is a need for a testing strategy – that is, an idea of how to tackle the testing. Often, a tester decides to test each module in turn and then test the program as a whole.

An example of how a set of tests might go and how to complete the test log is shown in Figure 3.5.

The tester decides that the first test run is for tests 1 to 20.
Unfortunately, the program crashes for each transaction.

Test no.	Date	Actual output	Comments on discrepancies
1 to 20	1/2/04	Program crashed. Output saved in file Crash20040201a.	Not applicable. Error log 1 raised.
1 to 20	2/2/04	All transactions rejected with message 'Transaction number error – must be numeric'.	All but one transaction should have had valid transaction numbers. Error log 2 raised.
1 to 20	3/2/04	Tests 4 & 7 worked correctly as expected. Tests 9 & 14 produced the expected error message. The rest of tests 1 to 8 were rejected. The rest of tests 10 to 20 produced the wrong error messages.	Error logs 3, 4 & 5 raised for tests 1 to 8. Error logs 6 to 11 raised for tests 10 to 20. There are fewer error logs than tests because some tests failed with the same error.
1	4/2/04	Correct record updated message and database changed correctly.	Error log 3 confirmed as now fixed.
2	4/2/04	'Invalid quantity' instead of valid transaction.	Error log 4 fixed, but this was hiding another problem. Error log 12 raised.

Once the developer fixes the program crash, then each transaction is rejected incorrectly.

On the third run, there is a positive test. Some of the tests run as expected. Others either fail when they should have worked or work when they should have failed. The tester produces an **error log** for each of these for later investigation and correction.

Figure 3.5 Example of a completed test log

Check your understanding

1 List the disadvantages of not using test numbers to cross-reference tests.

2 By mistake, two different sets of tests for one program were created with the same test numbers. List the problems that this could create.

2.3 Testing in the target environment

The developer normally develops a program in a very different technical environment from the user of the software. The developer has software tools that help him or her to design, write, test and document the program. These tools often:

◆ include debugging and tracing features

◆ are able to stop the program at any point

◆ can change any variable in the program

◆ can change where the program will next execute

◆ have a set of supporting software libraries that are consistent with the code the developer wrote.

To run these powerful tools usually means that the developer has up-to-date system software, running on powerful modern hardware. The developer can rely on having supporting libraries and programs. In contrast, the user will often have only as much as is needed for the job the computer has to do!

For example, an early model Pentium running *Windows 95* can still provide good response times and functionality for all of these activities:

◆ word processing using *Word 95* and spreadsheets using *Excel 95*

◆ presentations using *PowerPoint 95*

◆ email using *Outlook Express 4* and Internet using *Internet Explorer 4*

◆ specialised database programs.

The major constraint of hardware and software from the Windows 95 era is that it is poor at running more than one major program at the same time.

Minimum system requirements

The developer should decide on the typical minimum hardware and software specifications for the application.

◆ If the developer is working on a video editing program, then the user is likely to need a fast processor speed, a large and fast disk drive, good video equipment and fast data transfer around the system.

◆ A high-speed action game has many similar needs. It does not need large and fast disks.

◆ At the other end of the scale, a multi-function calculator, a specialised database program or a PC utility may need less than 10 per cent of any of a modern computer's resources. These programs are ideal for running in many computer environments from Windows 95 onwards.

Even where there is a real need for powerful modern hardware and software to run an application, similar functions may be found in older environments. It may be commercial considerations that have made the older program obsolete.

◆ In the games field, there are programs such as *Sim City* that has developed into *Sim City 2000*, *Sim City 3000* and *Sim City 4*. The underlying theme is still the same, but with better, more powerful graphics and computing.

◆ Many sports games produce a new game for each season. Often the major change is to the data for the simulated players or teams, rather than any major new functions.

There is little functional difference for the average user in most desktop business software. Updated versions bring impressive new functions for 'power users'. They may also increase the volume and size of data that the program can cope with. However, the developer should consider carefully the target audience when trying to set the minimum specification of computer that the new program needs.

◆ Most spreadsheet users are not professional accountants or financial analysts.

◆ Most word processor users are not professional writers producing complex documents all day long.

Testing for different environments

The approach uses the same form of test plans, test logs and error logs as the tester used in functional testing.

First, the tester checks that all the functions of the program work on the developer's hardware and software. Then the tester moves to a more typical modern user environment and repeats the tests. While the program usually still works, some features may work either unacceptably slowly or not at all. The program may even fail to load or crash with a system error message. The tester should record these tests on the test plan and test log and raise error logs if any problems arise.

The tester then tests the program on examples of the rest of the computer hardware and software that they expect the program to run in. The results of these tests are not likely to be functional problems. They are more likely to be that the program needs certain software version levels, minimum hardware requirements and other software for the program to work. Sometimes, the developer needs to change the way in which parts of the code have been written. This is so that the program can use optionally older support software that is available on older computers.

PRACTICAL TASK 3.5

This activity shows how similar functions are delivered by different versions of software for different environments. You should work in pairs or small groups. You will be looking at what *Office* software is installed on several PCs. Pick PCs that are of different ages and specification. For each PC:

1 List the hardware and system software specification.

2 List the name and version number of each item of *Office* software installed.

3 Where different versions of the same applications are installed, compare their functions.

4 List the functional differences between these versions.

5 Estimate what percentage more functions there are in the newer versions.

6 Calculate what percentage more power, by processor speed, amount of memory or some other factor, there is in the newer larger computer.

7 List how often you might use each of these new features. What conclusions can you draw from this?

Chapter summary

The following have been covered:

◆ test log essential features

◆ cross-referencing of tests

◆ testing in the target environment.

3 Analyse test results

This chapter shows how to use the test log to produce a testing report. This analysis of the test results:

◆ specifies the presence or absence of errors

◆ makes proposals for rectifying errors

◆ reports on the success of the test against the original software specification.

3.1 Types of software error

Several forms of error can occur in a computer program. The first – and most serious – is that program does not meet the business needs. Perhaps the program does meet the specification and the specification was at first correct, but now the needs have changed. This may mean changes to the modules, to the sizes of some of the data fields, or even to the structure of the programs.

At the programming level, a correct program is one that conforms to (is in line with) the program's written specification and good computing practice. The program should validate or check input so that it tries to process only valid data. It should also detect and correct errors, and not crash under unexpected conditions.

Compliance with specification and good programming practice

A program specification at most contains the structure of the solution. The developer needs to write code that is in line with that specification. He or she also needs to write code that is in line with good programming practice.

The program should validate input so that it processes only correct values. The program should reject incorrect values with an error message that means something to the user. This error message should also tell the user what needs to be done to correct the error. For example, if the user attempts to enter '32' as the day of the month, then the error message should say something like 'Invalid day: day must be 31 or less'.

For an updating program, the program should explicitly test for valid transactions or values. It should reject them gracefully if they are not correct.

Programming errors

Sometimes a program just does not work. Programmers can make two types of programming error: **logic errors** and **syntax errors**.

All languages, both spoken and computer, have rules of grammar and spelling. A syntax error is made when the developer has broken one of these rules.

A logic error is made when the program may appear to run successfully, but the results are not what the developer or user expects. There is an error in the 'logic' of the program.

If the developer makes a syntax error, then the computer is not sure what the developer wants it to do. The computer may detect this when:

- the developer is writing the program
- the program is compiled
- the developer or tester is running it during testing
- the user runs it in production.

For an **interpreted language**, the computer detects a syntax error only in the last two cases.

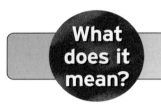

What does it mean?

*In a visual programming environment, the program is usually **interpreted**. This means that it is converted into what the computer understands only when you run it.*

It is more difficult for the computer development system to help to find out logic errors. Most testing therefore aims to find out and correct logic errors.

Runtime errors

When there is a runtime error, the program works successfully most of the time, but occasionally fails. This is the hardest type of error to sort out. It is difficult to catch in the first place. It is even difficult to make the error happen over and over again. It is often then hard to find out what is causing the problem and it may never be solved. It is sometimes only partly solved by a 'workaround', such that the user does not put the program into the position that causes the error to occur.

CASE STUDY

Café Theresa

Café Theresa's stock control update program is specified to receive two types of transactions to change the stock database.

- Credit transactions add to the quantity and value on the stock database.
- Debit transactions subtract from the quantity and value on the stock database.

The easiest and quickest way to code this program might be to test for a credit transaction and treat anything else as a debit transaction. This might appear to work, but give results that are in error when a new transaction type is introduced.

Better coding would be to test separately for credit and debit transactions. If the transaction was neither, then the program could report an error message. An even better and more robust solution would be to log the unexpected transaction type to a form of error log and continue processing.

1 List the advantages of just testing for a credit.

2 List the advantages of testing for a credit and a debit and, if neither, reporting an error message.

3 List the advantages of having an error log here.

4 Discuss as a group each of these advantages.

5 Produce, as a group, a set of guidelines for Café Theresa developers stating when they should use each approach.

PRACTICAL TASK 3.6

Look back at the last program you wrote.

1 How many syntax errors did it have?

2 How many compiler runs did it take to find these?

3 How many logic errors did that program have?

4 How many test runs did it take to find the logic errors?

5 What conclusions can you draw from the answers to questions 1 to 4?

3.2 Common causes of runtime errors

There are many ways in which a program can fail at runtime. Here are some examples that happen very often, with suggestions as to what the developer can do to avoid these errors.

Forever loops

The simplest example is of this form:

```
Label: DO X;
DO Y;
GO TO Label;
```

With structured programming, the programmer is unlikely to write code exactly like that, but he or she might write slightly more complex examples.

```
I = 1;
DO WHILE I > 0;
Code;
END;
```

Here, the variable I is always greater than zero and never changes, so the loop never ends. Here is a variation of the same problem:

```
I = 1;
DO WHILE I > 0;
Code;
I = I + 1:
END;
```

In that example, the loop counter changes but still never goes to zero. Here is yet another variation on this:

```
I = 1;
DO WHILE I > 0;
Code;
J = J − 1:
END;
```

In that example, the programmer has used two different variables, I and J, as the loop counter and still the loop never ends.

Illegal file operations

When handling files, there are many ways in which a program can fail, or not produce the expected results. The most simple is the file handling equivalent of 'Web page error 404 – page not found'. This unit uses the terms from database processing of 'row' and 'table', but similar errors apply to file handling with 'record' and 'file'. Here are some of the most common errors that the developer may come across when a table is being read.

◆ Allow for a 'row not found' status even if it is expected that the row always exists.

◆ Allow for a 'row not found' status, but processing as if a row had been found. This gives unpredictable results and it is often very difficult to find out what has happened.

◆ Try to read a row before a database has been opened.

◆ Try to read a row after a database has been closed.

◆ Reread the same row, instead of retrieving the next row.

What can a developer do to avoid these pitfalls?

1 When updating a row, make sure that the row does exist.

2 On the other hand, when inserting a new row, make sure that the new row does not already exist.

3 When deleting a row, make sure that the row being deleted exists before trying to delete it. In other words, make sure that the right row is deleted.

Sometimes in a large, highly secure system, physical deletion of some records is not allowed in an online transaction. Any attempt to do so causes a file error exception. The online transaction may only set a 'delete requested' flag. Some later batch process then comes along, performs the necessary security and consistency checks and writes audit records. Only then does the batch process do the physical row deletion.

Dividing by zero

Division by zero is not defined as a mathematical function. If the developer writes code that tries to do this, the computer will throw an exception. Best not to do it!

CASE STUDY

Café Theresa

Café Theresa sells one sandwich at £2, one at £2.50 and one at £3. They sell one coffee at £1.50, one at £2 and one at £2.50. They price teas at £1.80, £2.20 and £2.60 but sell no teas.

1 What is their average price for each product type?

2 Write a well-defined specification for the calculation routine.

Answers

Question 1:

Sandwiches $(2 + 2.50 + 3.00) / 3 = £2.50$

Coffees $(1.50 + 2 + 2.50) / 3 = £2$

Teas $(0 \times 1.80 + 0 \times 2.20 + 0 \times 2.60) / 0 =$ undefined

Question 2:

Incorrect solution:

FOR each product type, add up the quantity sold multiplied by the price of each product.

THEN divide by the total number sold of that product type.

Correct solution:

IF the total number sold is non-zero, THEN

FOR each product type, the average price is calculated by adding up the quantity sold multiplied by the price of each product.

THEN divide by the total number sold of that product type.

ELSE average price is undefined.

3.3 Testing and debugging

There is a difference between testing and debugging.

- ◆ **Testing** is the process of making sure that a program works in the way everyone expects it to. This includes the user, the people who specified the program, the developer and the tester. Sections 3.1 and 3.2 have shown how to tackle this. The result of these testing activities gives the developer a set of error logs to fix. These show where the program does not work in the way that the tester expected. These error logs do not say *why* the program does not work as it should. The developer uses these as the input to debug the program.

- ◆ **Debugging** a program is to first find out why a program does not work in the way that the tester, user or developer expected it to work – and then fixing or correcting the program so that it does work as specified and expected.

Debugging

Bugs can be consistent, frequent, occasional or once-only.

◆ If error Y *always* occurs when situation X occurs, the tester describes this as a **consistent bug**.

◆ If error Y *usually* occurs when X occurs, this is a **frequent bug**.

◆ If error Y *sometimes* occurs when X happens, this is an **occasional bug**.

◆ If error Y occurred *just once* when X occurred, it was a **once-only bug**.

The developer should be able to fix consistent and frequent bugs because they can be repeated and cured. This means that the developer or tester can create again and again the situation for the bug. When the developer thinks the bug has been fixed, he or she can set up situation X again and make sure that the correct result now happens, rather than error Y.

Finding occasional and once-only bugs is more difficult. As the developer often cannot repeat the situation that produced the bug, he or she cannot prove that the bug has been fixed. It is often possible to try to fix them only if there is a large amount of evidence.

*The evidence for occasional and once-only errors is usually in the form of a **trace** so the developer has something to look into. A trace identifes the path a transaction takes through a program.*

Debugging first has the developer copying into his or her own environment the bug that the tester has found. This is because sometimes the tester makes a mistake in describing the bug. It could also be that the tester and the developer understand differently what the specification means. The bug may be caused by technically different test and development environments.

Debugging a program is a mixture of logical analysis, experience, technical knowledge and intuition.

How to debug

When a bug report lands on a developer's desk, the bug should be investigated in a logical manner.

◆ In a well-structured program, if there is a fault with the validation of the input fields then the bug is in the relevant input module. If the output format does not look right, the bug is in the output module for that screen or report.

◆ If the program is not well structured, then the fault could be anywhere. It will be very much harder to find.

The developer starts by **desk-checking** the part of the program where he or she thinks the fault lies. This means looking at the code on the screen 'at the desk'. The developer tries to follow the path through the code that this error takes. Sometimes, it is then clear where the bug lies. If it is not, then it is time for the developer to call on help from the development environment.

The developer reruns the program under the control of the development environment. He or she sets **breakpoints** and **traces** at the part of the program where things may be going wrong. When the program reaches these points, the developer can:

◆ display and change the values of variables

◆ change the path through the program

◆ look in much more detail at what the program does while it runs.

Experience often plays a large part in debugging. Once the experienced developer has found the easier bugs, he or she can think back to when a problem like this was last seen. Some developers keep a notebook of unusual testing problems and what caused them. The notes can be consulted when a bug is elusive.

Figure 3.6 shows part of an error message produced from a website to a commercial user when the site had gone through testing and was in production. This error message did not mean anything to the user. It probably did not even mean much to the maintenance developers who received this message attached to a bug report!

Fault (4) : Cast from type 'DBNull' to type 'String' is not valid.

Description: An unhandled exception occurred during the execution of the current web request. Please review the stack trace for more information about the error and where it originated in the code.

Exception Details: System.Exception: Fault (4) : Cast from type 'DBNull' to type 'String' is not valid.

Source Error:

```
An unhandled exception was generated during the execution of the
current web request. Information regarding the origin and location
of the exception can be identified using the exception stack trace
```

Stack Trace:

```
[Exception: Fault (4) : Cast from type 'DBNull' to type 'String' is not valid.]
_30.fbAirport.ActiveTo(fbUser user) +338
_30.sda.Page_Load(Object sender, EventArgs e) +242
System.Web.UI.Control.OnLoad(EventArgs e) +67
```

Figure 3.6 Example of a poor error message

Intuition or luck occasionally plays a part in finding a difficult bug. Typical problems where this might happen are:

◆ missing language punctuation, such as full stops, semi-colons or comment markers

◆ duplicated language punctuation, such as brackets

◆ wrongly spelt variables

◆ a variable with the wrong initial value set

◆ a variable with no initial value set.

Some developers have the intuition to find bugs caused by this sort of error very quickly. They are often in great demand by their colleagues to look at their code to find difficult bugs and to see whether they can spot the problem quickly.

PRACTICAL TASK 3.7

Look back at the last program you wrote and tested.

1 List each bug that you found during testing.

2 Classify each of those bugs as either consistent, frequent, occasional or once-only.

3 Classify each bug that you found as simple, medium or difficult to find and fix.

4 What can you say about the type of bug and how easy or not it was to find and fix?

CASE STUDY

Minimum system requirements

A developer might use a *Windows XP*-based computer with a large amount of memory. The program is meant to run on all machines running *Windows 95* and later version of *Windows* with a limited amount of memory. If there is something wrong with the way the program uses memory, then it may fail to run on an older and/or smaller computer, while on a large modern computer it runs happily but inefficiently.

◆ As a group, discuss how you might work out what the minimum system requirements are for a program you are writing.

3.4 Test plans, test logs, test results and tests reports

It is important for you to understand what each of these four pieces of documentation is and what each is used for (see Figure 3.7).

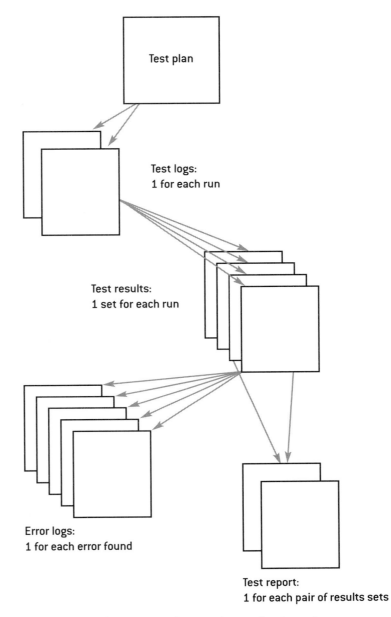

Figure 3.7 Test logs, test results, error logs and test reports

- The purpose of a **test plan** is to identify what parts of the program functions to test, how to test them and the expected results. The tester writes this before any test runs take place. It is a static document. At a big site, it is often signed off by all working with this program as a plan for a thorough test.

- The tester records on **test logs** what actually happens on each test run. The aim is for the final test run to record successfully that all parts of the program perform as expected. However, in both the student and business environments, time-scales sometimes overtake the developer. The test logs are a way to record how far the testing has gone at the end of the project. The program might not be fully correct, but may be good enough to regard as finished.

◆ The tester records one entry on the **error log** for each error found. This says what should happen and what actually did happen. The error log is then given to the developer to start the debugging process. When the bug has been corrected, the developer completes the error log. This is returned to the tester who then checks that the bug really has been fixed.

◆ **Test results** are the computer output from each test run. They are used directly at first to check that the actual results are the same as the expected results.

◆ **Testing software** is available to compare two sets of test results. This produces a **test report** on the differences between the two sets. This test report is used in the later stages of testing, when almost all the program works and there are only a few bugs left to fix. The tester uses this software to look at the differences between one test run and the previous run. What the tester is expecting is that the bugs that should have been fixed in this run now produce the expected answers. The tester also wants to be certain that the parts of the program that worked on the previous run still work now! The bug fixes should not have introduced any new bugs.

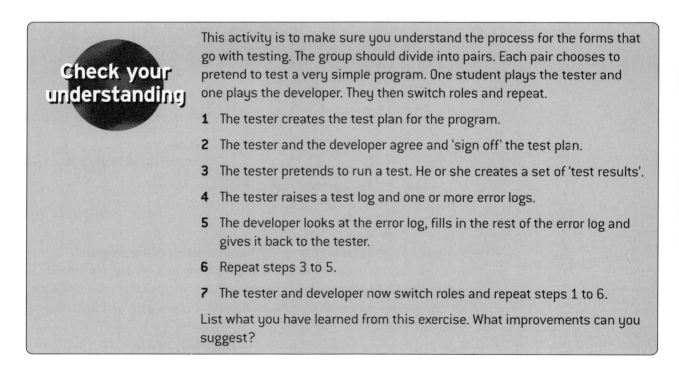

Check your understanding

This activity is to make sure you understand the process for the forms that go with testing. The group should divide into pairs. Each pair chooses to pretend to test a very simple program. One student plays the tester and one plays the developer. They then switch roles and repeat.

1 The tester creates the test plan for the program.

2 The tester and the developer agree and 'sign off' the test plan.

3 The tester pretends to run a test. He or she creates a set of 'test results'.

4 The tester raises a test log and one or more error logs.

5 The developer looks at the error log, fills in the rest of the error log and gives it back to the tester.

6 Repeat steps 3 to 5.

7 The tester and developer now switch roles and repeat steps 1 to 6.

List what you have learned from this exercise. What improvements can you suggest?

3.5 Testing and software quality and maintenance

Both the developer and tester need to know what quality of program the user needs before they start their work. If the program is a simple game to keep the developer amused, or a utility to help make a computer task easier, then the program only has to be good enough. If the program does not work under some conditions, then this is only a problem for the developer, who can perhaps achieve the necessary results in another way.

Sometimes, **speed of development** is a high priority compared with program quality. A business may suffer a lot if the deadline for delivery of a new program is not met. In this case, it may be acceptable that an early delivery date is more important than time spent on development and testing. This certainly leads to a lower quality program or system. This is only acceptable if the cost of this quality loss is much less than the benefit from fast delivery.

For some types of program or system, though, the developer and tester should not compromise on program quality.

◆ **Safety-critical systems** should be fail-safe. The tester must be able to show and document that the system continues to work safely at all times and in all situations. Some businesses that this applies to are nuclear, medical, airline engineering and railway signalling.

◆ **Mission-critical systems** exist in most businesses. A business may have just one or two systems without which it cannot work properly. Before making large changes to these systems, the changes must be rigorously tested. There must be a fall-back plan in place in case things do go wrong.

◆ **High-volume desktop software** is an example of a type of software in which a bug might have a small impact but on a larger number of people. If a company sells high-volume desktop software and it fails to test it enough, then it annoys many thousands of users. This poor reputation spreads rapidly to other products that the company makes. It quickly leads to a great loss of business to the company. This is one of the reasons why small IT companies can bring to market new software very much more quickly than the large companies with a large user base.

For many selling organisations, the IT system that supports telephone sales is the most critical system. For a retailer, the till or point-of-sale system is the most critical. Without this, they cannot sell goods or take money from their customers, For an airline, the most critical system is the passenger check-in system, not telephone sales. This is because a check-in system failure at once drives their customers away to other competing airlines. If the telephone sales system does not work then there are still several ways to carry on selling tickets to the customer, such as through the Internet or travel agents.

There are some types of system where maintenance and its ease or speed is the most important element of quality.

◆ *Multi-lingual systems*. These should allow easy introduction and change of language-dependent features. This is because it is known that frequent changes are needed to introduce new languages or to improve on the existing message wording.

◆ *Long-life systems*. Some systems may cost so much to either build or implement that it is not cost-effective to redevelop them very often. Code in these systems should be designed for ease of maintenance since, without this, the total cost of ownership will be even higher.

◆ *Systems for a fast changing business*. The business systems to support a sales or marketing part of a business are likely to change faster than those to support engineering or finance. This is because the way the sales or marketing part of the business works usually changes much faster. If the software developer knows that frequent speedy change is likely, then it is good to design that system for ease of maintenance.

PRACTICAL TASK 3.8

1 As a group, list different sorts of computer program.

2 Working on your own, give a rating of needed software quality, in the range 1 to 10, to each of these programs.

3 Working on your own, give a rating of speed of development needed, in the range 1 to 10, to each of these programs

4 Working on your own, give a rating of ideal cost of development, in the range 1 to 10, to each of these programs

5 As a group, discuss your answers to the above rating tasks and calculate the average rating for each program.

6 List where you have answers that differ greatly from the group. Justify your reasons for giving different ratings.

3.6 Regression testing

Regression testing was first introduced on page 167. This section describes how to reuse well thought-out test plans and test data for repeat testing after fixing errors or making maintenance changes. This form of testing is to make sure that new bugs are not introduced into a working program when the developer makes a change to it. The reason for the change can be:

◆ the program does more things

♦ maintenance (continuing to do the same things as the user makes minor changes to the way of doing things)

♦ fixing a problem.

A regression test runs a test against both the old and new versions of a program. The tester makes sure that they still produce the same answers. This checking is done either manually or by using testing software. Both methods identify where there are changed results.

The tester then goes through the changed records to see whether what has changed is what was expected. If it is not, then the tester raises an error log to have the problem fixed. The tester also needs to check that any of the outputs that were expected to change with the new version of the software did actually change.

In the business world, what happens in practice is that a regression test plan and test data may be produced as part of delivery of the original system. It is formed from a subset of the full data used to originally test the system. As new features are introduced into the system, the tester adds a few test transactions for these new features to the regression test plan and test data.

PRACTICAL TASK 3.9

Draw up a list of situations when you would *not* use a regression test when you change an existing program.

3.7 Version control

This section describes the purpose of version control procedures when developing, testing, amending and maintaining software and documentation with reference to quality assurance.

If the developer is writing a program that will not be upgraded there may be no need for **version control**.

CASE STUDY

Café Theresa

Café Theresa organises sales areas by county. They needed a new sales area reporting program. Their IT department wrote this report, it was tested and went into live running. However, they found that it was producing several total lines for each county.

The developer looked into this bug and found that the stores database had inconsistent names for counties. For example, the store in Preston had a county of 'Lancashire', the Blackburn store had a county of 'Lancs', while the Blackpool store had a county of 'Lanc'. A program was needed to change the contents of the 'county' field. The user wanted the abbreviation 'Lancs' to replace 'Lancashire' or 'Lanc' (and the incorrect 'Lancaster') whenever they appeared in the county field. The developer wrote the code to do this and fixed any bugs as they were found during testing. When the program was complete and approved, it was run just once in production to correct the database.

1 What else should this database correction program do as well as changing the Lancs county names?

2 What other changes should the developer make and to which part of the system to stop this problem happening again.

The staff in an IT organisation and elsewhere need version control for several reasons.

◆ *The developer*. During development, changes can be made that are wrong. The developer wants then to return (fall back) to the previous version.

◆ *The developer and the maintenance programmer*. Both need to be able to identify when new features were added or bugs sorted out.

◆ *The tester and the developer*. Both need to identify which version of the program produced which set of test results.

◆ *The person responsible for documentation*. It is essential to produce documentation that is in line with a certain version of the program.

◆ *The users*. They want to know what the version that they are using does. They also need to know what changes a new version of the program brings and how to use these features. Programs that run under Windows usually provide their version number to the user from the *About* button on the Help main menu.

When a developer releases or promotes a new version of a program into production, the use of a version number can make sure that the production program is the right one. The developer may be working on new features for the *next* version, or be trying to fix some minor bugs in an older version. These versions would not be put into production.

Version control systems can have up to three sets of numbers.

CASE STUDY

Version coding

The text of this unit was first written using Word version 9.0.3821.

◆ The first number indicates the major version of the program. The vendor will often use it in their technical marketing, although there may be a more user-friendly or marketing version of the name. So *Word* version 6 for the PC went with *Windows 3.1*, *Word 7* was better known as *Word 95*, *Word 8* was *Word 97*, and *Word 9* was marketed as *Word 2000*. The vendor will sometimes give a new product version a code name and decide on the marketing name close to production release. This may change only every two years or so.

◆ The vendor uses the second number to show new features of technical value but not large enough to need marketing. For example, the *Oracle* database went from 7.1 to 7.2 to 7.3 before moving to 8.0 and then 8.1.

◆ The final number has two uses. For the vendor and user technical support, it shows in production the exact set of code that the user is running. In development, it lets the developer to know the status of the code.

1 List the marketing names and version numbers of *Excel*.

2 List the marketing names and version numbers of Windows.

For the developer, version numbering is often automatic. The development environment will often identify versions by a sequential number, or by a date, or a combination of both of these. The developer will often want to use versions together with **program status**.

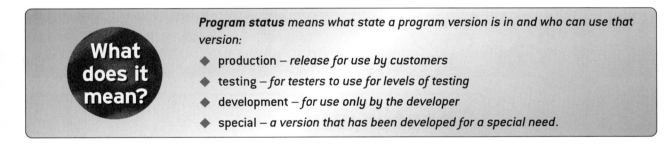

What does it mean?

Program status means what state a program version is in and who can use that version:

◆ production – *release for use by customers*

◆ testing – *for testers to use for levels of testing*

◆ development – *for use only by the developer*

◆ special – *a version that has been developed for a special need*.

Once a new version of a program is in production, there is still a need to keep securely all versions of the program that any customer might use. However, there is a high maintenance cost in keeping old program versions and their documentation. Most vendors therefore have a policy whereby they stop actively supporting older program versions at a suitable time after their new program versions are available. This time is often 18–24 months. They may leave their technical support program knowledge base available, but will not look at any bugs that users find. This sometimes leads to conflict between vendor and user. Why?

◆ The newest version of the program may not work for that user.

◆ The user may have no need for the newer features of the program.

◆ The user may not have been affected by the bugs that the new version corrects.

◆ The new version of the program may need a higher equipment specification than the user has installed.

◆ User priorities are elsewhere and so the user does not have the IT effort available to make the changes.

◆ The vendor might charge for the move to the new version, sometimes a lot of money, and the user does not see the benefit for this cost.

The technical support maintenance programmers who work for the vendor may make changes based on many production versions. They need to keep under control all of these changed versions while they test minor changes. Once this testing is successfully completed, these minor changes need to be released to the users. This is often in the form of **patches**. The user can download them from the vendor's website. Patches are small pieces of code that include only changes to another version.

The developer may be controlling several versions of the same program. Often, when a program moves into systems testing and beta testing, the developer starts to work on the next major version of the program. The system testing needs minor changes to one version, while major changes are going on in parallel to another version. For some programs, there may be different versions that run on different technologies, but deliver the same function.

Go out and try! Search for a program that has many versions. You could do this by using the Internet or by using your site software library and documentation. *Windows*, *Word* or *Excel* are examples. For your chosen program, list the main differences between the versions.

Chapter summary

The following have been covered:

◆ types of software error

◆ causes of common runtime errors

◆ testing and debugging

◆ test plans, test logs, test results and test reports, and the relationship between them

◆ software quality and maintenance

◆ regression testing

◆ version control.

4 Identify health and safety requirements

This chapter explains how to maintain a safe working environment for the user and others. It stresses the use of **safe working practices** at all times. It is important to operate equipment in line with suppliers', manufacturers' and workplace needs. It describes how to use and maintain equipment, materials and accessories to a safe standard. To head off problems, it tells how to use reporting procedures to report any hazards.

4.1 Good working environment

Three major factors lead to a good working environment for computer work:

◆ frequent breaks away from the computer

◆ correct positioning of screens, chairs and keyboards

◆ adequate lighting and ventilation.

Frequent breaks away from the computer have a number of good effects (see Figure 3.8).

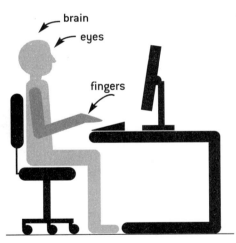

Figure 3.8 The major bodily strain points for computer users

◆ The first benefit is for the **eyes**. Looking at a computer screen for a long time means that the eyes are focused at the same distance during that time. Normal office or college work has variation between close work in reading a document or a book and long-distance work such as looking towards a colleague or teacher or across the room. Leaving the screen allows your eyes to exercise.

◆ Other parts of the body to benefit from a break away from the screen include your **muscles**. While at the keyboard, your **fingers** are working very hard but the rest of your body hardly moves at all. This means that the muscles associated with your fingers have too much strain, while the rest of your body has no exercise at all. A break away from the screen allows your fingers to have a rest while the rest of your body starts to move a bit.

◆ Another last part of your body to benefit from a break from the computer is your **brain**. There is usually a lot of concentration when a user is busy at the keyboard. While this is good for short periods, with most people there is a great loss of concentration after between 30 minutes and 2 hours. This means loss of productivity in a business environment. In a learning environment, it means a loss of effectiveness. The amount of this effect depends on the person and the type of work. A break and perhaps a brief talk to a colleague means the brain can relax for a short time. It then becomes much more effective again.

The **physical environment** — such as computer screens, chair and keyboard — has to be correct if a computer user is to be at his or her most effective.

It is often difficult to position a computer, its screen and keyboard in exactly the right position. This is because the rest of the furniture is usually there first and the **computer screen** is put where it can then fit. What is the best position for a computer screen?

- If possible, position it side-on to any nearby window, to minimise **reflections** on the screen.
- Often there is a wall or physical screen behind the computer. This can provide the right level of **light contrast**.
- The computer screen should not be at the same height as the user's eyes, but at a *slight angle*. This is also to prevent **glare**.
- The screen should *swivel* and *tilt* to make it easier for the user to adjust it to prevent glare.

What features does the ideal **computer chair** have?

- An *adjustable back* will help to prevent back strain and provide a comfortable support while working.
- An *adjustable height* will allow the user to view the screen at a slight angle and to comfortably use the keyboard and mouse. If one person only ever uses a chair then the screen height could be changed to do this. However, in most cases, there are many users, so the chair height needs to be changeable.
- *Armrests* are usually provided as an aid to use of the keyboard. They are useful during user thinking time and while waiting during a long response time.
- Easily movable *feet* (e.g. on castors) can make it easier to have frequent breaks away from the computer.

The computer **keyboard** has been developed from the 'QWERTY' typewriter, but with a lot of improvements for computer usage. The first computer keyboards were similar to typewriters, but today's ergonomic keyboards are a great improvement.

Adequate **lighting** and **ventilation** is important for the most effective use of a computer system. Lighting should:

- be good enough to read non-computer documents easily
- not give glare against the computer screen
- provide enough contrast between the computer screen and its office background.

Ventilation should have enough airflow to:

◆ keep the computing equipment at temperatures within their operating specification

◆ provide a comfortable working environment for the computer user

◆ meet at least the minimum requirements of the **Offices, Shops and Railway Premises Act** or similar legislation (for example a temperature of at least 16 degrees Celcius from an hour after the normal work start time)

◆ not be so hot as to reduce the computer user's productivity.

Check your understanding

1 List the features that are common to the typewriter and today's ergonomic keyboard.

2 List the new features of the modern keyboard compared to the typewriter.

3 Explain the benefits or reasons for introduction for each of the new features.

4.2 Health and safety precautions

Under normal operating conditions, computers are one of the safest items of equipment that can be used. There are, however, some health and safety precautions that all users should follow – see Figure 3.9.

Figure 3.9 Hazards!

Electrical hazards

The necessary electrical precautions are similar to those when using any electrical or electronic item.

1 Make sure that all power cables are safely secured.

2 Do not overload a power point with lots of plugs or extension points.

3 Do not probe the inside of computer equipment. The user should leave this to a qualified computer technician.

4 Do not spill liquid or food into a computer or any other equipment.

5 Do not block any vents in the equipment – they are there for cooling purposes.

Failure to follow these precautions can lead to various failures, such as:

◆ temporary failure of the equipment

◆ permanent failure of part of the equipment, leading to replacement of the failed part

◆ complete failure of that computer

◆ smoke and fire – in an extreme case spreading beyond the failing computer.

Tripping hazards

How do tripping hazards arise? Most personal computers have lots of wires attached to them, such as power cables to the computer, monitor, printer and many other attached devices. There are also data cables between the computer and all of its attached devices.

Many computers also have a network connection. At home, this is through a modem attached to a telephone line. In an office, college or school, the network connection is likely to be a local-area network (LAN).

Any of these wires could present a tripping hazard, especially as they have to be firmly attached at both ends to make good connections. It is therefore important not to have loose cables lying about. They should be carefully secured, bundled together and not run across the floor where the users or others could trip on them.

Weight hazards

Attempting to carry heavy items presents a weight hazard. Computers in the 1960s were so large that it seemed that the computer room had been built around them. Computers today have shrunk so that one technician can usually lift, handle and install them. Large monitors can still be awkward, however, so special care should be taken with them.

All people must follow standard good practice rules for lifting heavy objects. This is particularly true for PC system boxes and monitors.

Note

Computer equipment is fragile. Circuit boards in particular are easily damaged by knocking or vibration. Dropping a piece of electronic equipment is very likely to break it or make it unreliable.

Before moving a piece of equipment:

◆ *switch off and unplug*

◆ *remove all attached cables between devices*

◆ *temporarily secure these detached cables so they do not become a tripping hazard.*

Check your understanding

Look at the area around where your computers are.

1 On your own, list any hazards that you find there. If there are none, make some up.

2 In a group, discuss these hazards.

3 Produce a list of the hazards, with what needs to be done to fix the hazard, how much this might cost, in time or money, and the risk if the hazard is not fixed.

4.3 Injuries

Three common injuries arise when using computers in a bad working environment:

◆ repetitive strain injury

◆ eye strain

◆ bad posture.

Repetitive strain injury (RSI) is a generic term that covers a range of musculoskeletal disorders. It can affect the hands, wrists, fingers and arms when a computer is used a lot with a bad way of working. Relief comes with a reduction in the use of the computer and a better way of working, such as:

◆ resting the hands when not using the keyboard

◆ placing the keyboard and mouse at the right distance

◆ using a chair and keyboard at the right height.

There are a number of bad working practices that can lead to **eye strain**:

◆ The screen may not be at the right distance from the user's eyes.

- There may be reflected glare from the sun or lights when the screen is not in the right position.
- Flicker from the screen can occur if it has not been configured correctly.
- The display may be blurred if the screen is set to use too high a resolution. For example, do not expect a 15-inch monitor to handle better than 1024 by 768 pixels.
- Failure to use glasses when prescribed for computer work can cause eye strain. Businesses are required to provide eye tests for employees who are frequent computer users.

Bad posture when using a computer can lead to pain in the back, neck, shoulders or arms. There are many causes.

- The user, the keyboard and the screen may not be in a line.
- The user may be sitting at an angle on to the screen and keyboard.
- There may be no footrest.
- The user may be sitting at the wrong height for the keyboard.
- The user may be sitting at the wrong distance from the keyboard.

If the user has a chair that has an adjustable height and can easily move, this helps him or her to change posture to a more comfortable one. The user should also swivel and tilt the screen to where it is comfortable. The law requires that all modern screens can do this.

4.4 Cleaning

In general, IT equipment should be cleaned and treated in a similar way to other electronic office equipment. However, there are some extra guidelines that the user should follow.

- Screens should be cleaned with anti-static wipes so that there is no grease on them.
- Particles of food and dust should be removed from keyboards so that they don't interfere with the electrical contacts betweens the keys.
- Occasionally, a wired mouse should be opened up and any dust removed from the mouse ball. This removes one cause of jerky mouse movements.
- When there is a paper jam in a printer, the cleaner should take care to remove all damaged parts of the sheet of paper before putting the printer back online.
- Do not attempt to clean inside the PC system unit. The user should only dust the outer casing to reduce the amount of dust that might be drawn into the PC.

Do this only if your site allows it.

1 Clean each of the parts of a PC that you have access to.
2 Produce a status report on how clean, or otherwise, each part of your PC was.
3 In a group, compare your reports to see whether there is a pattern.
4 As a group, recommend whether there should be any change to your site's cleaning practices.

4.5 Ergonomics

Ergonomics, when used with computers, is about making the physical computer environment as easy and healthy to use as possible. There is no one right ergonomic design. This is because all people are different. Some are short and some are tall. Some have long arms and some have short arms.

People have different uses for their computer and so different ergonomic factors become important. Table 3.4 shows examples of the top ergonomic priority item for each type of use.

Table 3.4 **Ergonomic priorities**

Type of use	Priority
Word processing	Keyboard/mouse
Surfing the Internet	Mouse
Graphic design	Mouse
Data entry	Numeric keypad or keyboard
Games	Keyboard/mouse/game peripheral

The International Ergonomics Association has produced this definition.

'Ergonomics (or human factors) is the scientific discipline concerned with the understanding of interactions among humans and other elements of a system, and the profession that applies theory, principles, data and methods to design in order to optimise human well-being and overall system performance.'

This is a group activity using one PC.

1 For each of you in turn, position yourselves most comfortably at the PC.
2 Measure the height of the chair, the distance from the keyboard and the angle to the horizontal between the screen and the eyes.
3 Discuss why each of you has different results.
4 Return to the PC. What does it feel like when you use the PC furniture set more appropriately for someone else?

4.6 Legislation

Over the last 40 years, many laws have been introduced to improve heath and safety at work. It is the law that the employer must ensure safety at work for all employees. Employees also have to do their part as well. They must not put themselves or their colleagues in danger.

There are four main Acts or Regulations that affect the computer world in the UK.

The Health & Safety at Work Act 1974

The Health & Safety at Work Act is the main piece of law in work safety. Under it, the employer has to take reasonable steps to ensure the health, safety and welfare of employees at work. If they don't, then they are breaking the law. An employee may also sue the employer for personal injury.

An employer has to assess the level of risk compared to the cost of eliminating that risk. This is to show whether the employer's action, or lack of it, is *reasonable*. The employer's responsibility is usually to provide:

◆ safe plant and machinery

◆ safe premises

◆ a safe system of work

◆ competent, suitably trained and supervised staff.

Some groups of employees may need more care and supervision than others. Examples of these groups are disabled workers, pregnant workers and illiterate workers. The employer must consult on safety matters with employees, either:

◆ directly

◆ or through an elected health and safety representative

◆ or through a trade-union appointed safety representative.

An employer should have a written code of safety conduct, rules regarding safety training and supervision, and rules on safety procedures. There must be a health and safety policy in place.

Electrical regulations

The electrical regulations that affect computer work are the **Electricity at Work Regulations 1989**. An employer must assess the risks involved in all work activities involving electricity. This includes PCs, computers and those devices that are attached to them. The laws even cover home electrical appliances used at work, such as kettles. All this electrical equipment must be properly maintained.

Working with VDUs

The **Health & Safety (Display Screen Equipment) Regulations 1992** are the rules that control working with VDUs. These are usually known as the **Display Screen Regulations**. The purpose of these laws was to do something to prevent injuries such as RSI, fatigue and eye problems in the use of computer equipment.

These laws say that an employer must look at each workstation and surrounding work environment. The employer must make sure that the workplace meets the specified ergonomic requirements. The employer must provide to the employee:

- eyesight tests for frequent users on request
- breaks from using the computer
- health and safety information about the equipment.

Hazardous substances or COSHH regulations

The use of hazardous substances can put people's health at risk. To prevent this risk, the COSHH regulations control their use.

Note

COSHH stands for the Control of Substances Hazardous to Health Regulations 2002.

COSHH requires employers to control exposures to hazardous substances. This is to protect both employees and others who may be exposed from work activities.

Hazardous substances are anything that can harm the health of an employee when working with them if the substances are not properly controlled. An example of this control is the use of adequate ventilation. Hazardous substances are found in nearly all workplaces – factories, shops, mines, farms and offices. They may be:

- substances used directly in work activities such as glues, paints and cleaning agents
- substances generated during work activities such as fumes from soldering and welding
- substances that are naturally occurring such as grain dust, blood and bacteria.

For almost all commercial chemicals, the presence or absence of a warning label will show whether COSHH is relevant. For example, household washing-up liquid does not have a warning label. Bleach does have a warning label. So when used at work, COSHH applies to bleach but not to washing-up liquid.

Government advice for employers is to comply with COSHH in the following ways.

◆ Work out what hazardous substances are used in the workplace. Find out the risks to health from using these substances.

◆ Decide what precautions are needed before starting work with hazardous substances.

◆ Prevent people from being exposed to hazardous substances. Where this is not reasonably practicable, the employer must control the exposure.

◆ Make sure that control measures are used and maintained properly. Make sure that safety procedures are followed.

◆ If required, monitor exposure of employees to hazardous substances.

◆ Carry out health surveillance where an assessment has shown that this is necessary or where COSHH has specific requirements.

◆ If required, prepare plans and procedures to deal with accidents, incidents and emergencies.

◆ Make sure employees are properly informed, trained and supervised.

Almost all the things that go with a computer are not hazardous substances. Laser printer toner and typing correction fluid are the only hazardous substances most computer and office users see near the computer.

Go out and try!

1 Look in your kitchen cupboard or in the cleaning department of a supermarket.

2 List those products that are hazardous substances.

3 List the type of hazard that they are, such as irritant.

4 What safety procedures would you follow at home when using each of these products?

5 Compare and discuss your answers with your colleagues.

4.7 Fire doors, exits and reporting

It would be rare for there to be a fire either in a computer room or in an office containing PCs. However, standard office fire rules must be followed. This will keep to a minimum the effect of any fire.

In the event of a fire, the most important things to do are:

◆ start to move everyone to a place of safety

◆ report the fire to the fire brigade

◆ only then, if appropriate, tackle the fire.

Fire doors are the normal first line of defence in preventing a fire from spreading through a building. They should open in the direction of the exit from the building. Fire doors should be kept closed at all times except when someone is walking through them. They must never be wedged open. If a technician is moving bulky equipment through them, then they should have a colleague help them in opening the doors. Fire doors must protect all dedicated fire exit staircases.

Green signs showing an icon of a running man, a rectangle representing a door and an arrow identify **fire exits** (see Figure 3.10). Where appropriate this sign should be lit with an emergency light. This is so that the way to the exit can still be seen, even if the fire has already destroyed the electric power cables and there is no lighting.

Figure 3.10 The standard fire exit sign, always in green

So that they can be used in an emergency, fire doors and exits must always be kept clear and unblocked. Where they lead to the outside, it is acceptable for security purposes to have them open only from the inside, preferably with a bar push rather than a handle. For internal fire doors and exits, it is best that there should be no locking.

Reporting a fire

As part of their health and safety policies, all organisations must make it clear how to report a fire. For a small organisation, this may be as simple as calling the fire service on 999. The caller must know the full address of where the fire has broken out. The person taking the call at the fire brigade may be at the other end of the county. He or she might not have local geographic knowledge either of your town or of the buildings on your site. If the caller just says that there is a fire in classroom 5 at the County College, then the brigade does not necessarily know the details of the town, the street address, the campus or the location within the campus.

For large organisations, there may be special procedures. These may be to call first the organisation's switchboard or to report the fire to a control centre.

Reporting a fire hazard

Most organisations are required to have a Health and Safety committee as described earlier. Part of their responsibility is to react to fire hazards. They should consider what to do to eliminate or minimise the risk of fires. There is often a procedure for drawing hazards to their attention. The hazard should be monitored until it is fixed.

Go out and try!

This is a group exercise to review the fire safety of your building.

1 Follow one or more fire exits from your room. Do all the fire doors open outwards, are they normally closed, and are they indicated with a green sign? Record any that do not conform to these rules.

2 Look at the lifts in your building. What fire precautions do they have?

3 Look at the staircases in your building. What fire precautions do they have?

4 Investigate the assembly instructions for your building in case of a fire.

5 Investigate the fire reporting instructions for your building.

6 Find out the full reporting address of your building in the case of a fire.

7 Discuss this fire safety as a group.

Write a personal report on the fire safety of your building. You should say what things are already good and what could be improved.

4.8 Fire extinguishers

There are four classes of fire extinguishers, A, B, C and D, each meant for a different type of fire. Class A and B fire extinguishers also have a number that serves as a guide for the amount of fire the extinguisher can handle. The higher the number, the more fire-fighting power there is.

◆ *Class A extinguishers* are for fires in ordinary combustible materials such as paper, wood, cardboard and most plastics. The number on class A extinguishers shows the amount of *water* it holds and the amount of fire it can put out.

◆ *Class B extinguishers* are for fires in flammable or combustible liquids such as gasoline, kerosene, grease and oil. The number on class B extinguishers shows approximately how many square feet of fire it can put out.

◆ *Class C extinguishers* are for fires in electrical equipment, such as appliances, wiring, circuit breakers and outlets. Never use water to put out a class C fire. The risk of electrical shock is far too great. There is no number on a class C extinguisher. The class C means the extinguishing agent does not conduct electricity.

◆ *Class D extinguishers* are commonly found in a chemical laboratory. They are for fires that involve combustible metals, such as magnesium, titanium, potassium and sodium. There is no number on a class D extinguisher. They do not have a multi-purpose rating. They are meant for class D fires only.

Obviously, some fires may involve a combination of these classifications.

Water extinguishers or air-pressurised water (APW) extinguishers are suitable for class A fires only. They must never be used on grease fires, electrical fires or class D fires. This is because the flames will spread and make the fire bigger. Water extinguishers are filled with water and pressurised with oxygen. They should be used to fight a fire only when one is certain it contains ordinary combustible materials only.

Dry chemical extinguishers come in a variety of types. They are suitable for a combination of class A, B and C fires. They are filled with foam or powder and pressurized with nitrogen. Dry chemical extinguishers have an advantage over carbon dioxide (CO_2) extinguishers in that they leave a non-flammable substance on the extinguished material, reducing the likelihood of re-ignition.

◆ *BC*. This is the normal type of dry chemical extinguisher. It is filled with sodium bicarbonate or potassium bicarbonate. The BC variety leaves a mildly corrosive residue. This must be cleaned at once to prevent any damage to materials.

◆ *ABC*. This is the multi-purpose dry chemical extinguisher. The ABC type is filled with monoammonium phosphate. This is a yellow powder that leaves a sticky residue. This may be damaging to an electrical appliance such as a computer.

Carbon dioxide extinguishers are used for class B and C fires. They contain CO_2, which is a non-flammable gas. They are highly pressurised. The pressure is so great that it is not uncommon for bits of dry ice to shoot out the nozzle. They do not work very well on class A fires because they may not be able to displace enough oxygen to put the fire out. This causes the fire to re-ignite. CO_2 extinguishers have an advantage over dry chemical extinguishers in that they do not leave a harmful residue. This means that they are a good choice for an electrical fire on a computer or other electronic device.

Check your understanding

1 If your PC starts to smoulder, what type of fire extinguisher should you use to put the fire out?

2 If a wastebin containing only paper catches fire, what type of extinguisher should you use to put the fire out?

Go out and try!

1 Find out where the fire extinguishers for your building are located.

2 What types of extinguisher are they?

3 What sort of fire is each one designed to tackle?

4 Investigate your local procedures for notifying colleagues and the fire brigade of a fire.

Chapter summary

The following have been covered:

◆ the importance of a good working environment

◆ essential health and safety precautions

◆ common injuries

◆ cleaning

◆ ergonomics

◆ legislation

◆ fire doors, fire extinguishers and exits

◆ the reporting of hazards in the workplace.

Website design

This unit covers the basic principles to enable you to create and maintain a set of web pages. Assessment will be by means of a set assignment.

Outcomes

◆ Describe and apply the basics of web page development

◆ Undertake user requirements analysis

◆ Use appropriate development tools to implement web pages

◆ Test websites

◆ Use graphics software to create and manipulate images on web pages

◆ Publish and maintain web pages

1 Describe and apply the basics of web page development

Most of this unit covers the skills and techniques that you need to create and publish a website. This chapter provides you with some underpinning knowledge. Without this, some aspects of web design will seem very puzzling. It is easy to assume that the process of designing and creating a website is very similar to desktop publishing, but you will discover that there are many important differences.

In particular, you need to be aware of:

◆ the technical issues and limitations in creating a website
◆ the constraints imposed by the screens and settings that website visitors use
◆ the variations in browsers.

1.1 Screen resolutions and colour depths

A screen displays many dots of colour, known as **pixels** (derived from 'picture cells'). The number of pixels that can be displayed – expressed as width × height – is known as the **screen resolution**. It is usually possible to change the screen resolution, although there will be a maximum resolution for each screen.

PRACTICAL TASK 4.1

Find out the resolution on a screen that you are using. If you are using Microsoft Windows, select *Settings* and *Control Panel* in the Start menu. Select *Display*, and in the dialogue box click on the *Settings* tab (see Figure 4.1).

Use the slider to change the screen resolution. As you move the slider, you will see the resolutions that your screen can support.

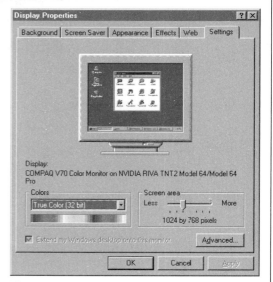

Figure 4.1 The Display Properties dialogue

Typical resolutions are 1280 × 960 ('high resolution'), 1024 × 768, 800 × 600 and 640 × 480 ('low resolution'). Note that they all maintain the ratio of 4:3. The 640 pixels width is rarely used these days.

Your choice of screen resolution will depend on the physical dimensions of the screen. For example, it is difficult to read text on a small screen set at high resolution. This is particularly significant for small laptop screens. A user with visual impairment might also choose a lower screen resolution to give enlarged images and text.

Designing websites for different screen resolutions

Websites should be designed to be viewable at all resolutions.

Scroll bars allow the user to reach the parts of a web page that are not displayed. But users are normally reluctant to use the horizontal scroll bar if a page is wider than the screen. For this reason, many commercial websites are still designed for 800 pixels width resolution. Other sites are designed on the assumption that most users have at least 1024 pixels width resolution.

Resizable web pages

The size of a **browser window** can be changed by the user, and it does not have to fill the whole screen. When a screen is set comfortably at a high resolution, many viewers take advantage of the extra space to display several windows at the same time. So they may well keep the browser window at a smaller size within the overall window.

This means that, even when used on a high-resolution setting, the actual display area of a web page cannot be predicted with certainty.

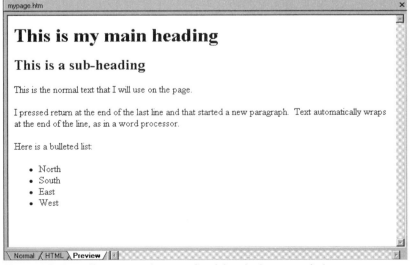

Figure 4.2 The effect on a web page of resizing the browser window

One solution to this problem is to design web pages that are **resizable**. Indeed, when you create a web page it is normally resizable unless you force it to fit into a fixed width. When the window is resized the text wraps around and images can be repositioned (see Figure 4.2). Many designers do not like working with resizable web pages because they cannot control the final appearance of the pages.

Colour depth

Figure 4.1 shows a control to alter the colours. The options are:

◆ true colour (32-bit)
◆ high colour (16-bit)
◆ 256 colours (8-bit)
◆ 16 colours.

True colour uses 32 bits (4 bytes) of memory to store the data about each pixel. Most screens today offer 32-bit colour. But when you design a web page you have to consider the needs of users who may be using lower colour settings.

1.2 Speed of Internet connection

Users connect with the Internet using either a **dial-up modem** or a **high-speed broadband** connection. The speed of the connection directly affects the time it takes for a page to be downloaded from a **webserver** to the user's system. If a broadband connection is shared by many users on a network, the actual download speeds may be much slower than expected.

Web pages should be designed bearing in mind the needs of the users with the slowest connections. The typical dial-up modem runs at a speed of 56 kilobits per second (kbps), which is equivalent to 7 kilobytes per second. This is the maximum speed that can be achieved by the modem, depending on the amount of traffic through the Internet service provider's servers and, in practice, many dial-up connections can be much slower.

When you download a web page you first of all download the actual page, which is a simple text file. The browser then interprets the code on the page, and downloads any images that are required. The images are stored as separate files on the server.

A typical simple web page may be 10 kilobytes in size and can download in a couple of seconds. The images on it can then take considerably longer to download. The process of requesting the image files itself adds extra time to the waiting period.

1.3 Web browsers

A browser is a piece of software which is used to view pages on the WWW. The most commonly used browser is Microsoft *Internet Explorer*, but other browsers, such as Netscape *Navigator*, are also used (see Figure 4.3).

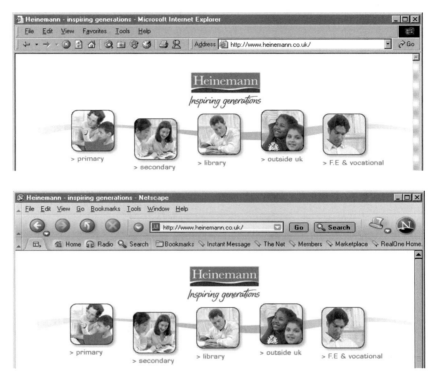

Figure 4.3 Internet Explorer *and* Netscape *web browsers*

Web pages are stored as files written in **hypertext markup language** (**HTML**). The HTML code is interpreted by the browser and used to generate a web page on the visitor's screen.

A browser does a number of tasks.

1 It sends a request for a page to the webserver where the website is stored. The request identifies the page by its uniform resource locator (**URL**) – often referred to as its 'web address'. The HTML code for that page is then transmitted over the Internet.

2 It interprets the HTML code and displays the web page.

3 It sends requests to the webserver for additional files that are referred to in the HTML code for the page. These could be for graphics or sounds. Each image or sound is transmitted as a separate file.

4 When the user clicks on a **hyperlink**, it sends a new page request to the webserver.

Browsers have been updated to match the developments in HTML, but it is important to realise that not all users use the latest versions. Web pages can appear differently in different browsers and in different versions of the same browser.

1.4 Hypertext markup language (HTML)

When you download a web page into a browser, the HTML code is transferred to your computer. This is referred to as the **source code**. HTML code is always stored and transmitted in a simple text file (an **ASCII** file). It usually has a filename with .htm or .html as its file extension – for example, homepage.htm.

In *Internet Explorer* you can view the source code by selecting *View + Source*. This usually opens up *Notepad* and displays the code (see Figure 4.4). *Notepad* is a text editor, and is the simplest means of viewing and creating text files. If you use a different browser, then you should also be able to view the source code from the *View* menu.

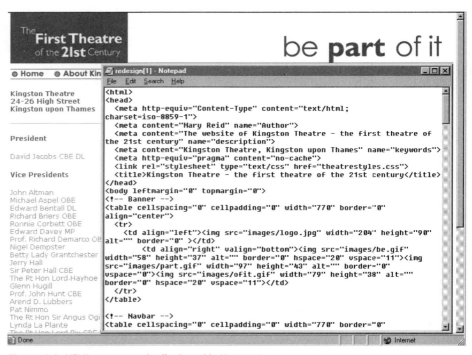

Figure 4.4 HTML source code displayed in Notepad

Checking the files used on a web page

If you scan through an HTML file, you will see references to other files that must be downloaded to complete the page. For example, you may see something like this:

```
<IMG src="http://www.thisismydomain.co.uk/pic.jpg" width=
          100 height=80 border=0 alt="My picture">
```

This tells the browser that it needs to download the picture stored as pic.jpg from the site www.thisismydomain.co.uk. You may also spot some links to other files that may be used, such as video or sound, or files that contain program code.

Web authoring software

Many websites are created using specialist web authoring software packages. These let you create a web page in much the same way as you would create a document in a word processing or desktop publishing package. The web authoring software then generates the HTML for you. You are free to look at the HTML code at any time, and to change or add to it directly. But it is perfectly possible to create a straightforward website, that meets its purpose, without knowing any HTML.

Macromedia *Dreamweaver* and Microsoft *FrontPage* are examples of web authoring software packages.

However, professional web developers often work directly with HTML. Some of the advanced features of websites can be created only in this way.

HTML editors

If you are a beginner then you are strongly advised not to use an HTML editor, but to use web authoring software instead. However, if you already have some skills with web authoring you may like to try writing HTML directly. You can do this in one of three ways:

1 *Use a simple text editor*. You can write HTML in a text editor such as *Notepad*. Each time you want to view the page you will have to save it, with the file extension .htm or .html. You can then view the layout of the page by loading it into your browser.

2 *Use the HTML editor in web authoring software*. Most packages allow you to edit the HTML code, and then switch to the page layout option to see what it looks like. This is the best way to experiment with HTML.

3 *Use a specialist HTML editor*. There are a number of packages on the market which make it easy to write HTML code quickly and accurately. These include Macromedia *Homesite*, *CoffeeCup HTML Editor* and *HTML-Kit*.

1.5 Pixels

Just like screen resolution, every image is measured in pixels. When you are preparing an image for use on a web page you should always be aware of its dimensions in pixels. Some graphical software offers you the choice of measuring the image in centimetres or pixels – always choose pixels.

You will also see that you can adjust many aspects of the layout of a page by referring to the size of components in pixels, such as:

◆ the thickness of borders and lines

◆ the width of cells in tables

◆ the margins around a page

◆ the spacing around an object

◆ the width and height of frames.

1.6 Graphics file formats

All images have to be prepared for web use, before they are inserted into a web page. Images are prepared by reducing them to the appropriate size, and by **compressing** them into one of the standard WWW formats.

When we use a computer graphic, we can refer to its size in two senses:

1 *The* **memory** *needed to store the image*. Most computer graphics use a very large amount of memory. For example, a photograph taken with a digital camera will be 2MB (megabytes) or more. On a slow connection, a picture this size could take half an hour or more to download from the Internet!

2 *The* **dimensions** *of the image measured in pixels*. It is important that an image created for a web page is exactly the right size for the space it is going to occupy. That ensures that it has no more pixels than it really needs.

Because of the memory requirements, all images used on websites are stored in a compressed format. Compression reduces significantly the amount of memory needed to store an image of given dimensions.

Two compressed formats are commonly used on the WWW:

◆ **JPEG** (usually shortened to JPG) is used mainly for photographs.

◆ **GIF** is used for most other images, but it is limited to 256 different colours.

Creating an image in a graphics package

There are many ways of finding or creating images to use on a website. You can use a simple package like Microsoft *Paint* or a more sophisticated one like Adobe *Illustrator*. As you will be saving it in GIF format, you should use only the preset colours that are offered to you. Once you have designed the image, you should reduce the dimensions (number of pixels) to the exact ones needed on the web page.

Figure 4.5 shows a simple image of a sprig of heather created as a **bitmap image** in *Paint*. *Image + Attributes* was used to set the page at 100 pixels by

100 pixels. The image was then reduced to 25 per cent of its width and height, by using *Image + Stretch and Skew*, before being saved in GIF format. The image can now be used as a small icon or bullet.

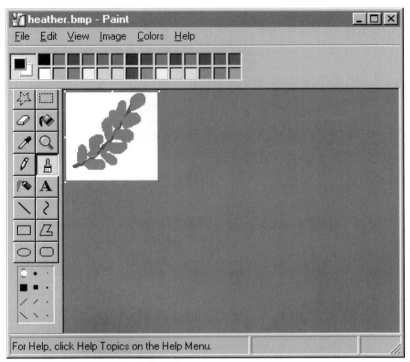

Figure 4.5 An image created in Paint

Using a photograph

You can either take a photograph with a digital camera or scan in a photo print. This will normally be stored as a bitmap image (.bmp), which is a non-compressed pixel format. You can then load it into a photo manipulation package, such as Microsoft *Photo Editor*.

Once again, reduce the dimensions to the number of pixels needed on the web page. Then save the photo as a JPG.

If you take a photo from a photo CD that was supplied when a film was developed, the images will normally be in JPG format already. You will normally need to reduce the dimensions of the photo, to something between 100 and 300 pixels wide. Save the image as a JPG again.

Figure 4.6 shows a photo loaded into Microsoft *Photo Editor* from a CD. The dimensions of the image are being changed using *Image + Resize*. The units should be displayed in pixels.

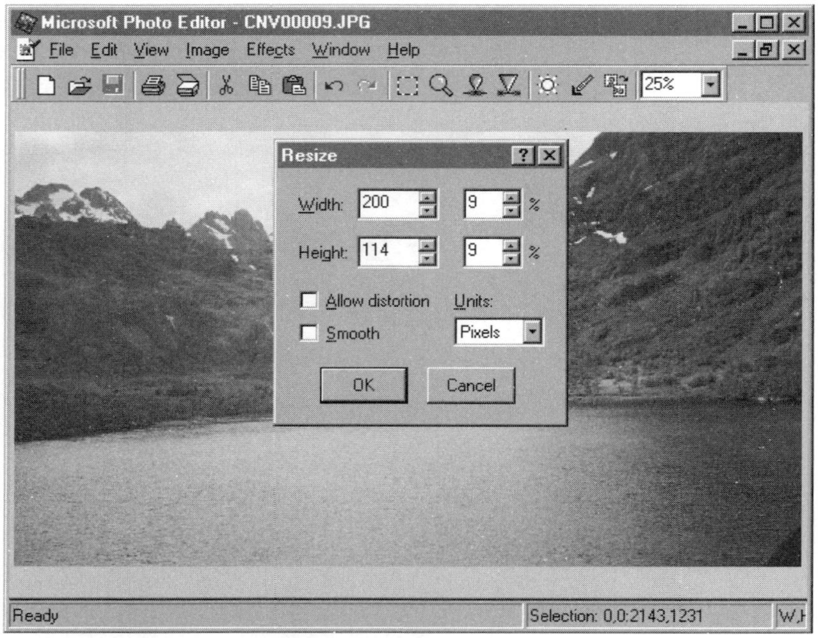

Figure 4.6 A photo being manipulated in Photo Editor

Obtaining an image from the WWW

You should never simply copy images on existing websites as the images will probably be protected by **copyright**. But fortunately, there are many sources of copyright-free images online. In many cases, the creators do ask you to acknowledge the source of any image you use. A search through a search engine will produce a bewildering choice, but you might like to start with www.freefoto.com and the portal site www.freegraphics.com.

1.7 Copyright issues

Writing, music, films and works of art are described as **intellectual property**, and the creators (or their employers) normally own the copyright to their work. This means that no one else may copy, print, perform or film work without the copyright owner's permission. In Britain, normally copyright extends for 50 years after the creator's death, and the rights extend to their heirs.

For many years, it was not clear whether copyright extended to software products. The **Copyright, Designs and Patents Act 1988** states that software (including websites) should be treated in the same way as all other intellectual property.

The copyright of a website belongs to the organisation that commissions it, not to the web designer.

Collecting and presenting information on websites

All content on a website should fall into one of these three categories:

◆ material created within the organisation

◆ material used with the permission of the copyright owner

◆ material that is free from copyright.

Permission must be sought before using text, photographs, images, videos, music and other sounds that have originated elsewhere. This applies whether they are found on a website or in books or recordings. Software used on websites, such as scripts in Java, Visual Basic and other languages, as well as Flash animations, are also covered by copyright. The copyright holders will usually charge for permission to use their materials.

Note

In general, it is wisest to assume that any material published in any format, including on the WWW, is covered by copyright, unless it explicitly states that it is copyright-free. Copyright-free material is not necessarily cost-free, but on the WWW there are many sources of copyright-free materials which can be downloaded and used at no charge.

There are several other terms used for software and other materials in relation to their copyright status.

◆ **Shareware** is software that has been copyrighted by the originator, but is sold (or given) to users with permission to copy it and to share with others. Sometimes, the conditions of use prevent the shareware from being used for commercial purposes. Shareware may be offered free on an evaluation basis, but with payment required for continuing use. Many scripts are offered as shareware.

◆ **Open-source software** is software that can be distributed without restrictions, so that all users can view and modify the code. Open-source software is not necessarily free of charge. Originally, open source was known as free software – in the sense of 'free to share' rather than 'at no cost'.

◆ **Public domain** materials are items that are completely free of copyright and can be used by anyone.

Go out and try!

Find sources of copyright-free, no-cost materials on the WWW that can be used legally on a website. You could look for images, photos, animations, literature, articles and music.

1.8 Example of web page development

This section is an introduction to creating a simple web page. Chapter 3 describes some more advanced techniques that you can use to enable you to develop a complete functioning website.

In a unit of this size, it is not possible to provide comprehensive instruction on web page design, but there are many books and online tutorials that can supplement your reading.

Selecting an appropriate web authoring package

Web authoring packages, or web page generating software, provide facilities that are very similar to desktop publishing (DTP) packages, but geared to the specific demands of the WWW. These packages give you a WYSIWYG (what you see is what you get) environment in which to develop web pages.

As you construct a web page in authoring software, the package generates the HTML source code. This code can be edited directly and can also be enhanced with **scripts** for dynamic effects.

There are a number of useful web authoring packages available, such as Microsoft *FrontPage* and Macromedia *Dreamweaver*. Another simple web authoring package, Netscape *Composer*, can be downloaded free with the browser, Netscape *Navigator*. These packages provide you with a complete environment which helps to automate the process of linking pages together to form a complete website.

Most of these packages provide useful page **templates** that can be used to lay out the content. A beginner can use any of these, although to gain a real understanding of how web pages are built it is better to start with a blank page.

Web authoring packages often provide **wizards** that can be used to create complete sites, with built-in themed graphics and page layouts. Although some of the results can be quite pleasing, they are rather limiting. Websites produced in this way are sometimes difficult to modify and update, and they do look very similar to each other.

Finally, the templates and wizards in web authoring packages are very useful for creating quick design **prototypes** of sites, even if the final site is developed using more refined techniques.

In this section, all the case studies are based on Microsoft *FrontPage 2000*. Similar features will be found in later versions of *FrontPage*, and in other web authoring packages.

PRACTICAL TASK 4.2

When you launch Microsoft *FrontPage*, it usually opens with a blank page. If anything else is displayed instead, then click on *Page* in the *Views* bar (see Figure 4.7 – the left-hand side of the window).

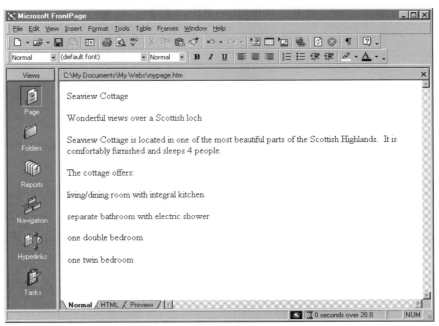

Figure 4.7 Entering text in page editor (normal) mode in FrontPage

Type in some text, as you would in a word processor, and then save the page, giving it a suitable name. All standard web pages are saved with either .htm or .html as the filename extension.

Notice that the text wraps at the end of lines, just as it does in a word processor. Also, as in most word processors, pressing *Enter* starts a new paragraph, whereas pressing *Shift + Enter* starts a new line omitting the paragraph spacing.

FrontPage, like most web authoring packages, will allow you to display the page in three modes:

◆ normal (page editor)
◆ HTML
◆ preview.

You create the page in the **Normal mode**, and then you can check what it will look like when displayed by a browser in the **Preview mode**. At this stage, they will look very similar, but differences will emerge as you use more advanced features.

A web authoring environment includes a page editor and an HTML editor. As the page is developed in the page editor, the HTML code is being generated in the background. Web designers can work in either editor and can easily switch between them.

The environment also provides a means of viewing the page in a browser. Some provide a built-in preview mode, which gives an immediate impression of how the page will be displayed. Some website design environments allow you to specify a standard browser that can be used for previewing the pages. However, there are some differences in the way different browsers (and different versions of the same browser) do interpret HTML code, so it is important to check web pages in a range of standard browsers before they are published.

Understanding the HTML

The HTML code for a page could look like this:

```
<html>
<head>
<meta http-equiv="Content-Language" content="en-gb">
<meta http-equiv="Content-Type" content="text/html;
    charset=windows-1252">
<meta name="GENERATOR" content="Microsoft FrontPage 4.0">
<meta name="ProgId" content="FrontPage.Editor.Document">
<title>New Page 1</title>
</head>
<body>
<p>Seaview Cottage</p>
<p>Wonderful views over a Scottish loch</p>
<p>Seaview Cottage is located in one of the most beautiful parts
    of the Scottish Highlands.  It is comfortably furnished
    and sleeps 4 people.</p>
<p>The cottage offers:</p>
<p>living/dining room with integral kitchen</p>
<p>separate bathroom with electric shower</p>
<p>one double bedroom </p>
<p>one twin bedroom</p>
</body>
</html>
```

The markup codes placed between triangular brackets are called **tags**. Tags are *not* case-sensitive (they can be in lower- or upper-case). Most tags come in pairs – the start tag (e.g. <p>) and the end tag (e.g. </p>).

This is the overall structure of the HTML code:

```
<html>
<head>
</head>
```

```
<body>
</body>
</html>
```

Lines of text placed between the head tags are hidden from the visitor, but can be used very powerfully, as we will see later.

◆ **<p>** and **</p>** mark the beginning and end of a paragraph.

◆ ** ** is an abbreviation for non-breaking space and is the code for a normal space character.

◆ **
** (not shown here) marks a line break.

If you press the *Tab* (indent) key on the keyboard it simply adds a fixed number of non-breaking spaces to the text.

Using heading and paragraph styles

The page editor allows the designer to highlight text and apply styles from a style list (see Figure 4.8). This list is similar to the style list found in word processing packages, but it is initially limited to a fixed set of styles. The list will always include 'Normal' (or default), headings 1 to 6, plus bulleted and numbered list styles.

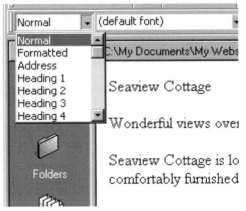

Figure 4.8 The style list in FrontPage

PRACTICAL TASK 4.3

In Normal mode, you can use pre-set styles with any of the text. The style list is found at the left end of the **formatting toolbar**, and the drop-down list displays the styles available (as in Figure 4.8).

1 Highlight the lines of text in turn and apply the Heading 1, Heading 2 and bulleted list styles from the style list as in Figure 4.9 ('Normal' is the default style for the page).

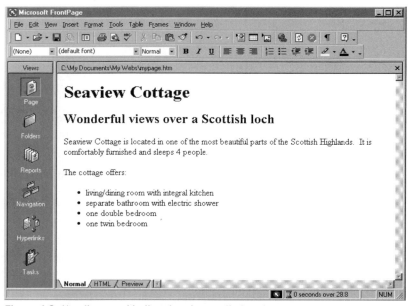

Figure 4.9 Headings and bulleted styles applied to the text

2 Check the HTML code to see what effect this has had.

3 In Normal mode, try replacing the bulleted list style with the numbered list style, and then check the HTML code again.

You may be tempted to use the other options in the formatting toolbar, and introduce other fonts, but try to resist this for the moment.

The HTML code for the body of the page uses a different tag for each style:

```
<body>
<h1>Seaview Cottage</h1>
<h2>Wonderful views over a Scottish loch</h2>
<p>Seaview Cottage is located in one of the most beautiful parts of
    the Scottish Highlands.  It is comfortably furnished
    and sleeps 4 people.</p>
<p>The cottage offers:</p>
<ul>
    <li>living/dining room with integral kitchen</li>
    <li>separate bathroom with electric shower</li>
    <li>one double bedroom </li>
    <li>one twin bedroom</li>
</ul>
</body>
```

◆ **<h1>, <h2>** etc. are the tags for headings 1, 2, ... in the style list.

◆ **<ul>** marks the beginning of an unordered (i.e. unnumbered) list.

◆ **<li>** is a list item.

All tags, such as <p>, use the 'Normal' (default) style from the style list, except those that have been specially defined.

Methods for formatting the text

There are several ways of formatting the text on a web page.

1   Using text formatting options on the formatting toolbar.

2   Using design themes.

3   Creating user-defined styles.

It is useful to know about all three methods, although the last method is by far the best.

A visitor's browser will be able to display a font only if it is already resident on the visitor's computer. So although a Web designer may want to use an attractive but obscure font for a heading, the visitor will be able to see the characters displayed in that font only if it is already 'on board'. If they do not have the required font then the browser will display the text in the **default font** for that browser. On a Microsoft Windows system the default font is usually Times New Roman, but the visitor can change the default font.

In web authoring packages it is possible to highlight some text and use the formatting toolbar to format it, making a selection from fonts, font styles, text alignment and colours. Unfortunately, if this method is used, every single paragraph and heading on every page of a website has to be individually formatted. This is a tedious process and some text can easily be overlooked. Worse still, if the web designer decides at some point to change the formatting – for example, to use a different colour for the main text – then every single instance has to be laboriously changed.

Figure 4.10 shows a formatted page. This is the HTML code for the body of the page:

```
<body>
<h1><font face="Tahoma" color="#0000FF" size="7">
   Seaview Cottage</font></h1>
<h2><font face="Tahoma" color="#008000">
   Wonderful views over a Scottish loch</font></h2>
<p><font face="Arial" color="#0000FF">
   Seaview Cottage is located in one of the most beautiful parts of
   the Scottish Highlands.  It is comfortably furnished and
   sleeps 4 people.</font></p>
<p><font face="Arial" color="#0000FF">
   The cottage offers: </font></p>
<ul>
```

```
<li><font face="Arial" color="#FF0000">
    living/dining room with integral kitchen</font></li>
<li><font face="Arial" color="#FF0000">
    separate bathroom with electric shower</font></li>
<li><font face="Arial" color="#FF0000">
    one double bedroom </font></li>
<li><font face="Arial" color="#FF0000">
    one twin bedroom </font></li>
</ul>
</body>
```

◆ **<font>** includes all the font properties that apply up to the next </font> tag.

Figure 4.10 A formatted page

Using design themes

FrontPage and other web authoring packages provide predesigned themes that can be applied across a website. These themes initially look pleasing, so they are very popular, especially on personal websites. They do appear again and again on the WWW, so it is not advisable to use them, unmodified, for serious web development.

However, most elements within a theme can be modified, and this technique can be used to give an acceptable and distinctive appearance to a simple site.

When a theme is used, the HTML may not appear to change much. For example, in *FrontPage* a theme is simply referenced by a tag in the head like this:

```
<meta name="Microsoft Theme" content="sumipntg 011">
```

However, this is a bit misleading because *FrontPage* does insert formatting codes when the page is uploaded to the webserver.

PRACTICAL TASK 4.4

1 Open the page you created.

2 If you have already applied text formatting to the page, select *Edit + Select All* then *Format + Remove Formatting*.

3 In *FrontPage*, select *Format + Themes*. Browse through the themes and select one. You will be impressed by the immediate improvement to all your pages (see Figure 4.9).

You can go back to the Themes dialogue to change a theme at any time. You can also modify any of the elements of a theme by clicking on *Modify* in the Themes dialogue.

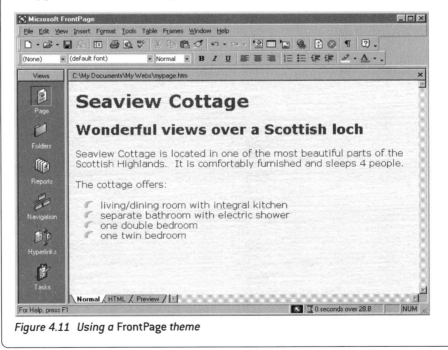

Figure 4.11 Using a FrontPage *theme*

Creating user-defined styles

FrontPage themes are useful for personal or very simple sites, but they should not be used for professional websites. Instead, you can define the styles for each of the styles that you use from the style list.

This process adds to the HTML code a list of the styles that you have defined. A list of user-defined styles is known as a **style sheet**.

PRACTICAL TASK 4.5

1 Open the page you were working on. If you have already applied a theme to the page, select *Format + Themes* and choose *No theme* from the list of themes. It should now look like Figure 4.9 again.

2 Select *Format + Style*. In the Style dialogue box (see Figure 4.12), select the h1 (heading 1) tag from the Styles list. Click on *Modify*.

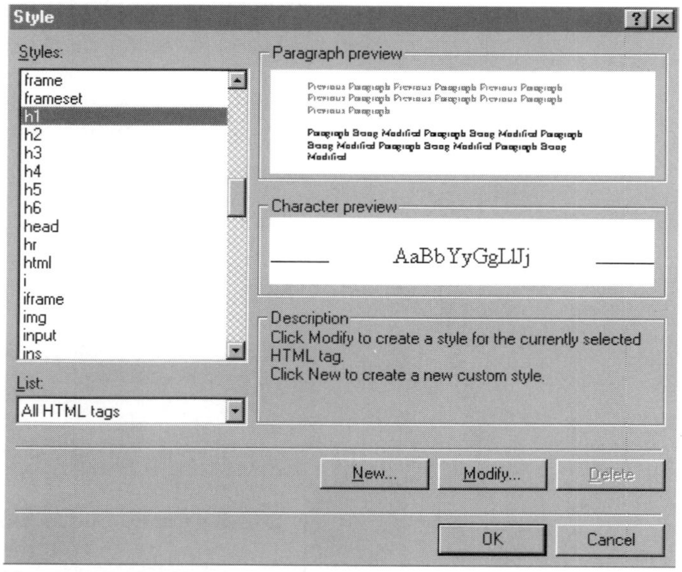

Figure 4.12 The Style dialogue box

3 In the Modify Style dialogue (see Figure 4.13), click on *Format*, then select *Font*.

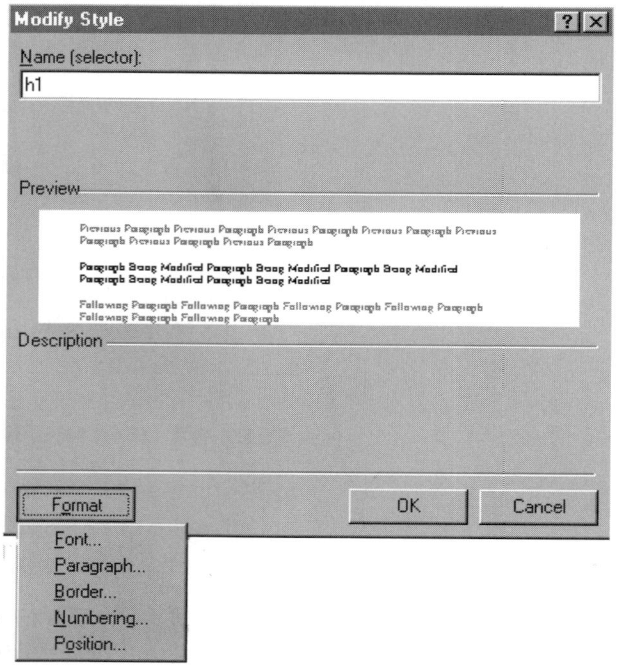

Figure 4.13 Modifying a style

4 In the Font dialogue box (see Figure 4.14), select from the font options that you want for h1, then click on *OK*.

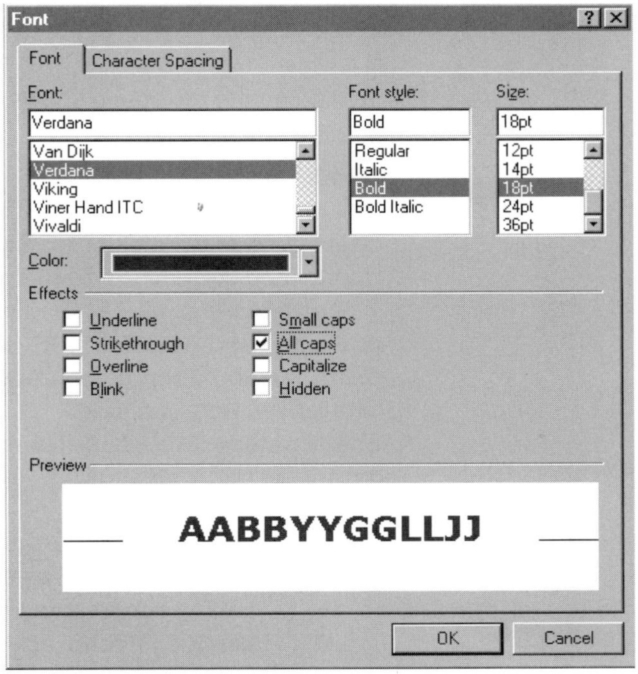

Figure 4.14 The Font style dialogue box

5 Back in the Modify Style dialogue, click on *Format*, then explore the other formatting options open to you.

6 When you have defined one style, you will observe h1 listed as a user-defined style (see Figure 4.15).

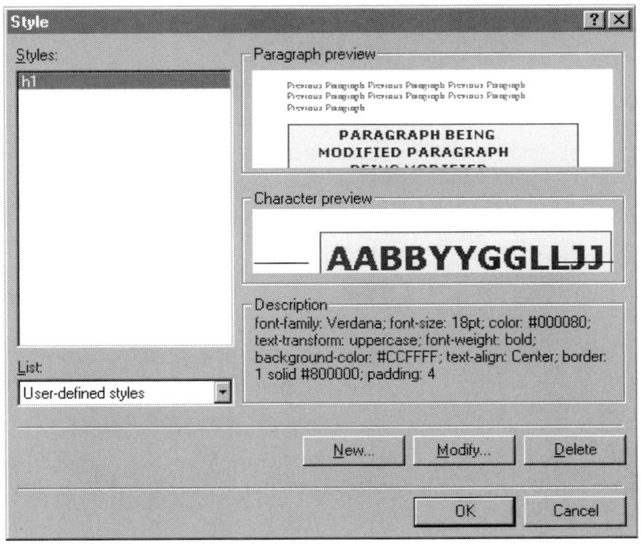

Figure 4.15 A user-defined style

> **7** To define another style, click on *List:* and select *All HTML tags*. Find the tag you want to define and repeat the process. Don't forget to format the styles for p and li.

Figure 4.16 on the next page shows a Web page with user-defined styles. The HTML for the page looks like this:

```html
<html>
<head>
<meta http-equiv="Content-Language" content="en-gb">
<meta http-equiv="Content-Type" content="text/html;
   charset=windows-1252">
<meta name="GENERATOR" content="Microsoft FrontPage 4.0">
<meta name="ProgId" content="FrontPage.Editor.Document">
<title>New Page 1</title>
<meta name="Microsoft Theme" content="none">
<style>
   <!--
   h1  {font-family: Verdana; font-size: 18pt; color: #000080;
           text-transform: uppercase; font-weight: bold;
           background-color: #CCFFFF; text-align: center;
           border: 1 solid #800000; padding: 4;}
   h2  {font-family: Tahoma; font-size: 14pt; color: #800000;
           text-align: center; font-weight: bold;}
   p {font-family: Arial; font-size: 12pt; color: #000080;}
   li {font-family: Arial; font-size: 12pt; color: #000080;
           text-align: left;  list-style-type: square;}
   -->
</style>
</head>

<body>
<h1>Seaview Cottage</h1>
<h2>Wonderful views over a Scottish loch</h2>
<p>Seaview Cottage is located in one of the most beautiful parts
   of the ScottishHighlands.  It is comfortably furnished
   and sleeps 4 people.</p>
<p>The cottage offers:</p>
<ul>
   <li>living/dining room with integral kitchen</li>
   <li>separate bathroom with electric shower</li>
   <li>one double bedroom </li>
   <li>one twin bedroom</li>
</ul>
</body>

</html>
```

The code between the <style> tags lists the chosen styles for each tag. You can edit this directly in HTML if you like.

A style sheet like this opens up many more possibilities, beyond the scope of this book. They can also be used with any web development software, whereas the themes were specific to *FrontPage*.

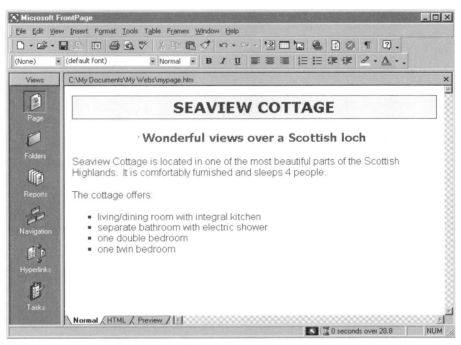

Figure 4.16 A web page with user-defined styles

Adding an image to the page

You can add an image to the page, provided it is already in JPG or GIF format. Some web authoring packages – including *FrontPage* – will convert the images for you, but it is much better to retain control over the process yourself.

Check that each image has the correct dimensions, in pixels, and does not take up too much memory.

PRACTICAL TASK 4.6

1   Open the page you are working on. In Normal view, click at the position on the page where you want to place an image.

2   Select *Insert + Picture + From File*. Find the prepared image and insert it (see Figure 4.17).

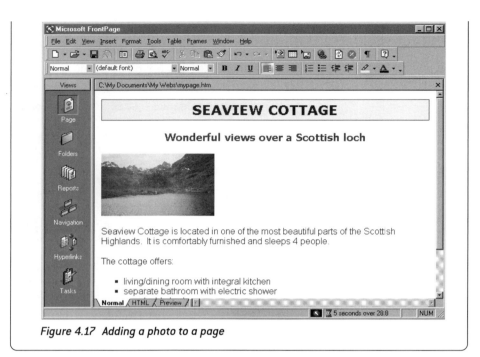

Figure 4.17 Adding a photo to a page

Adding a horizontal line and a background colour

A **horizontal line** can be added to the page, usually using the Insert menu on the web authoring package. The tag for this is simply **<hr>**, for horizontal rule, and there is no end tag in this case. The colour of the line can be set up in a style sheet, so will apply to all the lines you insert.

The colour of the **background** can be changed. This can often be done through a Page Properties dialogue, but in general it is better to do it through the Style dialogue.

Most web authoring packages offer a palette of colours. The HTML adds the 'bgcolor' attribute to the <body> tag:

```
<body bgcolor="#FFFF00">
```

◆ **bgcolor** gives the background colour, with the value expressed either as a six-digit hexadecimal code (e.g. "#FFFF00"), or as an RGB code (e.g. "rgb(255, 255, 0)"), or as a standard colour word (e.g. "yellow").

PRACTICAL TASK 4.7

1 In *FrontPage*, use *Insert + Horizontal Line* to add a standard grey line that extends across the page.

2 Use *Format + Style* to change the colour of any lines you insert. Select the <hr> tag. Use the *Border* option and select the *Shading* tab. The Foreground colour will give the colour of the line.

3 To change the colour of the background on a page, select *Format +
Style*, then select the body tag. Again, use the *Border* option and
select the *Shading* tab.

Figure 4.18   Background and a horizontal line inserted

Chapter summary

◆ The appearance of a web page is affected by the screen resolution,
colour depth and the size of the browser window on the visitor's
system. The speed of the Internet connection determines the time
taken for the page to appear.

◆ Web pages are coded in HTML, and you can create pages using an
HTML editor or by using web authoring software which generates
the code for you.

◆ Images should be prepared for use on websites, by reducing the
dimensions to those needed on screen, and by compressing the
image.

◆ Most material used on websites is subject to copyright legislation.

◆ Web authoring packages provide a page editor, plus templates,
wizards and design themes to help you create pages. A style sheet
can be used to define the styles used on a web page.

2 Undertake user requirements analysis

As with any other software project, the development of a website must be taken through the usual stages of analysis, design, implementation and evaluation (review). **User interfaces**, which are of particular importance for websites, are usually developed with **user-centred design** methods.

> ## What does it mean?
>
> **User-centred design** is an approach to the design and implementation of software, especially the user interface, that involves the user at every stage of the project. At the design stage, a **prototype** is created which is reviewed by the user and alternative designs developed in response.

The term 'user' is a bit ambiguous in this situation. It can refer to both the client who commissions the website, and the end user who visits it. In practice, both are involved, although the client is the main 'user' who is considered. At the final stages of evaluation, typical site visitors can also be asked to assess the site.

The design process usually follows this pattern:

◆ user requirements analysis, which leads to a **design specification**

◆ prototyping and implementation

◆ evaluation against the specification

◆ technical testing and publishing.

In the first of these stages the designer must establish – possibly by means of interviews with the client – the purpose of the website and the target audience. The designer then creates a design for the project for approval. This chapter looks in detail at the first stage, with some final comments on the other stages.

2.1 Functions of websites

The first task within user requirements analysis is to establish the purpose and function of the proposed website.

Websites can be developed for a variety of purposes, and many sites have more than one purpose. Here are some possibilities:

◆ *To inform*. All websites provide some information, which is one reason why the Internet became known as the information superhighway.

◆ *To promote and sell*. Websites can be used to promote products and services to visitors.

◆ *To interact*. Websites can easily offer interactivity, allowing the visitor to send information and ideas back to the organisation and engage in dialogue.

e-Commerce is the term used to describe sites that offer online sales.

Types of website

Websites can be developed by a number of different types of organisation. Each will have their own combinations of purposes.

◆ Educational organisations create websites to inform and interact. One of the earliest uses of the Internet was by universities to circulate academic papers.

◆ Governmental and other public service organisations create websites to inform the public, and increasingly to provide a space where citizens can interact with decision makers.

◆ Commercial organisations use websites to promote themselves and also to offer online selling.

◆ Community organisations use websites to inform people and to interact. Some communities of people with a common interest exist entirely within the WWW.

Using a website to inform

Websites are an ideal means of providing information, so it is not surprising that some of the most visited sites are those that specialise in giving information to the general public.

External communications are those directed primarily at people outside the organisation.

Information sites include the traditional media such as newspapers and magazines, which have developed their own online versions, and television and radio channels. While it is possible to listen to radio and watch television over the Internet, these sites have taken on a life of their own, exploiting the specific qualities of the new medium.

CASE STUDY

BBCi

BBCi (www.bbc.co.uk) has become a channel in its own right and does not simply repeat material broadcast by the BBC. In addition to live radio and streaming video, it provides interactive features such as webchats and message boards, as well as up-to-date information on a huge variety of subjects. It is the most visited website in the UK.

You might like to look at BBC – iCan (www.bbc.co.uk/ican) which offers information and guidance for you to start a campaign, or join an existing one, about something that concerns you.

Figure 4.19 BBCi's logo

Many public services have sites, such as the well-used NHS-Direct (www.nhsdirect.nhs.uk), which specialise in communicating information to members of the public.

There are also a few online organisations that have built huge databases of articles and external links, which they then provide as a service to visitors. One example is About (www.about.com).

You may wonder how an organisation can afford to provide a free information service. You will usually find that these sites are sponsored by other businesses, and the advertisements they have paid for will appear in **banners** and **pop-up screens**. Some information sites, such as the government's DirectGov, are paid for out of public taxation.

Using a website to promote and sell

Many websites promote a service or product but without actually offering online sales. For example, most rock bands have websites that promote the band and their music, although visitors may not be able to buy albums directly from the site.

Many tourist attractions use the Internet to give people information about location and opening times and to encourage people to attend. Similarly, hotels often provide basic information even though you may have to phone to book a room.

CASE STUDY

Disneyland Paris

Disneyland Paris uses its website (www.disneylandparis.com) to show what it offers and to encourage people to visit (see Figure 4.20).

Try to find a few other leisure attractions that market their services on the Web. Here are some hints:

◆ schools, colleges and universities

◆ charities

◆ political parties

◆ churches and other religious organisations

◆ theatres and cinemas.

All these organisations are trying to persuade the visitor to do something in response and are not simply providing interesting information.

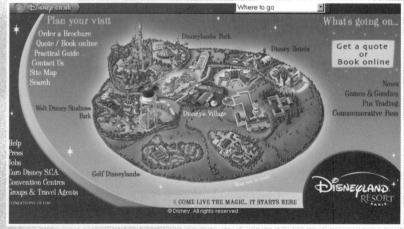

Figure 4.20 Marketing Disneyland Paris

Some promotional sites also offer online sales, and start to develop an e-commerce angle. The dividing line between promotion and e-commerce sites is not precise – the category depends on the *main* purpose of the site.

As the Internet has grown, so more and more businesses have emerged that exist only on the WWW. There are many examples of online banks, shops, travel agencies and insurance companies. These companies sell goods and services directly to the customer.

Customers normally pay for products online with a credit or debit card, and they need to be reassured that their payments will be safe. Online payments are usually routed through a **secure server** which **encrypts** all the data.

*Data is **encrypted** when it is converted into a secret code. Encrypted data is decrypted when it is converted back to ordinary text.*

Goods have to be sent to the customer either by post or using a distribution company, and successful online businesses usually guarantee delivery in 24 hours or a few days.

CASE STUDY

Amazon, the online bookstore

Amazon describe themselves in this way:

'**Who We Are** Amazon.co.uk is the trading name for Amazon.com International Sales Inc. and Amazon.com International Auctions Inc. Both companies are subsidiaries of Amazon.com – a leading online retailer of products that inform, educate and inspire. The Amazon group has stores in the United States, Germany, France, Japan and Canada. Amazon.co.uk (see Figure 4.21) has its origins in an independent online

Figure 4.21 Amazon's e-commerce site for the UK

store — Bookpages — which was established in 1996, and subsequently acquired by Amazon.com in early 1998.

'What We Do Amazon.co.uk offers a catalogue of more than 1.5 million books, thousands of CDs, DVDs and videos, a wide range of software and PC & video games and a great selection of children's products in Toys & Kids! The site also hosts online auctions and brings independent buyers and sellers together in zShops, our online marketplace. In addition, customers have access to a variety of other resources including customer reviews, e-mail personal recommendations and gift certificates.'

◆ Use your usual **search engine** (e.g. Google) to find other e-commerce websites. Can you work out which types of business mainly have gone in for e-commerce? What types of business are rarely to be found on the WWW?

Some Internet businesses offer services which avoid the need to deliver goods. For example, online banking has grown very rapidly, and customers can view their balance, make payments and generally manage their accounts at any time of the day. Similarly, travel companies can send documents, such as ticket confirmations, by email and may not need to use the post at all.

In addition, many high-street chains now have online e-commerce operations as well. Large supermarkets offer a home shopping service which can be very helpful for people who are housebound, have young children, or lead busy lives.

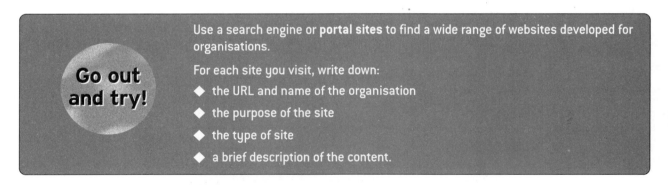

Go out and try!

Use a search engine or **portal sites** to find a wide range of websites developed for organisations.

For each site you visit, write down:
◆ the URL and name of the organisation
◆ the purpose of the site
◆ the type of site
◆ a brief description of the content.

2.2 The target audience

User analysis for a website includes an assessment of the target audience. The intended audience may be the public in general, or it may be targeted at specified age bands (children, the elderly), communities of interest (members of a club, people who enjoy a leisure activity, researchers, political and pressure groups), geographical communities, shoppers, travellers, etc. Most sites are built with a typical visitor in mind.

One particular consideration is whether the site is intended for internal use only — by members of a company or organisation — or is intended to reach the general public.

Using an intranet

One way of restricting access to a website is to create an intranet. An intranet (note the spelling) is a closed system that has many of the features of the Internet but which is accessible only *within* an organisation.

An intranet is created on the organisation's own network system and can be accessed by users who log on to stations on the network. It will normally include email services and an internal 'website'. Strictly speaking we should not really refer to the pages as a 'website' as it does not appear on the WWW.

An intranet can hold confidential information that should not normally appear outside the organisation, as well as day-to-day administrative arrangements.

By definition, members of the public do not normally have access to intranets, but you may find that you have an intranet at your place of study.

Many employees travel around the country on business or work from home. They also need access to the company's intranet. The organisation may make it possible for them to access the intranet over an Internet connection, using an ID and password system to gain access. This is sometimes known as an **extranet**.

2.3 House style

The house style of an organisation is a key factor in determining the visual design of a website. Most organisations have a style guide which lays down the correct use of company logos, and specifies the colours, fonts, etc. to be used on all publications – including letters to the public. This ensures that the organisation's communications with the public have a consistent look and feel to them.

Most organisations want to carry the style guidelines through to their website. This can usually be achieved although there are sometimes some constraints on the use of specific fonts or exact colour matching.

2.4 Page layouts

There are several ways of controlling the layout of text and images, although it is not always easy to arrange items on the page where you would like them to be.

Using the picture properties

If you click on an image in the page editor view, you can usually display the image (picture) properties either by right-clicking or by selecting from the main menu. The alignment of the image can be set as 'right', left', 'top', etc. –

these are in relation to the text (see Figures 4.22 and 4.23). You can also set a border, or create horizontal or vertical spacing around the image.

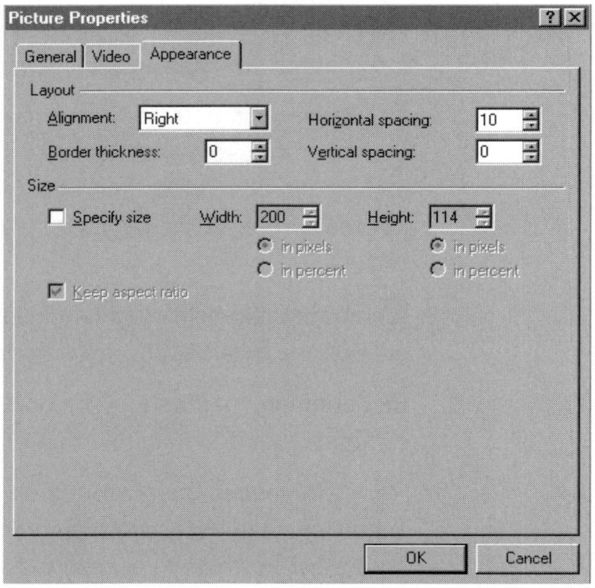

Figure 4.22 Setting the picture properties in FrontPage

Figure 4.23 Using picture properties to lay out a page
(compare this with Figure 4.18 on page 229)

Using a table

Tables can be created on a web page, just as they can in a word processor. But although a table can be used to display data in boxes in the traditional way, tables are more commonly used on web pages as a way of arranging text and images on screen. Often the tables are created without borders, so when the page is viewed in page preview the dividing lines are not visible. You can specify many of the properties of a table by clicking on it, then right-clicking or selecting the table properties from the main menu.

Using frames

The display in a browser can be split into two or more frames, each of which holds a separate web page (see Figure 4.24). This technique is often used so that constant information is shown in one frame while the contents of another frame may change. For example, a main navigation bar can be displayed in a narrow frame at the top or side of a page, with the main page contents varying according to which link has been selected.

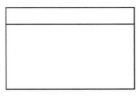 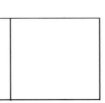 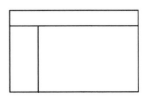

Figure 4.24 Three common frame configurations

*A **frame page** is a separate web page which will not be visible to the visitor. Instead it describes the structure of the frames in the window and assigns initial pages to the frames.*

2.5 Maintenance and future development

A website should always be designed with maintenance in mind. A community site that is run by volunteers should not aim to update the site on a daily basis, as that is unlikely to be sustainable. So, the site should be designed to look interesting without necessarily carrying immediate news.

On the other hand, an organisation might have ambitious plans for a site that will be updated several times a day. The organisation has to ensure that enough staff are trained to provide material and to upload pages, and that **fall-back options** are in place in case of staff absence.

Many large sites use **content management systems**, which allow non-technical staff to prepare web pages by simply copying text and images from elsewhere on their computers. These systems are often based on databases, which generate web pages automatically on demand, drawing on the data held in the database.

Major websites are usually redesigned every year or two, to take advantage of the progress of technology and the addition of new features to browsers. If old material is still going to be accessible from the site, there is sometimes a problem creating a new design that incorporates old material. Again, the use of a database that holds the raw content can solve this problem as the page design is handled separately from the content.

2.6 The essentials of designing a website

Based on the analysis, the designer draws up a **design specification** which is agreed with the client. The design requirements of a website can be broken down into three areas:

◆ content

◆ visual design

◆ technical design.

The **content** of a site covers all the information that it will contain, together with any interactive features. Certain information is essential:

◆ *How to contact the organisation.* This information should always be provided somewhere on the site. It may be offered through an online form, or an email address may be given.

◆ *Basic details about the organisation.* Visitors need to know something about the activities of the organisation.

◆ *Privacy policy* (if personal data is collected from the visitor). This is a statement about how the organisation will handle any information given to them by a visitor. This is necessary to comply with the Data Protection Act and to give the visitor the confidence to do business with the organisation.

The content part of the design specification should describe certain other features in outline.

◆ *The information that should be provided.* This should include text, visual information (charts, photographs, video, etc.) and sound (music, etc.)

◆ *The main categories of information.* These will identify the headings that will appear in the main navigation bar.

◆ *The style of language appropriate to the subject matter.* Business sites will tend to use more formal language than sites devoted to leisure interests. The age of expected visitors is also relevant.

As a general rule, visitors should not be overwhelmed with information that they do not want. **Links** can be given to allow visitors to **navigate** to more in-depth coverage of a topic.

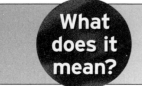

What does it mean?

Navigation refers to the way a visitor finds his or her way around a website, using links provided on the pages. Text or images can act as navigation links, and image links are often called 'buttons'. Some of the most important links may be positioned together in a navigation bar.

The **visual design** of the site should specify:

◆ *overall impression* – it could be businesslike, friendly, busy, formal, casual

◆ *required components* – such as company logo or corporate colours

◆ *colour scheme* – background, text and spot colours

◆ *appearance of text* – consistent text styles, length of paragraphs

◆ *use of images* – for information, as decoration, or to create a mood or style

◆ *use of animation and video* – appropriate use to entertain and inform

◆ *layout* – of the '**home page**' and of subsequent pages.

*Most websites open at an organisation's **home page**. This will set the scene for the visitor and provide essential links to the content of other pages.*

A website should use all its visual elements *consistently*. The main navigation bar should be accessible throughout the site, and should appear in the same position on each page.

The **technical design** concentrates on a number of usability issues.

◆ *Navigation*. Links are chosen for the main navigation bar, and a linking structure for all other pages.

◆ *Use of search tools*. List boxes, keyword search boxes and site maps can help the visitor to navigate.

◆ *Download speed*. A web page should download to the visitor's computer within an acceptable time. The page itself as well as all the images on it have to be downloaded individually from the webserver, so altogether they should not usually take longer than one minute to download using the slowest communication link. Larger files can be made available provided the visitor is warned about their size.

◆ *Browser compatibility*. A web page can change in appearance when viewed with different browsers. The designer will try to minimise these variations through his or her knowledge of the characteristics of each browser type.

◆ *Maintenance.* The site should be straightforward to maintain – that is, to update the content. The frequency of maintenance will depend on the purpose of the site.

Navigation issues

Internal links allow the visitor to find his or her way around the site. Unless the site is very small, you cannot provide links from any one page to *all* the other pages, so you have to design a **navigation structure**. You must consider how the pages are related to each other and work out what pages a visitor might want to see next.

Visitors can be divided into two types: those who are looking for specific information, and those who just want to browse. A site must provide links to suit both.

The website may naturally fall into a number of main sections, and links to the first page in each section should be given in the main navigation bar. This is an example of **linking by structure**. The structure of a website can often be represented in a tree diagram (see Figure 4.25). Here, a page is the **parent** to each of the pages below it in the structure, and is the **child** of any page above it. The child pages of the home page are particularly important, as they will always appear in the main navigation bar.

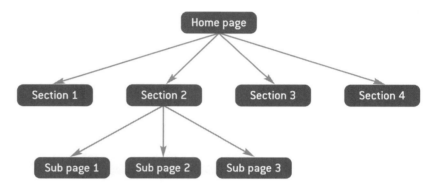

Figure 4.25 Tree diagram showing the structure of a website

CASE STUDY

Supermarket websites

Tesco (www.tesco.com) uses a strong structure to link its pages. The main navigation bar is shown as a series of tabs along the top of the screen and it appears on every page. In Figure 4.26, the shopping link has been selected and the first page of this section is displayed. The secondary navigation bar is down the left side of the screen and shows the links within the shopping section. The secondary bar is displayed on every page in the shopping section.

Visit www.tesco.com to see this for yourself. Also visit the websites of Tesco's main competitor supermarkets (use your favourite search engine) and look for common features they might have. Do their home pages provide clear links to what a typical visitor (or shopper) will be looking for?

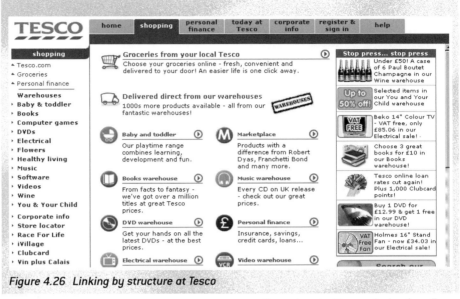

Figure 4.26 Linking by structure at Tesco

The WWW also allows visitors to browse to any page they like and in any order they like, so it is sometimes helpful to provide links to other pages that cover similar topics. This is called **linking by theme**. The diagram representing this type of linking will look like a random and rather messy network (see Figure 4.27). However, linking by theme helps the visitor who just wants to surf.

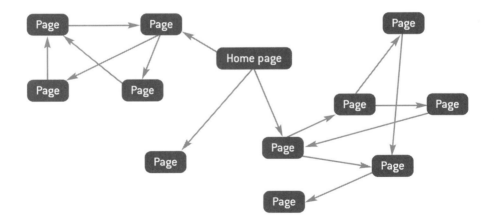

Figure 4.27 The random look of a diagram representing linking by theme

Many sites use a *combination* of linking by structure and linking by theme. Often a selection from the main navigation bar on the home page leads to a page that holds both the main navigation bar and a secondary navigation bar. The page also holds thematic links to other pages elsewhere on the site that contain content that might also be of interest to anyone who visits that page.

CASE STUDY

Combining linking styles

The page shown is from a community site, which features news, events and comments about the local area. It has a main navigation bar along the top, but it also has some thematic links in the right-hand column. These link to other news stories about crime and policing.

Check other news sites, such as online newspapers or TV channels, to see whether they use a combination of linking by structure and linking by theme.

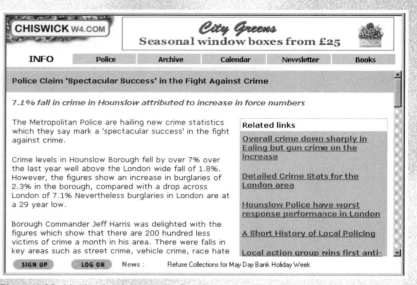

Figure 4.28 Linking by theme as well as by structure on a community website

A navigation bar can be placed anywhere on a web page. The main navigation bar is often placed horizontally across the top of the page, or alternatively vertically down the left side.

◆ If the main navigation bar is horizontal, then a secondary navigation bar can be placed immediately above or below it. Alternatively, the second bar could be placed vertically in this case.

◆ If the main navigation bar is vertical, it is quite difficult to place a secondary navigation bar alongside it. One solution to this problem is to use an **expanding navigation bar**. When an item is clicked a space opens up below the item revealing the secondary links.

Both horizontal and vertical navigation bars can be designed in **menu style**. When the mouse clicks or passes over the item, a drop-down menu reveals the secondary links.

A large site may need a handful of pages that contain little more than links to other pages. An **index** will list links to all the pages of a certain type. If the content of a site is managed by a database, then these indexes may be generated automatically. A **site map** is an index listing every page on the site.

Note

The 'three-click rule' is a good guideline to follow. A visitor should be able to find any piece of information being sought on a site with no more than three clicks of the mouse. That can be quite a challenge on a large site, but can be achieved with a combination of navigation bars, indexes and thematic links.

Prototyping and implementation

A **prototype** is a cut-down version of the site which can be used as the basis for a design review with the client.

The first prototype – known as a **storyboard** – is created on paper to match the design specification. The storyboard is usually sketched by hand. It should indicate:

◆ the layout of the home page and other pages
◆ the links on the main navigation bar
◆ the user of colour for background and text
◆ the use of images for information and decoration.

When the storyboard is reviewed with the client, discussion will often highlight aspects of the design specification that were overlooked or not specified clearly enough. At this stage, the client will often be inspired with new ideas for the site, and these can also be incorporated into the design specification.

The designer next creates a **computer-based prototype**, based on the agreed storyboard, using web design software. The design is then subject to review and amendment, and this is repeated until the client is satisfied. The prototype will normally consist of the home page plus a small number of sample pages (which may simply be in outline).

Once the client has approved the prototype, the remaining pages can then be fully implemented. The finished site must be subjected to a final review with the client against the original specification. At this stage any errors that emerge can be dealt with.

Technical testing and publishing

The website goes live at the moment when it is published – that is, when it is uploaded to a webserver and becomes accessible to visitors. Before that happens, the site should be subjected to thorough technical testing.

Chapter summary

◆ A design specification for a website identifies the type, function and target audience of the site. It should list the contents of the site, and describe the visual design, which is often determined by the house style of the organisation.

◆ The style and structure of navigation within a site should be covered by the technical aspects of the design.

◆ Page layout can be controlled using picture properties, tables or frames.

◆ Prototypes are used to demonstrate the design to the client.

3 Use appropriate development tools to implement web pages

3.1 Site management software

You need to be able to use appropriate software to manage the development of a site. It will be an advantage to learn how to use the software at this stage.

A website consists of pages that are linked together. A number of single pages can be created in a web authoring package, and the hyperlinks can be added manually. Alternatively, the website management tools that are built in to most web authoring packages can be used to automate some of the processes.

Site management software

The site management tools in web authoring packages do vary, but they often enable the designer to:

◆ manage the folders and files for a site

◆ view and modify the navigation structure of a site

◆ create and maintain navigation bars automatically

◆ check all the hyperlinks

◆ create a site map

◆ create a design theme for a site

◆ publish the site to a server

◆ manage a website project.

Setting up a website

All websites include one page with a filename **index.htm** (or index.html). This is the first page that any visitor will download. When a URL such as http://www.yahoo.com is entered into the address box of a browser, the browser actually searches for the index page, which in this case is http://www.yahoo.com/index.htm. On many sites, the index page holds the home page, although it can sometimes hold instructions for downloading other pages.

Note

A modern browser will add the 'http://' part of the address for you when it detects that 'www' has been entered.

PRACTICAL TASK 4.8

FrontPage provides a number of tools in the Views bar that help you to construct and manage a site. To see how they work, use one of the website templates or wizards to create an instant site. You should not use these whole-site templates for assessment work, but they are a quick way of demonstrating the principles.

In *FrontPage* each website that you create is stored on your system in a separate web folder. FrontPage refers to these as **webs**.

You should close a web folder by selecting *File + Close Web* or by simply exiting from *FrontPage*. To open a web folder, select *File + Open Web*, and select the folder name.

To get started, first close any pages or webs that are open. Select *File + New + Web*, then select *Personal Web*. To the right you will see a text box in which you can specify the location of a new web (see Figure 4.29). The default location for all *FrontPage* webs is in a folder called My Webs. The default name for a web folder is 'mywebnn', but you should change this to a meaningful name, such as 'personal'. *FrontPage* will create the folder for you.

The structure of the site will be created for you. The tools (or views) for developing the site are displayed in the Views bar.

1   Click on the Folders icon in the Views bar. *FrontPage* creates a new web folder and generates five web pages in the Personal website. It also creates _private and images folders specifically for this website.

2   Double-click on index.htm, then view the page in Preview mode. You can now explore the website. It is not finished, of course, but do not edit the pages. Close any open pages before the next steps.

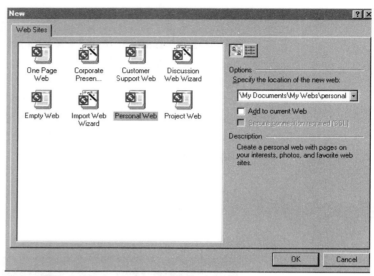

Figure 4.29 Setting up a new web in FrontPage

3 The Reports view on the Views bar lists some statistics about the site which will become more significant as your site grows.

4 You can see how all the pages are linked together by selecting the Navigation view (see Figure 4.30). You can edit any page by clicking on it in Navigation view, and this is usually the most convenient way of accessing pages. The Navigation view can be used to add new pages to your website structure.

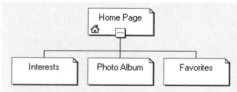

Figure 4.30 Navigation structure of a personal website in Frontpage

5 The Hyperlinks view displays links between pages (see Figure 4.31). Note the direction of the arrows in the diagram. On the left end of an arrow is the page which carries the hyperlink, and on the right end is the page or external website that it links to. Click on the '+' buttons to expand the diagram.

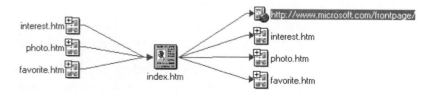

Figure 4.31 The Hyperlinks view of a website in FrontPage

6 The Tasks view allows you to list all the tasks that you have to complete and is a very useful planning tool.

3.2 Creating style templates

Well-designed sites have a consistent look, with the same textual and graphical elements repeated across all the pages. In creating a consistent design, the following design components should be considered:

- font type, size, style and colour
- background colours and images for page, table and cells
- graphic elements such as lines, buttons and images.

As we saw on page 221, the implementation of the visual design can be approached using three distinct methods – text formatting, themes (provided by web authoring packages) and style sheets. Of these, **style sheets** are by far the most flexible. They can also be created in any web development environment, whether you are working directly with HTML or using a full web authoring package.

Style sheets are particularly important for sites that have been designed in a specific house style. The pre-set themes that can be found in web authoring packages are not suitable. The style sheet should be set up at the beginning of the process, not added in later.

Using cascading style sheets (CSS)

You have already created an embedded style sheet, which contained the style definitions between the <head> and </head> tags (see page 226). This method is suitable for styles that apply to one page only.

When you create a full site, you will want to apply the same styles consistently across all the pages. To do this, the best approach is to create an external style sheet document that is then used by all the pages.

A style sheet is a separate page, hidden from the visitor, which is uploaded to the server along with the web pages. It contains a set of definitions for the styles used in the style list. In fact, any tag in the HTML code can have its own style definition.

The style definitions in a style sheet can be applied to all the pages on a site. That means that a simple change to the style sheet can have an effect right across a large site, and in this way visual consistency can be maintained.

A style sheet can be created in a web authoring package or in any simple text editor, such as *Notepad*. Sample style sheets are often provided as well, and these can be a good starting point.

Note *External style sheets are referred to as **cascading style sheets** and have the file extension '.css'.*

If you are not using web authoring software, then you can simply type in the style sheet code in *Notepad* (or other text editor). Remember to save the file with the filename extension '.css', *not* '.txt'.

PRACTICAL TASK 4.9

In this activity, you will set up a web and create an external style sheet.

1 In *FrontPage*, close any open webs. Select *File + New + Web* and choose the Empty Web template.

2 Specify the name of this web in the *Options* box. In the example shown in Figure 4.32, 'sportsclub' is chosen as the name. Click on *OK*.

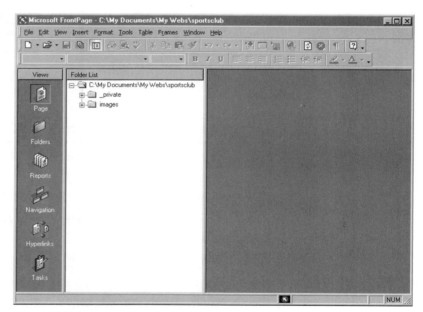

Figure 4.32 A new empty web

3 It is useful to be able to see the list of files while you are working on a page. Click on the *Folder List* button in the top toolbar. You can make the folder list wider or narrower by dragging on its border. You will see that the _private and images folders have been created for you, as in Figure 4.32.

4 Close the blank page called new_page_1.htm.

5 You will now begin to create a style sheet. Select *File + New + Page*. Click on the style sheets tab. Select one of the pre-designed style sheets, such as 'Capsules' (see Figure 4.33).

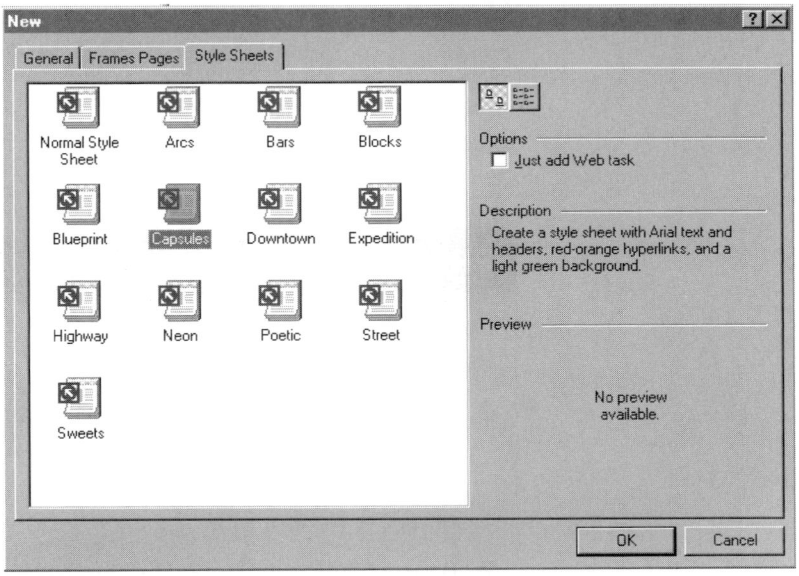

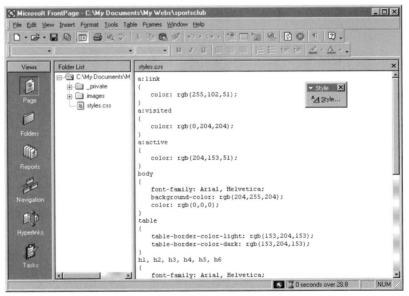

Figure 4.33 Selecting a pre-designed style sheet

6 The style sheet code appears, with a floating toolbar (see Figure 4.34). Have a look at the style definitions, but don't change them for now.

Figure 4.34 A style sheet

7 Save the style sheet as 'styles.css'.

Creating a template

A template is a pre-designed page that can be used as the basis for all the pages in a web. Web authoring packages provide you with a number of templates that you can use, but you can also create your own. These are all stored in a system file and are displayed whenever you create a new page.

If you are working in an HTML editor, then you can simple create a page, linked to a style sheet, and save it with a name like 'mytemplate.htm'.

PRACTICAL TASK 4.10

In the same web as before, you can now create a template that you will use for all the pages in the web.

1 Start by creating a blank new page. To do this, select *File + New + Page*. In the General tab, click on Normal Page. This is the standard page template. You are going to adapt it and then save your own template for this web.

2 On the blank page, type in some basic representative text. Apply the heading styles from the style list. Then add any text that will appear on every page in the web (see Figure 4.35).

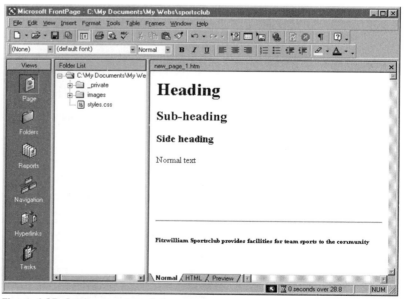

Figure 4.35 Setting up a template

3 Now save this page as a template. Select *File + Save As*. In the Save As dialogue that appears, select *FrontPage Template (*.tem)* in the Save As Type box. Click on *Save*.

4 In the Save As Template dialogue (see Figure 4.36), 'Title' will be the name of the template as it appears in the New Page dialogue. 'Name' is the actual filename (*FrontPage* will add the correct filename extension). 'Description' will also appear on the New Page dialogue.

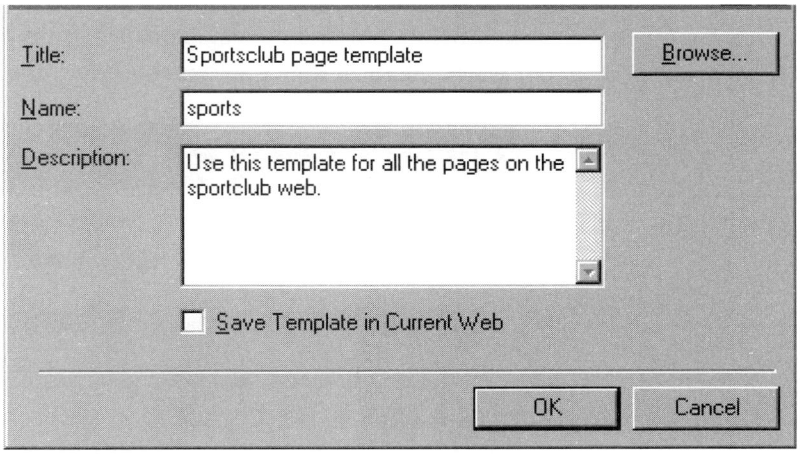

Figure 4.36 The Save As Template dialogue box

5 You now need to create a link to the style sheet from this page. Select *Format + Style Sheet Links*. Click on *Add*, then click on *styles.css* in the file list. Click on *OK*. Back in the Link Style Sheet dialogue (see Figure 4.37), click on *styles.css*, then on *OK*.

Figure 4.37 Linking a style sheet to a page

6 Click on *Save* to save the template linked to the style sheet. Close the template.

Using a template

When you create a template in a web authoring package, your new template will appear along with the pre-designed ones. Whenever you want to add a new page to your website, you should use this template.

In other environments, you can load up the template page and save it with a new name each time you create a new page.

PRACTICAL TASK 4.11

1   In the same web as before, select *File + New + Page*. Your template will be among the pre-designed ones (see Figure 4.38).

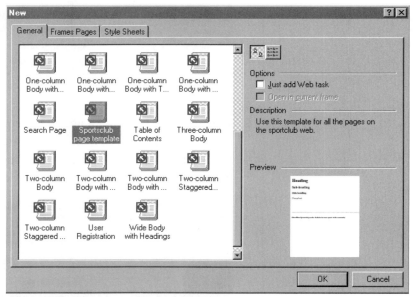

Figure 4.38 Using a template that you have created

2   Select this template. You now have a new page based on the template (see Figure 4.39). This will be the home page for the web. Add suitable text and save this as 'index.htm'.

Choose this template whenever you want to add a new page to this web.

Modifying the style sheet

If you check the HTML for a page created with a template, you will find this line inserted within the head of the page:

```
<link rel="stylesheet" type="text/css" href="styles.css">
```

You can make changes to the style sheet at any time. You will not have to change the template as it is permanently linked to the style sheet.

PRACTICAL TASK 4.12

1 In the same web as before, open the file 'styles.css'.

2 Click on the *Styles* button in the Styles floating toolbar. You can now modify any of the styles in the style sheet. You can also add new style definitions from the list of HTML tags. You will notice three tags called a:link, a:visited and a:active. These format your hyperlinks. Do not change them as you will meet them again later.

3 Save the modified style sheet.

3.3 Embedding images

Images should always be prepared in advance for use on a web page. There is more detailed advice on this later in the unit.

Images viewed on web pages are stored as independent files. This means that when a page is downloaded into a browser, the browser then has to download each of the image files from the server as well. So all the image files that are used on a web page are stored on the server alongside the page files.

It is common practice to store all the images on a website in a folder called 'images'. A web authoring package always provides a means of inserting images on a page, usually from an Insert menu.

PRACTICAL TASK 4.13

1 Open the web that you created before (Figure 4.39).

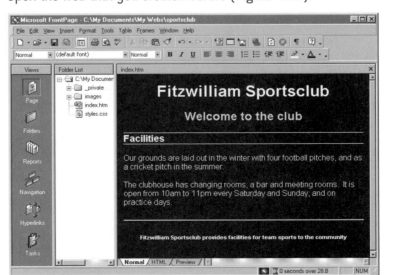

Figure 4.39 A page based on a template and style sheet

2 In *FrontPage*, in Normal mode, place the cursor at the point where you want an image to appear, then use *Insert + Picture + From File*. You will have to click on the folder icon in the dialogue box in order to navigate to the location where the image is stored on your system The image should appear on the page, as in Figure 4.40.

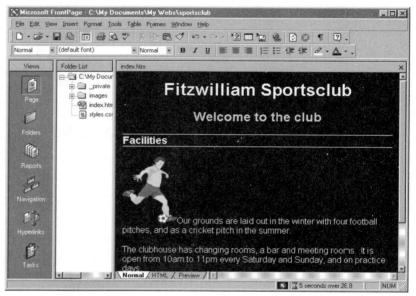

Figure 4.40 An image inserted on to a page

3 *FrontPage* has already created an image folder for you. When you next save the web, *FrontPage* prompts you to save the image as well, with the dialogue shown in Figure 4.41. The image should be saved in the images folder. If 'images/' does not appear in the Folder field, click on *Change Folder* and open the images folder.

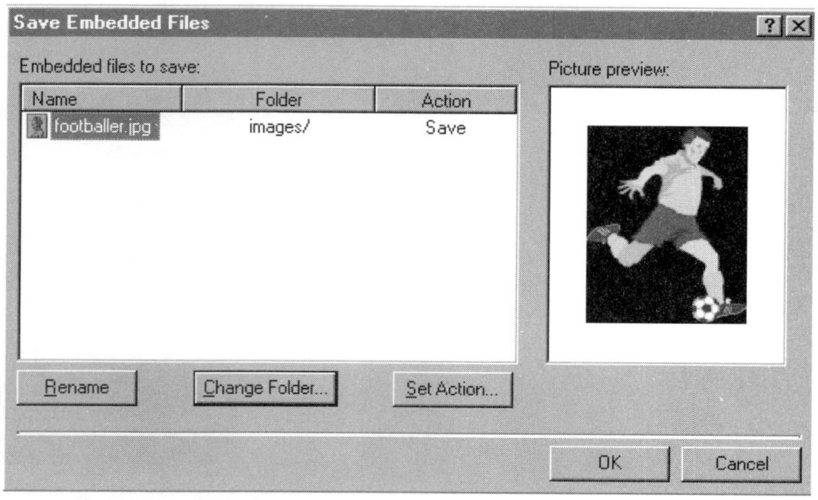

Figure 4.41 Saving an image for a page in FrontPage

Changing the image properties

Once an image has been placed on a page, the HTML coding includes an **<img>** tag, such as:

```
<img border=0 src="images/footballer.jpg" width=100
  height=127>
```

Border, source (src), width and height are all **attributes** of the <img> tag. Attributes are HTML's way of listing the properties of the image.

◆ **src** is the filename of the image and its location relative to the page.

◆ **width** and **height** are the dimensions of the image. Altering these values will distort the image but will not change the memory needed.

Images cannot be manipulated as simply as they can in desktop publishing (DTP) packages, but further attributes can be added to the <img> tag. Most web authoring packages provide an image properties dialogue, usually accessed by right-clicking the image in Page Edit mode, and this generates more attributes, such as:

```
<img border=0 src="images/footballer.jpg" alt="A footballer"
  align=right hspace=10 width=100 height=127>
```

See the effect of these in Figure 4.42.

Figure 4.42 The effect of changing the properties of an image

◆ **alt** text appears as a screen label in a browser, when the mouse is held over an image (see Figure 4.42). This acts as a marker if an image is slow to download and it also provides a useful description to the visitor. Alt text is essential to make a site accessible to blind visitors, who will use **text readers** to understand the content.

◆ **align** positions the image relative to the text next to it. The effect depends entirely on where the cursor was placed when the image was inserted.

◆ **border** values greater than zero draw a border around the image, with the given thickness measured in pixels.

◆ **hspace** (horizontal) and **vspace** (vertical) create space around the image.

PRACTICAL TASK 4.14

1 In Normal mode, right-click on the image and select *Picture Properties*. Any changes that you make to the properties of an image will be listed as <img> attributes in the HTML code.

2 In the Picture Properties dialogue box, enter some descriptive text in the Alternative Representations text box. This is the 'alt' text for the image.

3 Next click on the *Appearance* tab. Do not alter the size properties, but experiment with the layout properties. All the values are in pixels. When you have made your selections, view the page in Preview mode.

Using animated GIFs

The GIF format can be used to create short, repeating animated sequences. Many examples of these are displayed on websites, and there are many free sources on the Web. Animated GIFs should be used, if at all, with very great care. The eye is drawn to an animation, especially if it lies on the periphery of vision, and can distract the visitor from the main content.

As a general rule, animated GIFs should be used only to draw attention directly to an item on the page, such as a warning, or to request a visitor to take an action straightaway (e.g. to confirm some input information), or for amusement.

3.4 Using tables

Tables can be created on a web page, just as they can in a word processor. A table can be used for tabulation – to display data in boxes in the traditional way. Tables are, however, more commonly used as a way of arranging text and images on the screen.

Web authoring packages provide dialogues for creating tables, usually from a Table menu. They also allow the designer to set the properties of tables and of individual cells, often by right-clicking on the table or cell in Page Edit mode.

It is useful to see how the HTML handles tables and their properties. The HTML code for a table has this basic structure:

```
<table>
    <tr>
        <td> </td>
        <td> </td>
        <td> </td>
    </tr>
    <tr>
        <td> </td>
        <td> </td>
        <td> </td>
    </tr>
</table>
```

Note the **<table>** opening tag and the closing **</table>** tag. This table consists of two rows each with **<tr>** and **</tr>** tags. Each row has three cells each with a **<td>** tag (for 'table data').

Note

The layout of the code is not important in HTML. What is important is not to forget to insert the closing </table> tag. Some very strange results will be seen without the closing tag.

Text and images can be inserted into any or all of the table cells, to give a layout like the one in Figure 4.43. This is the HTML code for that table:

```
<table width=600 border=1>
    <tr>
        <td>First cell in the top row</td>
        <td>Second cell in the top row</td>
        <td>Third cell in the top row</td>
    </tr>
    <tr>
        <td>First cell in the second row</td>
        <td><img border=0 src="images/car.gif" width=83
                                    sheight=30></td>
        <td>Third cell in the second row</td>
    </tr>
</table>
```

The <table> tag can take a number of attributes.

◆ **width** is the width of the whole table, in pixels.

◆ **border** fixes the thickness of the border around the perimeter of the whole table.

First cell in the top row	Second cell in the top row	Third cell in the top row
First cell in the second row	![car]	Third cell in the second row.

Figure 4.43 A table with a border

If the border is given the value 0, not only does the outside border disappear but so do the boundaries of the individual cells. This technique can be used to create a page layout in which the text and images are arranged in columns with invisible borders.

Individual cells can be given their own properties, as in:

```
<td align="center" valign="top">
```

◆ **align** is the horizontal alignment (the default value is "left").

◆ **valign** is the vertical alignment, in this case placing the contents of the cell at the top (the default value is "middle").

Using tables for layout

Background colours and images can be set up for a whole table or for individual cells. In *FrontPage*, right-click inside the table, then select *Table Properties* or *Cell Properties*.

A group of cells can also be merged together for layout purposes. To merge cells together, highlight them in Normal mode, right-click and select *Merge Cells*.

Using these techniques you can create page layouts with columns, as in Figure 4.44. The HTML for this is:

```
<td colspan=3 bgcolor="#COCOCO" align="center" valign="top">
```

◆ **colspan** (column span) identifies the number of columns that a merged cell spans across.

◆ **rowspan** is used when cells in the same column are merged together.

This is a heading

First cell in the second row.   Third cell in the second row.

I can add lots of text to this cell and it will simply expand to take it.

I can add lots of text to this cell and it will simply expand to take it.

This is a good way of laying out a page in three columns.

Figure 4.44 A table has been used to create this layout of heading, text and graphic

Understanding the width of tables and cells

You may want to control the behaviour of tables by fixing the size of various components. The <table> tag can be given a number of size attributes, as in Figure 4.45. The HTML code for this is:

```
<table width=600 border=1 cellspacing=3 cellpadding=5>
```

◆ **width** is the *total* width of the table.

◆ **border** is the width in pixels of the border around the outside of the whole table.

◆ **cell spacing** is the width in pixels between the border and a cell, or between one cell and another, and is shown shaded in Figure 4.45.

◆ **cell padding** is the width of the space inside a cell between the edge of the cell and the text. The limit of this is shown by a dotted line in Figure 4.45, although usually it is invisible on the screen.

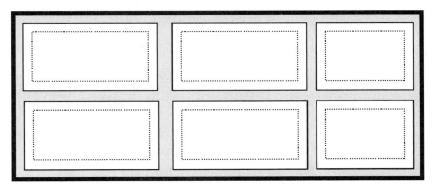

Figure 4.45 How the attributes of a table are set

In *FrontPage* you can set all these attributes by right-clicking inside a table in Normal mode, then selecting *Table Properties*.

The width can also be set for an individual cell in a table:

```
<td width=200>
```

or

```
<td width=40%>
```

Here, 'width' means the width of the cell *inside the cell padding*. It can be given in pixels or as a percentage of the total width of the table.

It is necessary to set the cell widths only for one row (any row) in the table, as all the cells in any one column will line up under each other.

PRACTICAL TASK 4.15

1 Open your web, and create a new page with the Sportsclub template. Save the page.

2 Select *Table + Insert + Table*, then enter values in the dialogue box as in Figure 4.46. Note that the width is given in pixels, not as a percentage. Check the HTML code.

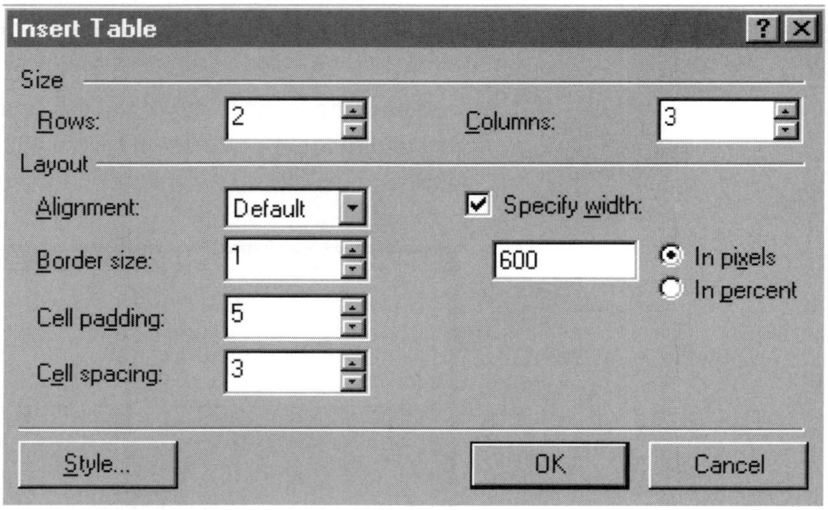

Figure 4.46 *Inserting a table in FrontPage*

3 In Normal mode, enter some text in each of the cells and place an image in one of the cells. Make sure that the image is a suitable width – preferably no more than 150 pixels wide. Then check the HTML code again.

4 Experiment with the table properties in Normal mode by right-clicking anywhere inside the table, then selecting *Table Properties*. You can add colour to the borders and change their appearance, and you can give the whole table a background colour.

5 You will probably have found that the individual columns varied in width as you entered the text. You can fix the width of each cell to prevent this happening. Right-click on a cell and select *Cell Properties*. Then specify the width as a percentage of the total width of the table – make sure that the percentages in a row add up to 100. You only need to do this across one row of a table, as all the cells in any one column will line up with the one that has a fixed width.

6   You can also fix the width of a whole column by dragging a column border to a new position. This action automatically adds a width attribute into every cell in the table.

7   Use *Cell Properties* to set the background colour for a cell in a table, and to align the text vertically (top, middle or bottom) and horizontally (left, centre, right or justified). Check the HTML to see how these are recorded in the attributes of the cells.

8   To add an extra row or column to a table, click where you want it to go, then select *Table + Insert + Rows or Columns* and make your choices. If you have added a column you should check the widths of the cells again.

9   You can merge all the cells in a row, but note that if you merge the cells where you have set all the width properties, that width data will no longer be valid. For example, you might want to merge all the cells in the top row to give a header that will span all three columns. Highlight the top three cells, right-click and select *Merge Cells*.

Using a table to fix the size of a page

All the web pages you have created so far are resizable. If you change the size of the browser window, the text rearranges itself to fit the window. This can sometimes have unexpected results.

You may want to have greater control over the layout of the page, so that all the elements remain in the same positions relative to each other. You can create a table with exactly one cell. This then holds the complete contents of the page. If the width of the cell is fixed in pixels then its appearance will be much more consistent.

The width of a page can be fixed, and the best width to use is 800 pixels. In practice, the width of the scroll bar to the right of the page uses up some of the screen width, so it is better to set the width at 780 pixels. A table of width 780 pixels can be used as a container for a full page.

When the page is viewed in a higher resolution, the table can either be positioned to the left of the window, leaving space to the right, or it can be positioned in the centre of the window with empty space on each side. Either solution is acceptable, but the preference should be set in the table properties.

PRACTICAL TASK 4.16

1 In *FrontPage*. start a new page. Insert a table 780 pixels wide and aligned to the left. It should have one row and one column. The border of the table should be of zero width. The cell padding and cell spacing can be any value (see Figure 4.47).

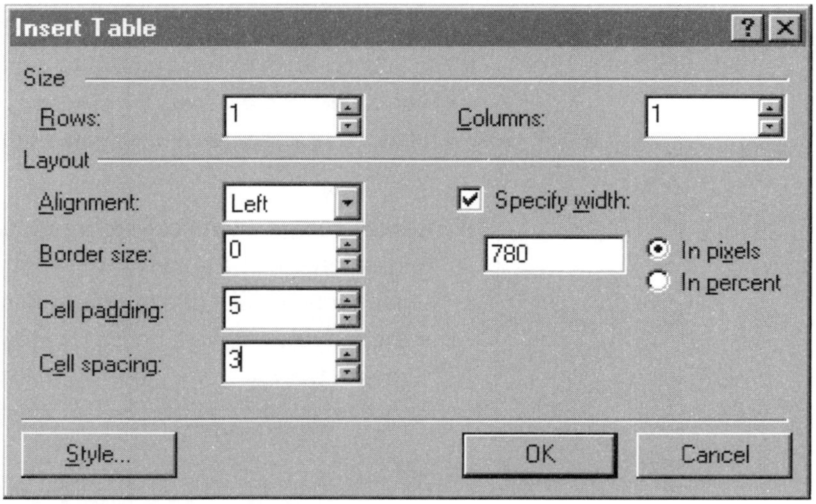

Figure 4.47 The Insert Table dialogue box

2 To see what is happening, use the Table Properties dialogue to give the table a background colour. In Preview mode, you will see that there are still white margins to the top and to the left side of the page.

3 Right click, select *Page Properties*, then click on the *Margins* tab, and set the top and left margins to 0 (see Figure 4.48).

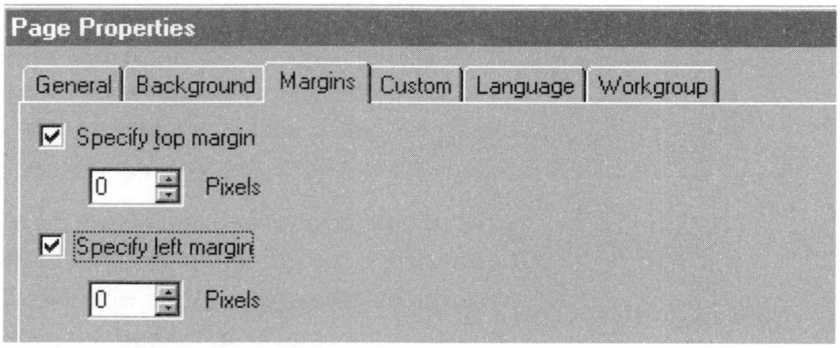

Figure 4.48 The Page Properties dialogue box

4 Although you have aligned the table to the left, you may prefer to align it to the centre. Try it.

You can now treat the single table as the boundary for the whole page. You may want to change the page background so that any extra space showing to the right of the table in higher resolutions matches the table itself, or you may prefer to use a contrasting colour.

Note

Tables can be placed within *the main table, but do make sure that they are not too wide to fit on the page.*

3.5 Using bookmarks

Hyperlinks can be used to link to:

◆ another position on the same page

◆ another page on the same website

◆ another website.

Creating hyperlinks to bookmarks

In a browser, a hyperlink can jump to an invisible bookmark placed elsewhere on a page. Using a page editor, bookmarks can be set anywhere on a page. In the HTML code a bookmark is denoted with the **<a>** tag (standing for 'anchor') which has a name attribute to identify it. In the next example, a heading with the title 'First section' has been bookmarked so that a hyperlink somewhere else on the page can link to it:

```
<h2><a name="First section">First section</a></h2>
```

The text that is to become the hyperlink is then highlighted by the browser and formatted as a link. By default, hyperlinks take on a familiar appearance, with underlined blue text, but that can be changed.

The HTML code for the hyperlink itself uses the **<a>** tag again and looks like this:

```
<p><a href="#First section">Link to first section</a></p>
```

href (standing for 'hyperlink reference') states the location that the hyperlink links to. In this case, '#First section' is the name of the bookmark where it links to, with the # (hash) used to identify it as a bookmark.

Images can also be used as hyperlinks – these are often referred to as **buttons**. The HTML for a graphical hyperlink looks like this:

```
<p><a href="#First section"><img border=0 src=
"images/mybutton.gif" width=120 height=30></a></p>
```

PRACTICAL TASK 4.17

1 Start a new web. For clarity, the examples are created without a style sheet or template, but you may like to add them.

2 Create a new page and enter text similar to that in Figure 4.49, with three distinct sections, each with a subheading. The three lines below the main heading will become hyperlinks to the content further down the page.

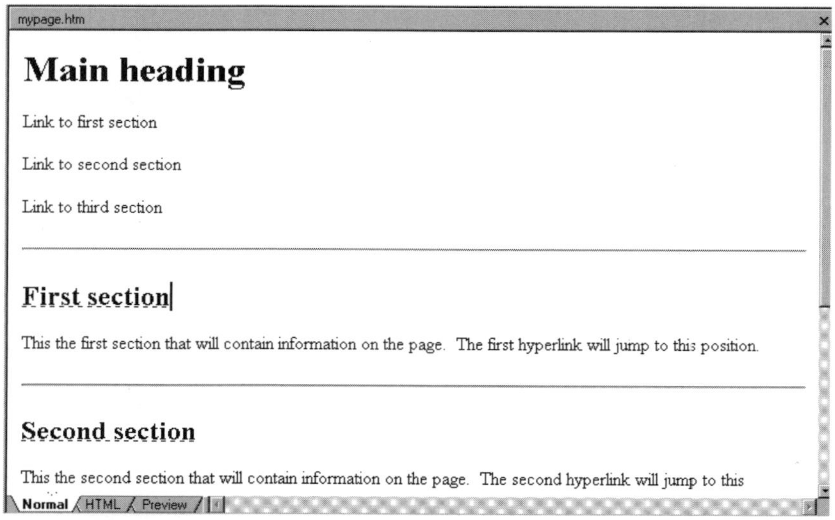

mypage.htm ×

Main heading

Link to first section

Link to second section

Link to third section

First section|

This the first section that will contain information on the page. The first hyperlink will jump to this position.

Second section

This the second section that will contain information on the page. The second hyperlink will jump to this

Normal / HTML / Preview / |‹

Figure 4.49 The subheading 'First section' has been bookmarked in Page Editor mode

3 To insert a bookmark, highlight the subheading to be bookmarked, then select *Insert + Bookmark*. By default, this gives the bookmark the same name as the subheading. A bookmark is displayed in Normal mode by a dotted underlining (as in Figure 4.49), but is invisible in Preview mode.

4 The hyperlink to a bookmark is inserted by highlighting the text – 'Link to first section' – that will act as the hyperlink, and then selecting *Insert + Hyperlink*. In the dialogue box, the relevant bookmark is selected from the Bookmark list, as in Figure 4.50.

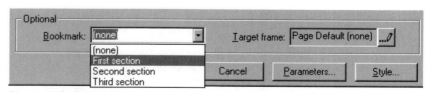

Figure 4.50 Selecting a bookmark that the hyperlink will link to in FrontPage

5 Add the remaining hyperlinks, and then try them out in Preview mode (see Figure 4.51).

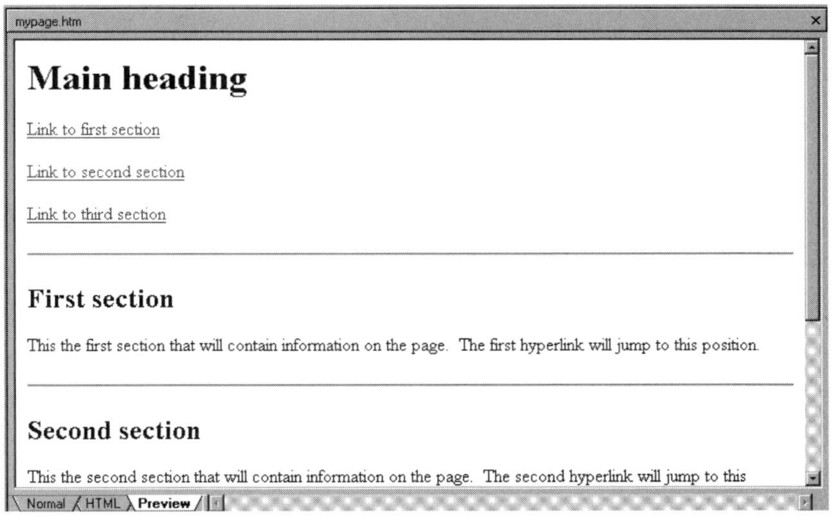

Figure 4.51 Hyperlinks to bookmarks on the same page

6 To make a graphical hyperlink, insert a suitable image, then highlight it and use *Insert + Hyperlink* in exactly the same way as you did with text.

3.6 Using hyperlinks

On the WWW, the links between pages create one vast global network. An individual site will ensure that the visitor explores what the site has to offer by offering internal links to other pages on the same site, and may have external links to other sites.

All web authoring packages allow the designer to convert text or an image into a hyperlink. Usually the Insert or Format menu includes a Hyperlink item which launches a dialogue box. The HTML code for a link to a page called 'news.htm' looks like this:

```
<a href=news.htm>Latest news</a>
```

When an image is used as a button instead of text for a hyperlink, the code will look like this:

```
<a href="news.htm"><img border=0 src="images/newsbutton.gif"
  width=120 height=30> Latest news</a>
```

PRACTICAL TASK 4.18

In this activity, you will create a web for a fast-food outlet using *FrontPage*'s site management tools. The home page will give basic information, such as the name, address and telephone number, and details of the delivery service.

A second page will contain the food menu, and a third page will list job vacancies in the company.

The examples are created without a style sheet or template, but you may like to add them.

1 Close any open webs, then select *File + New + Web* and create a new One Page Web. If you cannot see the folder list, click on the *Folder List* button. The index (home) page has been created for you. Double-click on the index page and it will open in Normal view.

2 Simply enter the name and address and any other text, as in Figure 4.52, and save the page.

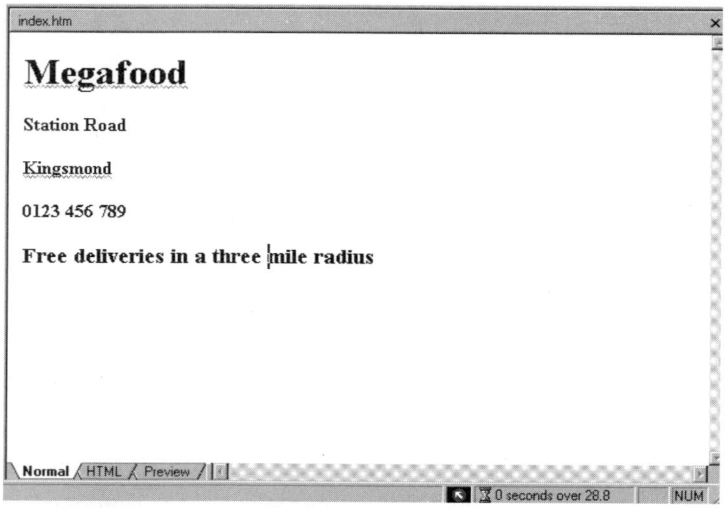

Figure 4.52 An index page for a site for a fast-food business

3 Now use *File + New + Page* to create two more pages in Normal view. Save them as 'menu.htm' and 'jobs.htm'. Add a small amount of suitable text to each and re-save them. You can use a table to hold the menu, as in Figure 4.53.

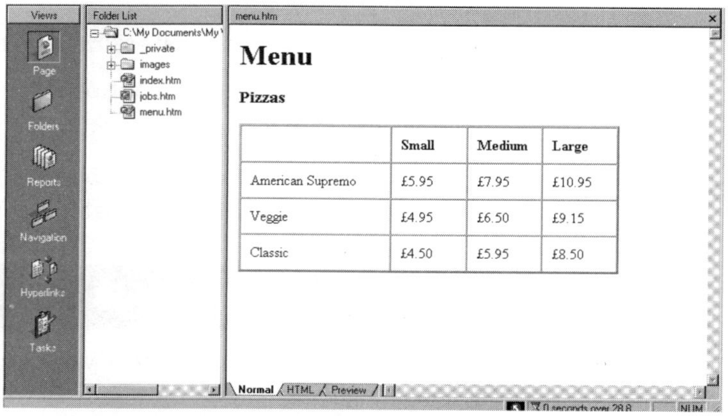

Figure 4.53 The folder list in FrontPage, and a basic page

Using site management tools to create navigation bars

Site management tools usually assume that the site has a **tree structure**. They can sometimes generate and insert one or more navigation bars on a page on demand. Any additional links must be created individually on the page.

Figure 4.54 shows the Navigation Bar Properties dialogue in *FrontPage*, which offers a number of options. The 'Child pages under Home' option creates the main navigation bar and this can be placed on each page, together with a link to the home page. A secondary navigation bar can be inserted using the 'Same level' option.

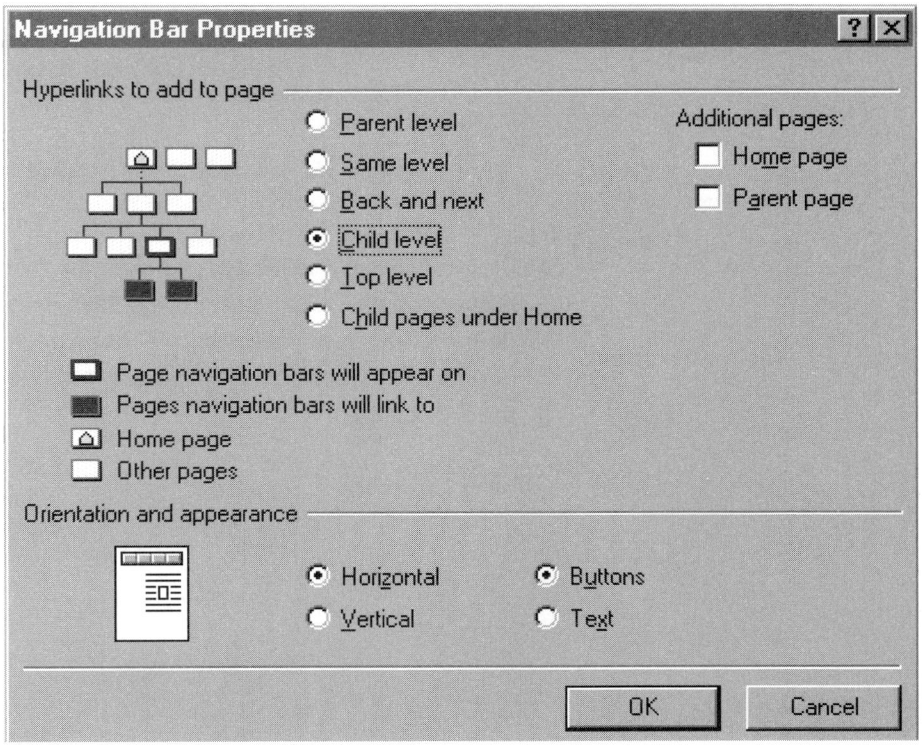

Figure 4.54 *Setting the properties of a navigation bar in* FrontPage

The navigation bar tool in FrontPage generates HTML code similar to this at the position where the bar is inserted:

```
<!--
webbot bot="Navigation" S-Type="children" S-Orientation=
"horizontal" S-Rendering="graphics" B-Include-Home
B-Include-Up U-Page S-Target
-->
```

This is not standard HTML code. It calls on a procedure – a **webbot** – *that is specific to FrontPage*. The navigation bar tool can create text or image hyperlinks.

PRACTICAL TASK 4.19

1 Open the fast-food site – or, if it is already open, close any pages.

2 Click on the Navigation view. An icon representing the index page will be shown (see Figure 4.55) with the title 'Home Page'. If the folder list is not displayed, click on the *Folder List* button.

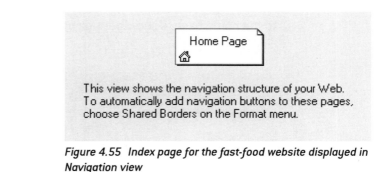

Figure 4.55 Index page for the fast-food website displayed in Navigation view

3 Drag the menu and jobs pages from the folders list on to the diagram to give the navigation structure shown in Figure 4.56. This has defined the relationships between the pages. The index page is the parent to the menu and jobs pages, and the menu page is a child of the index page.

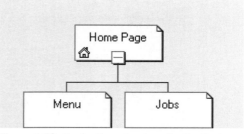

Figure 4.56 Navigation structure for the fast-food website

4 The site management tools can now create the navigation bars on the pages. Open the index page by clicking on its name in the folders list or on the page icon in Navigation view. Place the cursor where you want the navigation bar to appear. Select *Insert + Navigation Bar*, and the Navigation Bar Properties dialogue will appear (Figure 4.54). Under 'Hyperlinks to add to page', select *Child level*. Under 'Orientation and appearance', select *Horizontal* and *Buttons*, as in Figure 4.54.

5 In Preview mode, the page should look similar to Figure 4.57. The buttons do not look very impressive, but they can be transformed by the use of style sheets or themes.

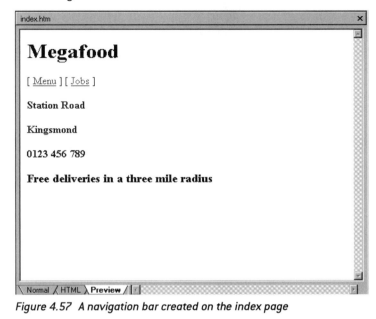

Figure 4.57 A navigation bar created on the index page

6 You now need to add navigation bars to the other two pages. Repeat the process that you used for the home page. This time provide links to pages at the same level as well as to the home page (as an additional page).

Note

When you try out the links in Preview mode you will see that the navigation bar includes a non-functioning button that refers to the page that it is on (see Figure 4.58). This is equivalent to a greyed-out item on a drop-down menu in Windows-based software. It is important to include this non-functioning button as it means that the navigation bar items appear in the same positions on different pages. FrontPage always places the Home button to the left of the others.

jobs.htm

Jobs

[Home] [Menu] [Jobs]

We often have job vacancies. If you would like to apply for any of the jobs listed below then please phone the manager on 0123 456 788

Delivery person

6.30pm to 10.30pm five evenings per week. Must have clean motorbike driving license.

Full-time counter staff

Hours to suit.

Normal / HTML / Preview /

Figure 4.58 The Jobs page with a navigation bar

Hyperlinks to other sites

When a hyperlink provides a link to a page on another website, the full URL must be given, like this:

```
<a href="http://news.bbc.co.uk/" target="_blank">BBC News</a>
```

◆ **target** defines the window where the page is opened. The default value is the same page.

◆ **_blank** opens the page in a new browser window.

Links to other sites can be added to any web page. Some sites provide no external links at all, because they do not want the visitor to leave the site once there. On the other hand, some sites contain very many links to other sites; where that is the main purpose it is known as a **portal site**.

Other uses of hyperlinks

A hyperlink can be used to encourage a visitor to send an email to the organisation's address, like this:

```
<a href="mailto://myname@thisismydomain.co.uk">Email me</a>
```

When this hyperlink is clicked, a new email window opens in the visitor's email client software, with the email address already inserted in the 'To:' field.

You can also create a hyperlink that will allow the visitor to download a file from the site. This can be any sort of file – a word processing file, program file etc. The file can be transferred using either hypertext transfer protocol (HTTP) or file transfer protocol (FTP). The HTML code in each case would be like these:

```
<a href="http://thisismydomain.co.uk/mydocument.doc">
   Download the document</a>
<a href="ftp://thisismydomain.co.uk/mydocument.doc">
   Download the document</a>
```

PRACTICAL TASK 4.20

1 Open the fast-food site – or, if it is already open, close any pages.

2 Create an external hyperlink. Add text to link to an external site on one of the pages. Highlight the text and select *Insert + Hyperlink*. In the URL box, enter the full URL of the website, including 'http://'. Alternatively, click on the web browser icon to the right of the URL box, and find the correct page with your browser. When you switch back to *FrontPage* the URL will be entered in the box.

3 Next create an email hyperlink. Enter text inviting people to email the manager. Highlight the text, and then select *Insert + Hyperlink*. Click on the email icon to the right of the URL box. Type in an email address.

4 Use Preview mode to check that these two links work correctly (see Figure 4.59).

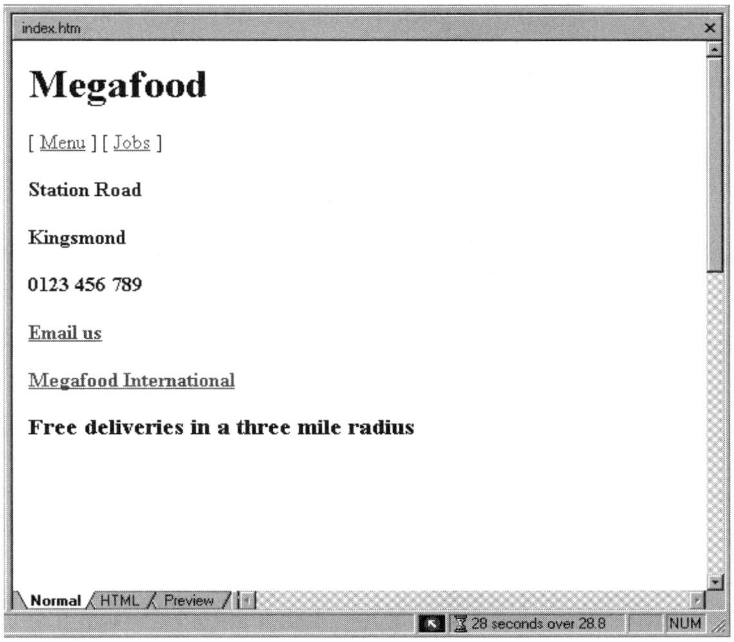

Figure 4.59 External and email hyperlinks

3.7 Creating image maps

A **hotspot** is an area of an image that acts as a hyperlink, and an image that has hotspots on it is known as an **image map**. Image maps can be used as highly graphical navigation bars. They can also be used to help the viewer identify items on a plan or geographical map of an area.

Web authoring packages usually provide an image mapping tool that you can use to develop them. They are a bit tricky to create directly in HTML, but again image mapping tools are available for HTML editors.

PRACTICAL TASK 4.21

You are going to create a map of an area which will show the delivery area for Megafood. This will be placed on the home page.

1 First create an imaginary map in a painting package (such as

Microsoft *Paint*). Alternatively, you could download a map from a website to experiment with.

2   Open the fast-food site you have created. Insert the map on the home page.

3   Click on the image and the Picture toolbar will appear at the bottom of the window. In the Picture bar there are four hotspot buttons, like this:

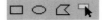

4   Click on the circular hotspot button. On the map, draw a circle centred on the shop location, as in Figure 4.60.

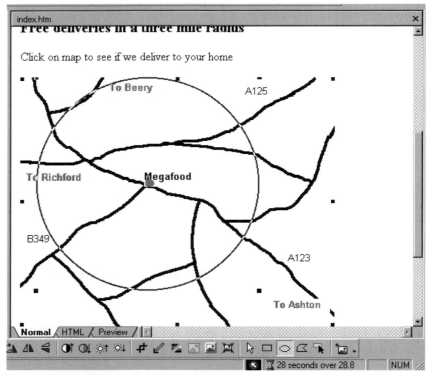

Figure 4.60 Outlining an area with the circular hotspot button

5   When you lift up the mouse button, the Create Hyperlink dialogue appears. From the list, click on the menu page and click *OK*.

6   You can now create hotpots for the areas outside the shop delivery zone. These could link to the websites of other shops, or to a new page that lists other shops.

7   Click on the Preview mode to check that it works correctly. If you click inside the hotspot area, the menu page appears.

3.8 Using metatags and other head tags

The HTML code between the **<head>** tags of a page, such as those below, contains some important information.

```
<head>
<meta http-equiv="Content-Type" content="text/html;
charset=Windows-1252">
<meta name="GENERATOR" content="Microsoft FrontPage 4.0">
<meta name="ProgId" content="FrontPage.Editor.Document">
<title>Menu</title>
</head>
```

These tags provide information about the page that follows, and a number of them are used by **search engines**. These can be edited directly in the HTML code, or web authoring tools can be used instead.

The **<title>** tag gives the title of the page, and this has two important functions. The title usually appears in the browser's title bar. Web authoring packages like *FrontPage* often use the first line of text on the page for the title, but it can be changed to something like:

```
<title>Pizzas, pastas and more to enjoy at Megafood</title>
```

Search engines display the title of a page when they list a site in response to a query, so that is good reason for making it meaningful.

The remaining tags are known as **metatags**. The default ones created by the web authoring package should not be changed. Two further very important ones are the **keyword** and **description** metatags.

◆ The keyword metatag contains a list of keywords that people might use in a search engine, like this:

```
<meta name="keywords" content="Megafood, fast food,
    pizza, pasta">
```

◆ The description metatag contains a description of the site, which may also be quoted by a search engine when it lists a site:

```
<meta name="description" content="Welcome to Megafood –
    where you can find the best fast food in Kingsmond. Pizzas,
    pastas and more.">.
```

3.9 Website development

The style sheet used in the example that follows is one of the samples provided with *FrontPage*, called 'Street'. The effect of this style sheet is shown in Figure 4.61.

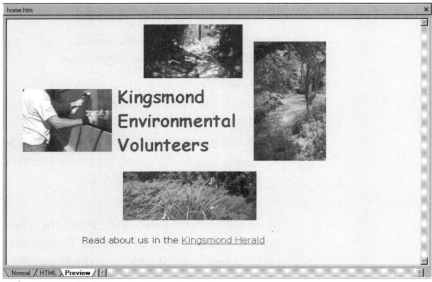

Figure 4.61 A page formatted by a style sheet

Each style definition refers to one or more of the HTML tags. This is the **body style** definition in the style sheet:

```
body {font-family: Verdana, Arial, Helvetica; background-color:
rgb(204, 255, 255); color: rgb(0, 0, 102);}
```

This defines some properties that apply to the whole page between the **<body>** tags. The Normal style that can be selected from the style list is the default style, and this is initially defined by the system settings for the computer. The body style definition sets up the basic style for the page, and a browser will use this as the default style for the page.

- ◆ **background-color** (note the American spelling of colour) applies to the background of the whole page.

- ◆ **color** defines the default colour for the text on the page. This is expressed as an RGB (red, green, blue) colour code. Each of the three colour numbers can take a value from 0 (none of that particular colour) to 255 (full colour)

- ◆ **font-family**, in this case, lists three fonts, although the list can be of any length. The browser works along the list until it finds a font that it can use.

The visitor can view a font only if that font is already resident on the visitor's own system. So although in this case the designer would prefer the visitor to view the text in Verdana, the other two fonts are listed as **fallback** options. Only widely used fonts should be included in a style sheet, but as a precaution two basic fonts can be added to each definition, one font for Windows systems and one for Apple Mac systems.

◆ If the preferred font is a **serif font**, then Times New Roman and Times should be included.

◆ If the preferred font is **sans serif**, then Arial and Helvetica should be added.

The next style definition applies to more than one tag:

```
h1, h2, h3, h4, h5, h6 {font-family: Comic Sans MS, Arial, Helvetica;}
```

The heading 1 style in the style list generates the **<h1>** tag in the HTML code, and so on. This style rule applies to all six heading tags and sets Comic Sans MS as the font for all the headings, with Arial and Helvetica as the fallback options.

The browser has to deal with the seeming contradiction between the font properties for the body and those for the headings. The font defined for the body is the default font and applies throughout the page except where another tag defines it differently. So the Verdana font is used everywhere except in the headings, where Comic Sans is used.

The next style rule defines the colour of one of the headings, and there will be similar rules for all the remaining heading styles:

```
h1 {color: rgb(153, 0, 0);}
```

The <h1> tag has been used in Figure 4.61 for the central text 'Kingsmond Environmental Volunteers'. By default, heading styles are always bold, and the sizes decrease from h1 to h6.

The next style rules define three states that the hyperlinks take. The **<a>** tag is used for both bookmarks and hyperlinks, but these styles affect only the hyperlinks themselves:

```
a:link {color: rgb(0, 102, 102);}
a:visited {color: rgb(0, 153, 153);}
a:active {color: rgb(255, 102, 0);}
```

◆ **a:link** is the normal style used for the hyperlink.

◆ **a:visited** is the style used for a hyperlink that has already been followed.

◆ **a:active** is the style used when the mouse button is held down on a hyperlink.

◆ **a:hover** (not used in this example) is the style used when the mouse passes over the hyperlink.

The link to the Kingsmond Herald at the bottom of the window in Figure 4.61 uses the <a> tag, and can take on one of three different colours.

PRACTICAL TASK 4.22

In this activity, you will create a website for a local group. You will use a cascading style sheet to give the page its style and will later add a separate side frame to hold the navigation bar.

It is a good idea to work in 1024 pixels horizontal resolution. The pages will be designed to be viewed at 800 pixels resolution, but by using a wider window in *FrontPage,* you will also be able to see the Views bar and the folder list at the same time as the page itself.

1 Create a new empty web. Select *New + Page*, then select the *Style Sheets* tab. Select the 'Streets' style sheet template and save it as 'mystyles.css'. Create and save a template based on it.

2 Use the template to create a new page and save it as 'home.htm'. Although this will be the home page for the site it will not actually be the first page that is loaded, so is not saved as 'index.htm'.

3 Set up a table to hold the contents of the page. It should be 600 pixels wide, and aligned to the left. Use *Page Properties* to set the page margins to zero. This ensures that the page takes up no more than 600 pixels width.

4 Use *Page Properties* to set the top and left margins to zero.

5 Now add some text and images to the page. Use the styles from the style list, such as heading 1. Include at least one external hyperlink.

Editing style sheets

A pre-designed style sheet can be modified. This can be done by simply amending the text in the style sheet file. In *FrontPage*, the process can be simplified by using the Style dialogues.

A new style sheet could look like this (note the American spellings):

a:link {font-weight: bold; color: gray; text-decoration: none;}

a:visited {font-weight: bold; color: gray; text-decoration: none;}

a:hover {font-weight: bold; color: silver; text-decoration: none;}

body {font-family: Verdana, Arial, Helvetica; font-size: 12pt; background-color: white; color: rgb(0, 102, 51);}

h1 {font-family: Comic Sans MS, Arial, Helvetica; font-size: 20pt; text-align: center; color: white; background-color: rgb(0, 102, 51); border-width: 5pt; border-style: double; border-color: white; padding: 3pt;}

Other style definitions for h2, h3 etc. can be added when needed. Note that a style definition for *a:hover* has been added, and that some of the definitions have been deleted from the earlier code.

The effect of this style sheet can be seen in Figure 4.62. The underlining on the 'Kingsmond Herald' hyperlink has been removed, but the use of a different colour and bold face indicates to the visitor that it is a hyperlink. This is confirmed by its hover state – when the mouse is passed over the link it changes from a dark grey to a light grey.

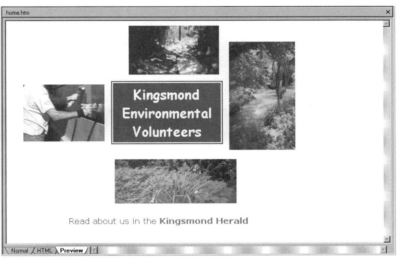

Figure 4.62 A new style sheet applied to the page

Fast and effective hover links can be created using a style sheet and without the use of images. The background, border and padding properties can be used to give a rectangular box around the text, which could change colour in hover mode.

Note

There are many properties that can be applied to tags in style sheet rules. You will need to consult a handbook on cascading style sheets to see them all.

PRACTICAL TASK 4.23

You can change the style sheet by clicking on the *Style* button in the Style floating toolbar. But you can also edit the style sheet directly.

1   In Normal view, first close any pages that are open, then open file 'mystyles.css'. Make changes and save it. A style sheet must be saved before any changes can be observed in a page.

2   If you amend a stylesheet while a page is open, when you switch back to the page you will have to click on the *Refresh* button to reload the page and view the effects of the changes.

3 Now use the Page template to create another page for the website, in which the content should also sit inside a table 600 pixels wide. Do not include any navigation links at this stage.

Creating frames

Frames can be created directly in HTML. The process is quite complex so there is much to be said for using a web authoring package.

Frames are created in a **frame page**, which sets down the sizes and properties of all the frames that are being used (refer back to Figure 4.24 on page 237). The frame page is always loaded first into the browser, so it is usually made the index page for a website. The frame page creates the empty structure and then loads the pages into each of the frames.

PRACTICAL TASK 4.24

Working with the same web as before, you will create a vertical navigation bar which will appear in a frame to the left side of the page. The side page will be 180 pixels wide, so that it will sit alongside the 600 pixels width main pages. The total width of 780 pixels allows for the scrollbar to the right side of a 800 pixels width window.

When using frames, you should not use the Navigation tool in *FrontPage*.

1 Create a new page, using the Page template, and save it as 'side.htm'. Use *Page Properties* to set the page margins to zero.

2 Create a table 180 pixels wide, with one column and one row. The cell padding should be non-zero, so that text is not pushed up against the sides of the frame.

3 Enter an image or some information at the top. Then add links to 'home.htm' and to the other page that you have already created. See Figure 4.63 for an example of how the side page might look.

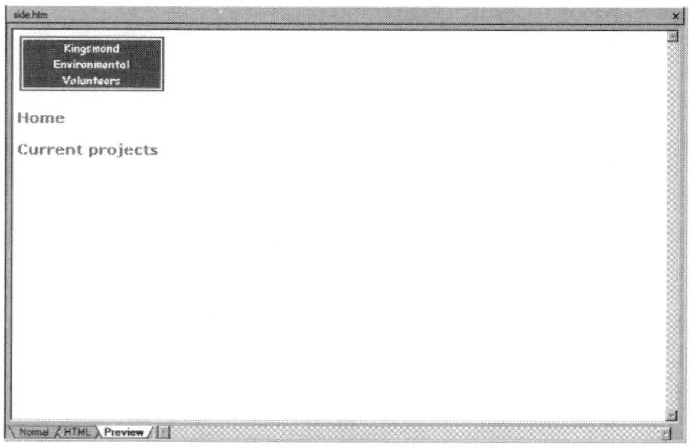

Figure 4.63 A navigation page before it has been integrated into a frame

4 Next the frame page itself will be created. Select *File + New + Page*, then click on the *Frames Pages* tab. Select the Contents template. The frame structure will appear as in Figure 4.64. Save the page as 'index.htm'.

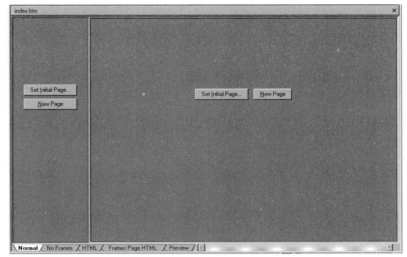

Figure 4.64 The frame structure displayed in FrontPage

5 Right-click anywhere in the left frame, and click on *Frame Properties*. In the dialogue box that appears, set the width to 180 pixels, and both the margins to zero. Under 'Options', you do not want the frame to be resizable, so remove the tick. You also do not want a scroll bar to appear in this frame, so for 'Show scrollbars' select *Never*. The dialogue should now look like Figure 4.65.

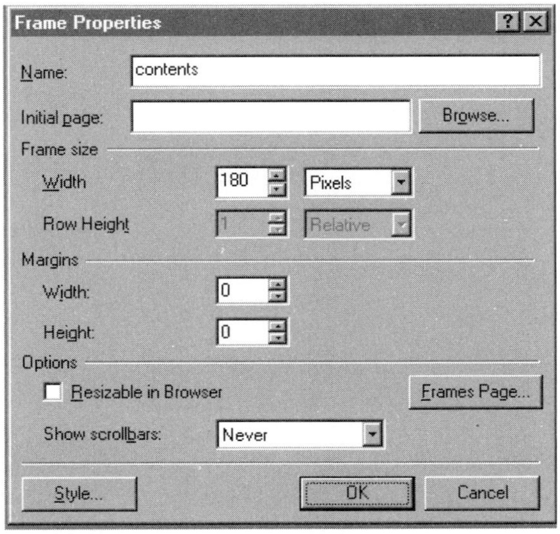

Figure 4.65 The Frame Properties dialogue box

6 In the right frame, simply set the margins to zero.

SOFTWARE DEVELOPMENT

7 In the left frame, click on *Set Initial Page*, then select 'side.htm'. Similarly, select 'home.htm' for the right frame. Save the frame page again.

8 View the whole frame page by selecting Preview mode (see Figure 4.66).

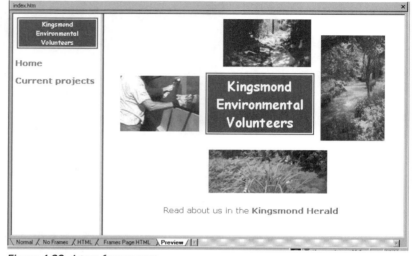

Figure 4.66 A two-frame page

9 The border between the two frames can be removed. Return to Normal mode on the index page, then right-click in the left frame and select *Frame Properties* again. Click on the *Frames Pages* button, and on the *Frames* tab set 'Frame spacing' to zero and make sure that the 'Show borders' box is not ticked.

10 Check the page again in Preview mode. Select the other page in the navigation bar and check that it loads into the main frame, as in Figure 4.67.

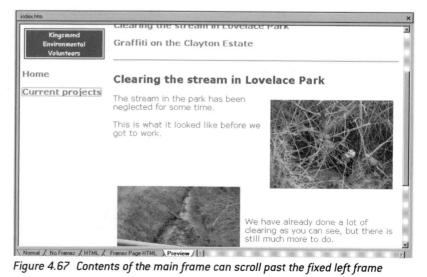

Figure 4.67 Contents of the main frame can scroll past the fixed left frame

Finishing the site

You might like to add an image map (see page 271), identifying the location of all the projects. Metatags (see page 273) should be added before publishing the site.

Chapter summary

You should be able to use web authoring software to:

◆ manage a complete website
◆ create an external style sheet linked to a page template
◆ embed and modify images on a page
◆ use tables and frames for layout
◆ create hyperlinks and navigation bars
◆ create image maps.

---

4 Test websites

4.1 Technical testing

Before a site is published on the WWW, it should be subjected to thorough technical testing, and the tests should all be repeated after the site has been published, along with additional tests. These tests should be constructed to check that the final website matches the original design specification, bearing in mind any amendments that may have been made to the specification during the prototyping stage.

The technical design of a website concentrates on usability issues:

◆ *navigation* – should be tested both before and after publishing
◆ *use of search tools* – best tested after publishing
◆ *download times* – best tested after publishing
◆ *browser compatibility* – should be tested both before and after publishing
◆ *maintenance* – best tested with the client after publishing.

All testing should be carried out in a browser, not in the Preview mode of a web authoring package. The site can be opened in a browser by navigating to the position of the index page on your local drive.

All websites should be fully tested before they go live. They should then be tested again after they have been uploaded to the Internet. Similar tests should also be done whenever a site is updated.

4.2 Style issues

Images

- Check that each image occupies the intended space on the screen and is positioned correctly.
- Select the properties of each image to check how much memory each uses. Do not forget to include any graphical buttons or bullets that you have used. Calculate the total memory used by all the images on each page. Aim to keep the total to under 60KB per page.
- If you want to use a larger image (for example, if you want to offer your visitor the chance to see a full-size photo), you should warn visitors before they link to the page that it will be a slow download.

Layout

- Check that each page appears as intended in your usual browser.
- Check the whole site on an earlier version of the browser you are using.
- Check the whole site on a different browser.

4.3 Verifying links

Before the site is uploaded, the home page should be opened in a browser. These tests should be carried out.

- Check that each of the links from the main navigation bar loads the correct page.
- Check that the links in the main navigation bar on all other pages behave as expected.
- Check all the internal links on each page.

It is important to document the tests carried out on a site as you do them. It is very easy to lose track of the tests you have done, and then to repeat tests unnecessarily, or even leave some out. When you check links you can create a chart like the one in Figure 4.68.

Page: products.htm

Link to:	OK?	Notes
contacts.htm		
home.htm		
cartridges.htm	Bad link	Update this

Figure 4.68 Keep a record of your checking of page links

4.4 Preview in different browsers

Web pages do not appear exactly the same in each browser, mainly because of the slightly different ways in which browsers interpret the HTML code attributes. *Internet Explorer* and *Netscape* are the most used browsers; others, such as *Opera*, are used by smaller numbers of visitors. Older versions of these browsers are still being used.

Your website should first be checked in your resident browser at both 800 and 1024 pixels horizontal screen resolutions. The full width of each page should be visible at 800 pixels without scrolling sideways. The site should also look reasonable when a full-size window is opened at 1024 pixels width.

The site should then be checked in the alternative browsers at both resolutions. If possible, the site should then be checked in the oldest versions of each browser.

The latest versions of both Internet Explorer and Netscape can be downloaded free of charge from their respective websites, which are www.microsoft.com/windows/ie and http://www.netscape.com.

Changes may have to be made to the pages to ensure that the displays in all cases are as compatible as possible and that any minor differences are acceptable.

4.5 Testing a website after uploading

Immediately after a site has been uploaded to the webserver, it should be tested by entering the URL in a browser.

The full set of technical tests should then be repeated. The most common errors found at this stage occur if a file has not been uploaded, or if one has been uploaded to an incorrect remote directory.

Additional technical testing can be carried out. The designer should:

◆ test each external link to ensure that it loads the correct site

◆ ascertain how long it takes to download each page, including all the images, using the slowest dial-up connections.

Chapter summary

◆ A website should be tested thoroughly both before and after it is published on the World Wide Web.

◆ The testing should check all internal and external links.

◆ Page layout and appearance should be tested in a number of different browsers and with different screen settings.

5 Use graphics software to create and manipulate images on web pages

5.1 Manipulating an image

If you want to prepare images for use on a web page, the best option is to use specialist graphics software. General painting packages, such as Microsoft *Paint*, can be used to create images and also to manipulate existing images. You can then save the images in JPG or GIF format.

Photo manipulation packages such as Microsoft *Photo Editor*, Corel *PhotoHouse* or Adobe *PhotoShop* provide a number of tools that help you to optimise the appearance of photos. They can also be used to work with any ready-drawn bitmap image.

Web authoring software sometimes offers you a limited range of image manipulation tools and these can be used if specialist graphics packages are not available.

PRACTICAL TASK 4.25

You can insert **clipart** on a web page in *FrontPage* just as you can in word processing or desktop publishing documents. You can then use the inbuilt image manipulation tools to change it.

1 Click on the page where you want the clipart to appear. Select *Insert + Picture + Clipart*, then choose the clipart image that you want. It will be inserted on the page.

2 The clipart image will probably have to be changed before it is right for your page (see Figure 4.69). Click on the image, and the Pictures toolbar will appear at the bottom of the window.

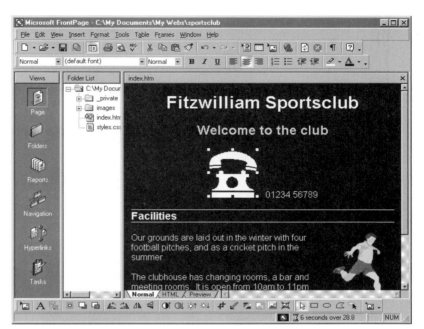

Figure 4.69   Clipart inserted on the page, with the Pictures toolbar

3   You can use the buttons on the Pictures toolbar to rotate or flip the image. You can also change the brightness and contrast of the colours.

4   If you want to go back to the original drawing, click on the *Restore* button.

The clipart image will look odd if the background colour of the page is different from the background colour of the GIF. A technique will be explained later for overcoming this by making the background of the GIF transparent.

5.2   Image file size and type

When you download a web page from the Internet, the browser first of all downloads the actual page file. It then downloads all the image files that are used on the page. If there are a lot of images this can take some time, especially on a slow dial-up connection.

Most of the image files that you use in word processing or desktop publishing take up a great deal of memory. The size of the image file can vary from a few kilobytes up to several megabytes.

For example, photos taken with a digital camera are often 2MB or 4MB in size. If you could put these on a website and then tried to download them, they would take many minutes on a slow modem. For this reason, all images on a website are stored in a compressed format which gives much smaller file sizes.

For most pages, try to limit the total memory size of all the images on a page to 60 kilobytes. Larger images can be used if the user is expecting an image-rich site, or if he or she is warned that the page may take a while to download.

You can find out how big an image file is. Click on the images folder in the folder list. Right-click on the image file, and select *Properties*. The Properties dialogue window tells you how big the file is in kilobytes (see Figure 4.70).

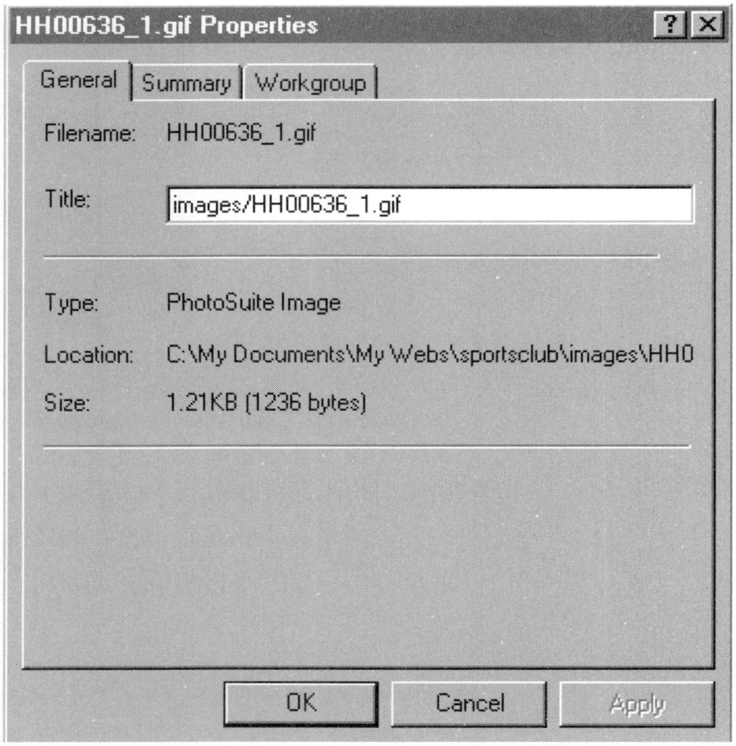

Figure 4.70 *The image Properties window*

Number of colours

We have already looked at the colour depth of screens. The two image formats that are used on the WWW use differing colour depth.

◆ **JPG** (or JPEG) can use 16- or 24-bit colour values.

◆ **GIF** uses only 8-bit colour values.

The JPG format usually uses 24-bit colour values. That provides over 16 million different colours, which is more than can be distinguished by the human eye. That is why JPGs are used for photographs.

The GIF format uses 8-bit colour values which provides only 256 different colours. GIFs are ideal for simple icons and line drawings.

File compression

The package will offer you some choice over the level of compression for JPGs. A more compressed photo will take up less memory, but will also display less detail. If a dialogue box asks you to chose the quality, select 75 per cent. On the other hand, if you are asked to specify the degree of compression, select 25 per cent. These two choices have exactly the same effect as each other, but unfortunately software packages are not consistent in the way they ask the question.

Manipulating compressed images

Once an image has been saved in a compressed form, GIF or JPG, you should not try to manipulate it any further. If the image is compressed for a second time the quality may suffer noticeably. Always go back to the original version before it was compressed if you want to make any more changes.

You may not have access to the bitmap version of an image but have it only in JPG format (e.g. if you use a photo from a CD). After you have reduced the size, save the image again as a JPG, but this time choose 100 per cent quality or zero per cent compression. If you compress the image a second time the image may become distorted. Check the memory used. If it is too large then experiment with a small amount of compression.

Dimensions of an image

Most photographs should be cropped before being used on a web page. You need to cut out the unnecessary parts of the picture and just focus on the key elements. Photos on a website do not have to conform to any of the standard picture ratios, so can be any shape. If you need to crop a picture do so before you reduce the dimensions.

Images are usually reduced in size before use on a web page. It is not a good idea to enlarge an existing image. Often enlarged images suffer from the 'jaggies', which is the nickname for the jagged edges that you sometimes see on graphics (e.g. Figure 4.71).

Figure 4.71 A case of jaggies in an image that has been enlarged

PRACTICAL TASK 4.26

FrontPage allows you to manipulate images to a certain extent, without using specialist graphics package. You can resize an image directly on the page, but you must resample it to save it again at its new dimensions. This ensures that the image file is no larger than it needs to be.

FrontPage will also convert an image to a GIF or JPG for you automatically when you save it.

1 Resize the clipart image you used before by dragging on the corner handles. If you drag on one of the side handles the image will be squashed in one direction only. If you drag on one of the corner handles the image will get smaller but still keep the same proportions. The image may look a little distorted at this stage.

2 Click on the image, then click on the *Resample* button in the Pictures toolbar. Not only does this reduce the size of the image file but it also improves the appearance of the image (see Figure 4.72). The button looks like this:

Figure 4.72 The handles have been used to resize the image

3 Save the page. The Save Embedded Files dialogue window will appear. The name of the images folder should appear under Folder. If the word 'Images' does not appear under Folder, then click on *Change Folder*, and select the images folder.

4 *FrontPage* will convert the image to GIF format and then save the image as a separate file in the images folder.

You can check which image files have been saved by clicking on the images folder in the folders list.

Background images

A background image can be applied to a page instead of a background colour. Backgrounds should be chosen carefully as too much detail can distract the visitor from the text, or even obscure it (see Figure 4.73). All backgrounds are automatically **tiled** – that is, repeated to fill the available space – so quite a small image can be used.

Figure 4.73 Use of an unsuitable background image (tiled)

Web authoring packages usually provide a selection of background images, which are defined in the HTML code like this:

```
<body background="images/ripple.gif">
```

PRACTICAL TASK 4.27

1 To change the background image on a page, select *Format + Style*. Select the body tag, then use the *Border* option and select the *Shading* tab.

2 In the Background Picture box, browse to find a suitable image. You will probably have some background images in your clipart gallery.

Note

The JPG format uses 3 bytes per pixel so takes up more memory than the GIF format. Also, the method of compression is rather different, and beyond the scope of this unit, but the effect is to make GIFs far more economical in terms of memory.

If you do need photorealistic images, or you need to match colours exactly, then you should use the JPG format. Otherwise, experiment with the GIF format to see whether it produces an acceptable image. Web pages download much more quickly if the images are in GIF format.

5.3 Transparency

In Figure 4.72 the telephone image has a black background so fits on the black background of the page. But most clipart and many other images have a white background, so the image can look very odd on the page (see Figure 4.74).

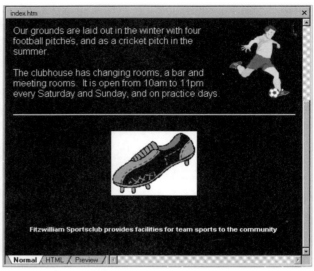

Figure 4.74 The boot image has the wrong colour background

In the GIF format you can make the background of the image **transparent** so that the background colour of the page shows through. You can do this in any full graphics package that generates GIFs. Some web authoring packages allow you to do this to the image directly on the page.

PRACTICAL TASK 4.28

You can experiment with transparency by inserting clipart.

1 Click on the page where you want the clipart to be placed. Select *Insert + Picture + Clipart*, then choose a clipart image that has a different colour background from the background on your page.

2 Click on the image, then click on the *Set Transparent Color* button. You may get a message at this point – if so, click on *OK*. The button looks like this:

3 Click on the background of the image. In the example in Figure 4.74 you would click somewhere in the white area around the boot. The background of the image will become transparent, and show the background colour of the page (see Figure 4.75).

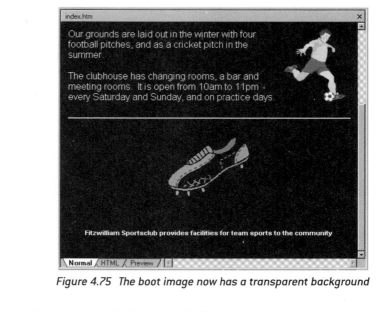

Figure 4.75 *The boot image now has a transparent background*

4   Save the page and the image as before.

5.4 Colour codes

24-bit colours, as used for JPGs and bitmaps, are stored in RGB (red, green, blue) format. Eight bits are used for each of the three colours, and combinations of these three primary colours give all the possible hues.

The **RGB codes** consist of three numbers, each of which has a value from 0 (none of that colour) to 255 (maximum colour). In a style sheet you will see that colours are expressed like this:

rgb(51, 102, 204)

Thus rgb(51, 102, 204) has some red, more green and a lot of blue, and displays as a strong mid blue.

Black is the complete absence of colour so has the code rgb(0, 0, 0), while white is created by combining all colours and has the code rgb(255, 255, 255). It can be quite tricky working out colour codes for a particular shade from scratch, but colour charts can be found on the WWW. Colours in graphics packages are determined in a similar way.

The **numerical value of a colour** can be expressed in decimal (0 to 255) or hexadecimal (#00 to #FF) numbers. Thus rgb(51, 102, 204) is the same as #3366CC (# is used to denote hexadecimal numbers).

Web safe colour codes

The appearance of colours does vary from screen to screen, even when set at the same colour depth. A limited number of colours have been found to appear clearly and without **dithering** on all screens. These are known as the web safe colours.

In *FrontPage* you may have noticed that only a limited number of colour values are used in the pre-designed style sheets – 0, 51, 102, 153, 204 and 255. The hexadecimal (hex) equivalents are 00, 33, 66, 99, CC and FF. Colours constructed with one of these values for each of the three RGB components make up the web safe colours. Thus rgb(153, 0, 51) is a Web safe colour, whilst rgb(57, 139, 17) is not.

That does not mean that you should never use colours outside the web safe list – indeed photos normally contain many more colours. But if a colour is to be used over a large area – for example, as a background colour – then you should choose from the web safe palette.

Chapter summary

You should be able to use graphics software (including tools within web authoring packages) to:

◆ reduce an image to the correct dimensions

◆ save it in either JPG or GIF compressed formats

◆ create a transparent area on a GIF image

◆ change colours in an image

◆ to select and use web safe colours.

6 Publish and maintain web pages

6.1 Publishing your website

To publish a website on the WWW a designer needs:

◆ access to space on a webserver

◆ a domain name that points to the website on the server

◆ the means to transfer the pages and other files to the webserver.

Webservers and web hosts

A webserver is a computer linked to the Internet which stores one or more websites. A web host is a company that owns one or more webservers, and rents out space on the webservers to others.

All the files and folders that make up a website must be uploaded to a webserver before they can be made available on the Internet. A large commercial organisation may own its own webserver, but the majority of websites are hosted by web hosts.

Most Internet service providers (ISPs) also act as web hosts, and many include a certain amount of web space with their accounts. Typically, the space will be 20Mb to 30Mb in size, and this is more than enough for a quite substantial site. Larger amounts of space can usually be acquired at additional cost.

There are also some specialist web hosting companies. These companies can be found easily by searching for 'web hosts'. Sometimes free space is offered, but this often carries the condition that the site must display some advertising for the host. It may be acceptable to display advertising of this kind on a personal website, but it is not appropriate on a website for a commercial enterprise.

Server-side scripts

Some sites can function properly only if they are hosted on servers that also store additional support software (or **scripts**). In each case, the designer must ensure that the webserver does support the requirements of the website.

Sites developed in *FrontPage* often include special functions that make use of additional software, known as **FrontPage extensions**, stored on the webserver. These are not made available by all webservers; in particular, a number of the major ISPs that include web space in their low-cost packages do not support *FrontPage* extensions.

CGI scripts are used on many webservers. FormMail.pl is a script that is used by many web designers to generate emails from data collected by an online form. The ISP will provide the URL of this script on their server.

Registering a domain name

A domain name, such as 'thisismydomain.co.uk', must be **registered** with one of the registration organisations. All domain names ending with .uk are registered with **Nominet**. There are a number of official registries for .com and other domains. A fee is charged for domain name registration.

293

Domain names are often registered through ISPs who then carry out the formal registration process on behalf of the organisation or individual. Once the domain name has been registered, the ISP will ensure that the domain name points to the correct web space on their webserver.

A **Whois server** can be searched to find out which domain names are currently registered and which are still available. Again, most ISPs provide a Whois search facility.

Choosing a domain name can be a challenging task, as many millions of names have already been registered. There have been some legal moves to protect commercial names from being registered by individuals who have no connection with the companies, as in the past so-called cyber-squatters have tried to charge well-known organisations large sums to transfer registered domain names to them.

Uploading files to a webserver

When a website has been tested it can be uploaded (published) to the chosen webserver. If the webserver is in-house – that is, owned by the organisation – then the system administrators will provide guidance to users about how to transfer the files to the webserver.

If an external webserver managed by an ISP is used, then all the files and directories will have to be transferred by the designer. This can be done either using the publishing tool built into a web authoring package, or by using file transfer protocol (**FTP**) software. In both cases the following data is needed:

◆ the domain name
◆ the user's name (as registered with the ISP)
◆ the user's password.

FTP shareware software can be downloaded from the Internet. To use it, the user must be online to the Internet. A dialogue window asks for the required data, then locates the web space on the remote server. Figure 4.76 shows a typical layout. The left side shows the files and directories on the home computer (**local system**) and the right side shows the files and directories already on the webserver (**remote system**). The user highlights the files and directories to be uploaded from the left side, then clicks on the right-pointing arrow to transfer them across.

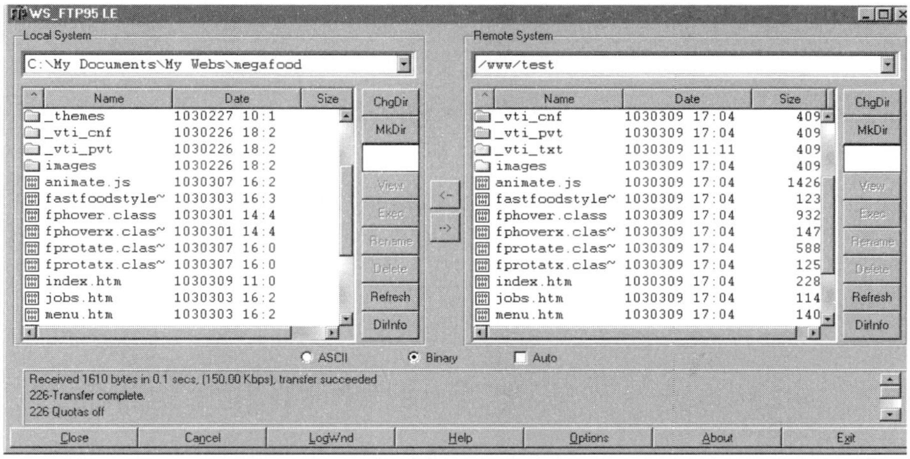

Figure 4.76 FTP software provided by Ipswitch

All the files that make up the site must be transferred, including page files, style sheets, any script files, the images directory and its contents, plus any folders and files that may have been created by the web authoring package.

PRACTICAL TASK 4.29

1 In FrontPage, select *File + Publish Web*. A dialogue box appears as in Figure 4.77.

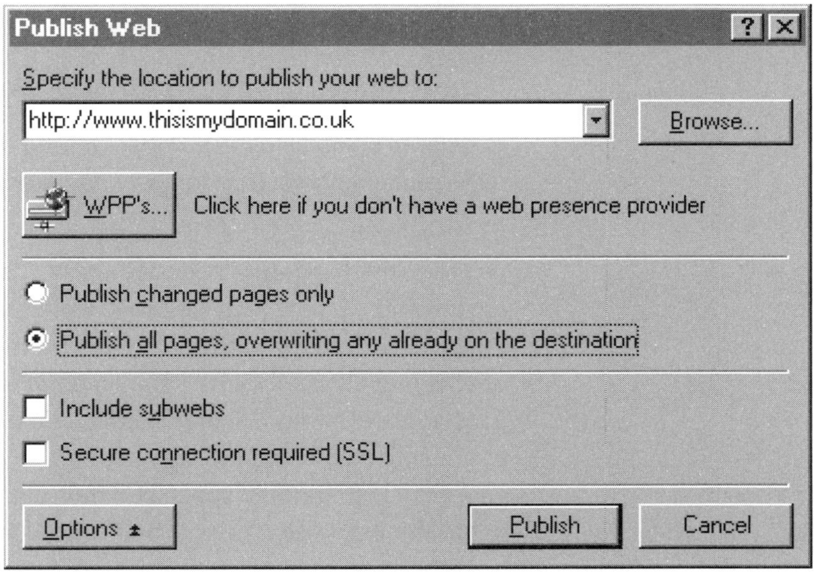

Figure 4.77 The Publish Web dialogue in FrontPage

2 Enter the URL of the domain, then click on 'Publish all pages' (if this is not visible, click on the *Options* button). Click on *Publish*.

3 You will then be asked for your user name and password, as used with your ISP.

An animation records progress, and when the site has been successfully uploaded you will be informed and prompted to view it in your browser.

6.2 Search engines

Search engines are continually crawling through the WWW by following all the links from one site to another. As they do this, they maintain huge indexing databases about the sites. In particular, they note the **keywords** and **descriptions** in the metatags (see page 273), and they also extract keywords from the text on pages. The indexes are then referred to whenever a user enters text in a search engine.

It can take some time for a search engine to discover a new website, but sites can be registered directly with them. Many search engines have UK versions which enable the visitor to restrict the search to UK sites if desired. The most widely used search engines are **Google** (www.google.co.uk), **AllTheWeb** (www.alltheweb.com), **Yahoo!** (uk.yahoo.com) which is powered by Google, **MSN Search** (search.msn.co.uk) and **Ask Jeeves** (www.ask.co.uk).

6.3 Internet security

Unauthorised access to the webserver

In order to upload files to a webserver the designer needs three items of data – the domain name, plus the user name and password for the account.

If the webserver is owned by an organisation and connected to its internal network, then unauthorised access may be possible from within the organisation. Employees who have legitimate access to the server can at times be careless with their user IDs. Even if confidentiality is not breached, user names usually follow a standard pattern within an organisation, and passwords can often be predicted. It can sometimes be easy for an employee who wants to damage the organisation, or who simply wants to play a joke, to gain access to the web space and then change the content. Of course, such behaviour would be traceable and would lead to instant dismissal.

Webservers located within organisations can be protected from external interference by **firewalls**. A webserver owned by an ISP is much more vulnerable. Someone who knows the user name and password for a domain can gain access to the web space from any computer that is connected to the Internet anywhere in the world.

Computer Misuse Act 1990

The Computer Misuse Act makes any unauthorised access ('**hacking**') to a computer system illegal. It defines three offences in increasing order of seriousness.

1 *Unauthorised access to computer material*. The key issues here are whether someone was authorised to access a computer system, and whether the person deliberately did something with the intention of gaining unlawful access. If someone accidentally gains access to a system then he or she is not guilty of an offence, although would be if continuing to explore the system once realising what had happened.

2 *Unauthorised access with intent to commit or facilitate commission of further offences*. This deals with cases where the person intends to commit another crime, such as theft or blackmail, and is gaining unauthorised access in order to do so.

3 *Unauthorised modification of computer material*. This section of the Act outlaws the intentional alteration or deletion of data when the person does not have authority to do so.

Someone who alters a website without authority would be guilty of the third, and most serious, offence.

Secure servers

A webserver may hold database files, containing information collected from the website through an online form. Organisations that collect personal data from customers in this way have to be particularly vigilant in protecting their webservers from unauthorised access. They need to do this:

◆ to comply with the **Data Protection Act**

◆ to reassure customers that personal data about them will be **secure**

◆ to encourage customers to provide credit card details for **online transactions**.

A secure server **encrypts** all the data stored on it (see page 233), so if anyone does gain illegal access he or she will not be able to understand or use the data. Secure servers are used for all financial transactions over the Internet, and increasingly for the collection of other personal data (see Figure 4.78).

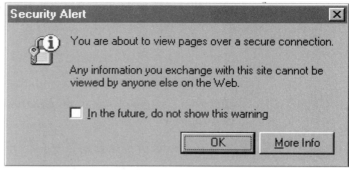

Figure 4.78 Message given when using a secure server

When a website is on a secure server you will see a small **padlock icon** at the bottom of the window as in Figure 4.79.

Figure 4.79 The icon to indicate that a web page is on a secure server

Chapter summary

◆ FTP software, or tools built into web authoring packages, are used to upload a website to a webserver. This process makes the site available on the WWW and is sometimes referred to as publishing a website. Secure servers are used for websites that capture confidential data.

◆ Sites developed in *FrontPage* need to be supported by scripts stored on the webserver.

◆ A domain name can be registered, and pointed to the site on the webserver.

◆ A site can be registered with a search engine, although the engines themselves find sites by crawling the WWW.

◆ Unauthorised access to webservers is covered by the **Computer Misuse Act 1990**.

Index

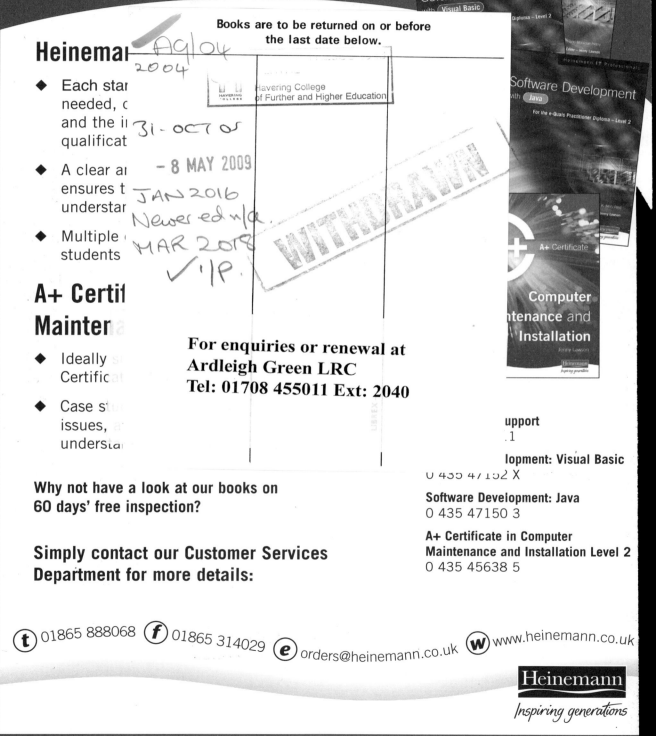